THE DEATH OF THE GODS

D1422076

THE
DEATH OF THE GODS

The New Global Power Grab

Carl Miller

WILLIAM HEINEMANN: LONDON

1 3 5 7 9 10 8 6 4 2

William Heinemann
20 Vauxhall Bridge Road
London SW1V 2SA

William Heinemann is part of the Penguin Random House group of companies
whose addresses can be found at global.penguinrandomhouse.com.

Penguin
Random House
UK

First published by William Heinemann in 2018

www.penguin.co.uk

A CIP catalogue record for this book is available from the British Library.

ISBN 9781785151330 (Hardback)
ISBN 9781785151347 (Trade Paperback)

Typeset in 12.5/16.5 pt Fournier MT Std
by Integra Software Services Pvt. Ltd, Pondicherry

Printed and bound by Clays Ltd, St Ives plc

Penguin Random House is committed to a sustainable future for
our business, our readers and our planet. This book is made
from Forest Stewardship Council® certified paper.

MIX
Paper from
responsible sources
FSC
www.fsc.org   FSC® C018179

[Dedication TK]

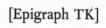

CONTENTS

INTRODUCTION

The Death of the Gods

———————————

A man is holding a knife to my throat as I hold a knife to his. I'm in a penthouse apartment, at the home of one of the world's leading technologists. Outside I can see the lights of south London glitter. A bolognese is quietly bubbling away in some kind of high-tech pressure cooker in the kitchen. And here we both stand, perfectly still. I was there because I was on a journey. It was one that would change my life in the months that followed, one that would take me across the world, and bring me face-to-face with both the best and the worst that humanity had to offer. It was a journey in search of a single idea. The knife was my first lesson.

Take a moment, and pause. Stock prices plummet with a tweet. Newspapers collapse. Giant corporations disappear overnight. Political parties that have stood for centuries struggle for survival Protests spill out of social media and onto the streets. Facebook has grown bigger than any country. Memes have managers, hackers advise governments, gamers are sports stars, and YouTubers are celebrities. 'Mines' produce crypto-currencies worth millions. New refineries enrich data. Cities are smart, intelligence artificial, data big and realities virtual. Governments the world over are losing control. On and on it goes. Technology is changing, people are changing, the world is changing around us . . . and in some way, as unique as your life is, I bet that you've experienced something that has made you stop. And think. And feel that the world is changing around you too.

For centuries, writers and thinkers have groped for an idea to interpret the world around them during moments of profound social change: Power. They ask how it is created, who has it, and why. They've tried to make sense of its shape, of its effects and consequences. As an idea it is sometimes mobilised to defend the status quo, sometimes to destroy it. But again and again it has appeared as the best possible prism through which to see and understand the world during moments of profound change.

Machiavelli began to define modern thinking about power as the world shuddered out of the dark ages and the politics, religion and philosophy of the Renaissance clashed with the old certainties that had stood for centuries. In *The Prince*, he urged rulers to see the pursuit of power as their highest moral goal, and he proposed that the use of fear, lies and pain were all justifiable means to get it. Harnessing power and taking control, Machiavelli believed, were the only ways to navigate through the chaos.

A hundred years after Machiavelli, Thomas Hobbes turned to the subject of power again after he had seen his own social order collapse. Seventeenth-century England had been ripped apart by civil war, and the king, Charles I, beheaded. In *Leviathan*, his greatest work, Hobbes argued that there is a restless striving for power in all men, a striving that has to be checked through a social contract in which we give up some of our own freedoms and rights in return for the protection of a greater power – the state, Leviathan – that must be sovereign.

Two hundred years later, another revolution, and the western world was launched once more into a new version of modernity. Karl Marx again used the idea of power to explain why this new society was one of unprecedented and great wealth, yet also one of immense inequality, with soot-blackened factories and terrible squalor.[1] Yet while Machiavelli saw concentration of power as the only way to achieve stability, for Marx it was the source of the problem. For him, power was economic rather than political, a material resource, something that arose from the ability to control labour and capital. The industrial revolution had caused it to concentrate into the hands of factory owners and financiers, and they had used it to wring profits from exhausted workforces, collapsing from cholera and crushed by machines. Material power also translated into control over ideas, weaving a 'false consciousness' over the working class that made them accept their misery. Machiavelli urged the rulers of his time to grasp power however possible; Marx believed that the examination of power would lead to a new class consciousness that would ultimately break the spell of capitalism.

Writing in the decades after the Second World War, Hannah Arendt challenged the assumption that power should be understood as a power over others. Power, she believed, was antithetical

---

1   It must be said that Marx never developed an explicit theory of power, but it is something is constantly and implicitly addressed in his work.

to violence. She saw it as something that could only be held by a group, never an individual. Power was in the ability of humans not just to act, but to act in concert. Power for Arendt was about persuasion, not violence.

Perhaps the most influential theorist on power of all was Michel Foucault. Writing through the 1960s and '70s, Foucault's was a time, like Machiavelli and Marx's, when taboos and conventions across the western world were being pulled down. Amid waves of protests against the Vietnamese and Algerian wars, for prison reform, for sexual liberation, Foucault too reached for the concept of power, but this time to insist that it was everywhere. For Foucault, it had nothing to do with Machiavelli's princes or Marx's factory bosses. Ignore power in politics and war, Foucault said, and look at power in sex, science and the arts. It is there, in the areas you least expect, operating through a complex web of norms, conventions, discourses, regimes of truth and rationalities. It is what forms the structure of life. What makes us who we are.

Philosophers have tried to logically define power. Social scientists have tried to measure it. Across feminist thought and post-colonial scholarship, thinking about power has been used to diagnose and challenge oppressions and inequalities. Yet for each of these writers and countless others, it has taken different meanings. For Robert Dahl, power is the ability to make somebody do what they otherwise wouldn't do. For Peter Bachrach and Morton Baratz, it is also about determining what was important and unimportant. Stephen Lukes added another dimension: power is also about convincing people to embrace ideas that are contrary to their own interests. Joseph Nye sought to explain American predominance in the latter half of the twentieth century through the idea of 'soft power' – the ability to make others want the same

thing as you. Judith Butler saw power as something we internal-
ised, where submission was as much a question of psychology as
external force. Simone de Beauvoir, Anthony Giddens, John
Gaventa, Pierre Bourdieu . . . each added additional layers to our
definition of power, exploring new dimensions of it. The concept
of power has become surrounded by a thick web of interpretation,
critique, re-interpretation and re-formulation. Power is a slippery
idea. It isn't an accident that power can't be easily defined. It's an
important part of the idea itself. Yet for each of these thinkers,
power provided the best lens through which to view their world,
and to discern its direction of travel. Power helped them interpret
the changes they were experiencing, it showed them what was
happening, and why, and whether it was good or bad. Looking
atpower stopped them from sleepwalking through a revolution.

I began this book convinced that we are living through our own
moment of flux and change. Across the world, again and again, I
could see old familiarities tumbling down and new social orders,
new hierarchies, new winners emerging that all, in one way or
another, traced back to digital technology. But I was also afraid
we were hurtling into a new social reality that we didn't really
understand and couldn't anticipate. Was all this technology making
each of us better able to lead the lives that we wanted to lead? Or
was it moving it further away? Were we more powerful as individuals than ever before, or more controlled? You could see the
rate of change increasing, but, I thought, it was hard to see whether
it was heading towards a new dawn of knowledge and opportunity,
or a nightmare of ignorance and oppression?

Now is a moment to, again, think about power. It could come
in many forms, from blunt force and coercion, to bribes and incen-

tives, the shaping of the moral codes we live by or the moulding our perceptions and preferences through a broad array of influence, manipulation, inducement, deceit, threat, encouragement and persuasion. But as I set out, the kind of power that I cared about was as a particular kind of influence like no other. It was the capacity to reach into and change the lives of others, to change the choices we make and and the choices we have. It was the kind of influence that shapes each of our destinies whether we like it or not. It is a form of rule.

This book is an account of a journey I took to search for the reality of this kind of power as it touches all of our lives today. A journey that has followed a strange and winding path. From that penthouse apartment in London, it took me to Mexico, to a colourful jamboree of inventors, merchants, architects and activists who mingle, drink, dance and argue about how the internet should really work. In freezing courtyards in Berlin I met techno-activists, hackers and cyber-pranksters. In South Korea I visited the most digital city on earth; a city full of screaming e-sports fans and invisible hikikomori – 'the departed' – who never leave their room and only live their lives online. I lived in a political-technology commune in east London (twice) with people for whom technology is a way of making society better. I went onto an army base surrounded by the rolling green hills of Berkshire where soldiers were fighting a war unlike any I'd heard of before, and in Prague I met NATO officials and possibly Russian spies to talk about how digital warfare has broken out between states struggling for control over what people see and believe. I found a fake news merchant in Kosovo, a legendary hacker in a deserted model railway club in Boston, and under the marbled edifice of Caesar's Palace, Las Vegas, I went to the largest annual gathering of the best hackers in the world (never take your phone there). In Silicon Valley, in the middle of a second gold rush, I found a place far stranger than most people suspect, where 'cool' ideas collide with bundles of money and power and powerlessness live side-by-side.

Wherever I went, I immersed myself in the murky waters of this brave new world. I went on a cyber-crime raid with the police, and became involved in a struggle for control of an online market selling murder. I peered into the mechanics of algorithms that have been kept secret; I built a 'bot' to keep the peace on Twitter. I crafted viral messages to infect online conversations. I hung out with citizen investigators in a struggle to expose truths and lies. I joined with journalists to investigate a shadowy new protocol that despots might be using to control the internet. I even tried to hack a hacker.

The cast of this book includes former presidents and digital ministers, spies, soldiers, criminals and police officers, investigative journalists, guerrilla viral artists, hackers, labour organisers, academics, algorithmists, entrepreneurs, activists and many others. Some I was determined to meet because they were newly powerful, others because they were newly powerless. Some were seeking to expose power, and others still were influenced by power in ways I thought important. They will be our guides and interpreters to the stories that expose the reality of power. They come from all over the world and different walks of life, as I tried – wherever possible – to see the changes that were happening from points of view across political, social, even moral lines.

I cannot remember a time when power has been spoken about more, than over the 18 months that this book was written. The allegations around Harvey Weinstein, the #MeToo campaign, Black Lives Matter, gender pay gaps in the BBC – it has been a time when the power that we experience has become more recognised to be intimately related to the identities we hold, and it is important to say a few words about mine. White, male, with an upbringing that certainly wasn't rich, but wasn't poor either, there are ways that power works, and is abused, that I have not experienced myself, and cannot hope to really understand. This book is an account of power told predominantly by someone who has not had to go through life and experience abuses of it because of my race, or been discriminated against because of my gender, or sexual orientation, my class, or indeed any other aspect of myself that I cannot change. You'll notice also that the people featured are themselves both disproportionately white, and disproportionately male. In part, this may merely reflect who I am and who I know. But in part it undoubtedly says something else about power: about the kinds of people involved in how it is changing. You might call it my failure, and also a finding.

Each chapter is a window into a different landscape, a different aspect of our lives, where power is being won, lost, fought over and transformed. I've selected some subjects because they seemed to show power at its newest and most exotic. Some because they seemed to show power at its least tamed and civilised; power in its purest form. Some simply because an opportunity arose and I felt able to add something new. Some of the areas are increasingly well known; others are, I hope, surprising and even unsettling. This is not a comprehensive account; such a thing isn't possible. But if I have succeeded, they are by shades entertaining and interesting as well as illuminating and instructive.

It has been a disconcerting, sometimes scary journey. There are people who have been arrested during the course of writing this book, and others who would certainly be dismissed, if not sued, if their employers find out who they are. I have had to take careful steps to protect the identities of many of the individuals I have interviewed for this book, and to honour the confidence that very different kinds of organisations and people have placed in me.

Standing there, with a knife against my throat, made me feel something that is really true for all of us. My life was in the hands of another. On forces outside of me and beyond my control. This was power, and it is something we have grappled with and tried to understand throughout human history.

Amongst the oldest stories about power that we have are from the ancient Greeks. They told stories about the Titans, the first gods, shapers of the world, and shapers of the lives of humankind. Cronus was the king of the Titans, a god who assumed power by overthrowing his father and the old order. His reign was known as the 'golden age', a time of peace and prosperity on earth. But Cronus alone was in charge. After hearing prophecy that one of his children, the Olympians, would usurp him, he set out destroy them – swallowing them all in a bid to secure his rule. Every child was eaten, except one. Zeus's mother handed Cronus a stone wrapped in a blanket in place of her son. Zeus was hidden away, and when he was old enough, he rose up against his father. He freed his brothers and sisters, and for ten years, the old and new gods fought a war. The new gods – these new shapers of destiny – then divided the world amongst themselves.

The story tells us something about the world today. About power being fought over, about some gods falling and others rising. The question is, who are we in the story? Are we newly freed by power? Or being consumed?

I

People

'They are the ones who translate human demands into code that the machines can understand and act on. They are legion. Fanatics with a potent new toy.'

> Stewart Brand, creator of the Whole Earth
> 'Lectronic Link (WELL)

The TMRC

Massachusetts is Old America. Middlesex, Suffolk, Plymouth, Arsenal Mall: it is a state filled with names dragged across the Atlantic by English settlers. Visit Cambridge – another old name – and you'll see the austere red-brick buildings and formal lawns of Harvard rising up on the north-western end of Massachusetts Avenue. Harvard is the oldest seat of learning in the United States, but follow the avenue as it cuts south and east through Cambridge, and you'll arrive at a very different kind of academic powerhouse. The Massachusetts Institute of Technology, founded 225 years after Harvard, was built to supply wisdom and learning for a new age of American history. The MIT was born into the dawning world of industrialisation, technology and engineering.

The campus of the MIT stretches along the north bank of the Charles River, as, meandering through the city, it begins to widen before spilling into the deep green-blue water of Boston Harbour. The centre of the campus is all sweeping treelined aspects, white colonnades and a large, central, white dome. But the building I'm after is set away and north of the grand MIT concourse. Building N52, 265 Massachusetts Avenue.

N52 is sat on a busy, dusty intersection, across the road from a beat-up Sunoco gas station. A smaller and shabbier outpost of MIT than its glamorous cousins stretched along the river, it looks like an old factory, a four-storey red-brick building, with box-like ventilators poking out of large window frames. A small silver door is set off to one side surrounded in chrome, and on the wall a grey plastic phone sticks out of the wall. N52 houses MIT's Environment Health and Safety Office, something to do with industrial hygiene and, alarmingly, the Hazard Assessment and Control Program. But I'm not here for any of those. It was late evening when I arrived, and through the door and up a dark empty corridor, I found what I'd been looking for. A small, white door with a sign that says T-M-R-C. Knock. No answer. I push it open.

'Hello?'

'I have a few criticisms,' a voice responds, from somewhere within.

As I step into the room, I can smell sawdust, or cut wood. A large extractor fan is droning loudly.

'You say in your talk',[1] the voice continues, 'that the reason for parliamentary democracy, as opposed to other forms of democracy, was the result of space and distance. And these aren't required any more. Well, wouldn't you say that it is also a question of time and judgement?'

Two men emerge from the back of the room and wave me over to an empty chair. One reaches to shake my hand. He is holding a clipboard, and on this clipboard seems to be written a series of questions. He doesn't wait for my answer before proceeding.

'The problem with tweets is that they can be done in a second . . .'

The man is probably in his seventies. He has neat white hair, spotless white trousers, a plaid shirt, and black shoes and socks. An engineer – you can tell. I guessed this was John McNamara, who'd invited me to drop by when I was in town. I spotted another man sitting nearby. He was taller, wearing large, old-fashioned brown glasses with two joins across the nose. Like John, he wore a neat button-down shirt. I wasn't sure who he might be. Neither me, nor they, had said who we were.

The room was large – a workshop, cluttered, low ceilinged, and dominated by a huge irregularly shaped table, about chest high. As I looked across it, I could see sweeping hills, a town, a lumber farm. There was an industrial area, a downtown area with shops and offices and off into the distance, a papier-mâché mountain. An enormous model railway set. Tracks swept out

---

[1] I had spoken at a TEDxAthens event some months before this trip, on the subject of digital democracy.

3

of a turntable at the railway depot, past the giant Gifford City Storage Fireproof Warehouse rising above the storefronts, past Anderson Lumber. They went past a church with a tiny working clock, overlooking a quiet car park. Figurines were frozen, strolling down the town boulevard, bent over a pile of tiny iron girders, or carrying a tiny body away from a tiny car crash. Buried away, here in building N52, is an institution of enormous significance: the Tech Model Railroad Club. The TMRC.

The TMRC was the home of a tiny, committed group of people that, perhaps for the first time, dedicated their lives to mastery of the computer. For almost all of us, the technology that we draw around us closer and more intimately with every passing moment is also something that we understand only more and more distantly. As it becomes smarter, better, more pervasive and more essential it also becomes more mysterious and arcane. The phones in our pockets are now so complex, to most of us they might as well be small black boxes of magic.

Yet for them, technology wasn't a mysterious black box. They understood it, bent it and forged it to do things that it had never done before. As each our lives is changed so much by the technology that surrounds it, it was the people at the TMRC that began to shape that technology.

Underneath the spray-painted trees and lovingly detailed street signs, you could still see the games and projects that this first generation of truly digital tinkerers had left behind. Under the table, strung through metal brackets, was a thick tangle of cables. Grey, yellow, purple, green, some threading off into the railway, some connected to circuit boards dangling below the surface. An old grey-plastic, green-screened computer monitor next to the track showed a schematic of how TRK1, TRK2, LEAD, IND and SCRAPYARD joined and split with each other. They called it 'The System'.

First, they had used computers to change how this model railway ran. But the TMRC was the origin of a mindset, a craft, a way of thinking that has significance far vaster than this room, this club, this university, or themselves. Theirs was an example that would stretch down through the decades that have passed since, but here was the origin. The TMRC was the home of the first people to taste the power of a new age.

The Computer Age

In the 1950s, computers were huge, fragile and ridiculously expensive. The few that existed were housed in a starched, controlled world where only a small and elite cabal of engineers, and only for legitimate purposes, might hope to operate the dials and blinking lights of these wondrous, towering new machines. Nobody else could get their hands on them, and certainly not for fun.

But this was about to change. In 1956, the MIT Lincoln Laboratory, funded by the US military, had made the 'Transistorized eXperimental computer zero' – the TX-0 – one of the first transistor-run computers in the world. In 1958, 'Tix oh' was sent out on indefinite 'loan' to another part of MIT, a research laboratory working on electronics, joined in 1961 by another computer, the Programmed Data Processor, or PDP-1, also designed at Lincoln Laboratory. Two computers! 'Tix oh' and 'the 'One', next to each other down the hall in MIT. There they were, when the two gentlemen I was sitting with – John McNamara and (I learned) Richard Greenblatt – turned up as fresh-faced, train-obsessed, young undergraduates.

'We joined in the early sixties,' John said, 'just at the right time. The primary thing was that there was hands on computers.' At MIT there was a huge number of different clubs to join, offering extracurricular activities in everything from chess to mountaineering, but both were drawn to the same: the Tech Model Railroad Club. It was a student-run club that had been set up just after the Second World War, to protect and develop a model railway that, over generations of MIT students, had grown larger and larger, more and more complex. Both were technically minded, and fascinated by The System – with its intricate networks of relays, points and interchanges.

As John and Richard arrived at the TMRC, they found themselves with something no one else in the world had: hands-on access to computers, freed from bureaucratic control. 'In the very earliest of days there was no time-sharing. So there was just a sign-up list that went up on Friday morning and within two hours that computer would be signed up twenty-four hours a day for the following week,' John explained. The TX-o and the PDP-1 were contrasts to the so-called glasshouse big IBM machines. 'On those, you submitted a deck of cards that described the program that you wanted to run – and maybe it ran and maybe it didn't. Some hundred hours later,' John continued, 'you'd get your deck of cards back together with a print-out of how you'd screwed up. Whereas with the PDP-1 and the TX-o you'd get the benefit of instant feedback. Momentarily, they'd be your personal computer.'

Suddenly, and for the first time, these men[2] found themselves with the opportunity for a very different kind of computing to the sanitised world of IBM machines, and it was centred around the TMRC. 'There was no such thing as a computer club. This club was the alternative to there being a computer club. Step out of here and step to your right. That's one of the birthplaces of American computing.'

'Fall of '62 was when I became a student. I got involved in computers, and was in quite deep after a year and a half,' Richard said. Flashback to 1962, and Richard Greenblatt, cherub-faced, dark-haired, awkward of speech, had just arrived at MIT. 'I would hang around the machine, and someone wouldn't show up for their time,' he said. 'Quite deep', I learned later, was an astonishing understatement. He never told me himself, but Richard Greenblatt was one of the most legendary, visionary members of the first generation to get their hands on computers.

Steven Levy wrote a famous history of the TMRC in the late 1950s and early 1960s, just when Richard joined. 'Some hackers recall that one of the things Greenblatt's hacking precluded was regular bathing and the result was a powerful odor,' wrote Levy. 'The joke around the AI Lab was that there was a new scientific olfactory measure called a milliblatt. One or two milliblatts was extremely powerful, and one full blast was just about inconceivable . . .' On one occasion, his friends manoeuvred Greenblatt to a lab equipped with emergency showers for cases of accidental chemical exposure, and just turned one on.

---

2   And, it should be said, it was a world almost entirely male.

This strange trail in the pursuit of power had led me to a room, but it was pointing to Richard, not the railway. He was one of the most enthusiastic devotees of a new way of life that was emerging around the club, one where humans and computers began to form a new, intense kind of relationship. They began to think in a different way, to live in a different way, all to make the computers do things no one had thought of before.

Richard would often be seen shuttling back and forth between the TMRC and the PDP-1 in the dead of the night, or building the system of relays under the TMRC layout, waiting for the next chance to get in front of the computer. Programming those early computers required a state of pure concentration: you needed to hold, if you could, the program in your head as you worked on it. You needed to maintain a mental picture of where all those thousands of bits of information were going, from one instruction to the next. When he reached that state, Richard lived thirty-hour days to create extended blocks of wakefulness in which to fever-ishly write code, try the code and rewrite it before reaching total exhaustion.

It was a monastic, devotional life that threw Richard and his TMRC friends at odds with the rest of the non-computational world – of classes, appointments and meals. They would 'vulture' around the computers in the dead of the night carrying a stack of print-outs, hoping someone wouldn't show up at their scheduled time. Richard slept through a final exam. He was placed on academic probation. His parents were summoned to MIT. His personal habits became a matter of concern. He was booted out of the Cambridge YMCA because he wouldn't keep his room clean – and ended up sleeping at the TMRC, near to the computers. He began to be paid to work on the computers, but sometimes would go six months without finding time to pick up his MIT pay cheque.[3]

'What did you actually study?' I asked him. None of what Richard was doing was actually, yet, on the academic syllabus at MIT. 'I didn't officially graduate,' Richard said. 'I dropped out, they let me in as a graduate, and I dropped out again.' He was, instead, part of building an entirely new discipline, with its own disciples, culture and language. To 'munge' something was to 'Mash Until No Good'. To 'gronk' something was to destroy an item. 'Losing' code was inefficient, inelegant. 'Winning' code was the opposite. But of all these coinages, one has stayed with us more than any other. 'Er, I guess I studied hacking?' he eventually volunteered, after a silence. Richard Greenblatt and his colleagues were the first hackers.

Hack: 1) an article or project without constructive end; 2) work undertaken on bad self-advice; 3) an entropy booster; 4) to produce, or attempt to produce, a hack.[4]

'Hacking' came to describe the new, smelly, dishevelled, obsessive kind of computing of Richard and the TMRCers that was a world apart from the sterile universe of IBM. Things like profit and practicality stopped at the door of the TMRC computer-monastery. Pioneering computing was joyous and hackers mixed technical virtuosity with playfulness and whimsy. 'Wouldn't it be neat if this could do that? Well, I think we can make it do that. You got some parts here? Oh, OK. It's ingenuity, I would say,' said John, trying to

---

3 See Steven Levy's *Hackers: Heroes of the Computer Revolution* for a much more extended description of the early TMRC hackers. Greenblatt was considered hardcore, but was by no means the only one.
4 tmrc.mit.edu/dictionary.html#ADVANCE

explain the word itself. The word has since come to suggest something shadowy and illegal. But in the beginning, it wasn't about breaking the law, it was about building a new way of thinking. The hackers didn't write their new creed down. They didn't take a vote, and didn't issue a manifesto. They had simply started to see the world in a new way. Hacking was art, science, engineering and play, where mastery of the computer was an end – the only end – in itself.

'Hacks' were often done for the wild pleasure of taking part rather than the end result. One of Richard's friends, Peter Samson, spent a night writing a program that would instantly convert Arabic numbers to Roman numerals. Why? Because it was difficult to do. Next Samson worked on a program to convert the Mayan calendar, and another to get the computer to play musical scores. Soon, the PDP-1 was playing Gilbert and Sullivan operettas.

One of their most ambitious hacks was to use the computer to work out how to travel across the whole of the New York subway in the shortest time possible. A program was designed that was fed all the train timetables, and would produce the specific route that was the shortest, and one day a team set off to actually try it out. 'My job', said Richard, 'was to call up the data centre from a payphone in New York. And I can tell you that in 1968, 1967, there weren't that many working payphones in Harlem. I did find one in the back of a record shop. If something had gone wrong [a delay, missed connection], the team back at MIT was to be alerted and they were to run a new version of the program. I was to give the riders of the train the next section of the route. There was me, this army of about a dozen people and a major computer, all working to try and save a few minutes on the subway. This was the kind of the challenge that MIT people found a suitable use of their time and the technology.'

Some hacks could start as a whimsical thought and quickly evolve into complex and potentially world-changing projects. MIT hackers used the One to program the very first computer game, *Spacewar!* Then they built the first gamepad to play it with. Many of the TMRC hackers became the core of the first group devoted to studying and building artificial intelligence, centred around the MIT professors Marvin Minsky and John McCarthy. Naturally, they saw, before anyone else, that computers were more than expensive number crunchers. Lurking in the machine, the hackers probably felt as much as knew, was the potential for machine intelligence. Richard was one of these AI pioneers. He wrote the Greenblatt Chess Program, the first computer program created to play tournament-level chess and to be granted a chess rating. In 1977, the chess Grandmaster Bobby Fischer played three matches against 'Greenblatt (Computer)'. (Fischer won all three of them.)

The hackers lived life according to a new ethic, one that better reflected the logic of the computer itself. No one was there to teach them anything about computers that they didn't know, so they pulled systems apart with their hands to teach themselves how they worked. They tweaked, reverse engineered, fiddled with and broke things until systems and programs became known to them. Even for obsessives like Richard, time on the computer itself was limited to a few hours a week, and there was no time to waste programming the same stuff – so they kept everything free for everybody else to use.[5] Hackers saw beauty in elegant, efficient,

5 Of *course* this was the correct approach. A computer is, by its nature, something that benefits from the free flow of information; of bits moving, unconstrained, in logical paths from here to there. Flows of information constrained only by logic, not ownership, were what computing needed, what computers themselves demanded in order to work.

well-executed code. They found thrill in hacks that tackled a well-known problem from a totally new direction. They found meaning in the firsts that they were making the computers do.

The hacker ethic wasn't only about building a new world, however; it was also about ignoring the old. Bureaucracies, academic qualifications, hierarchies meant little to the early TMRC hackers. Only one thing could really matter: demonstrated skill in front of a computer console. Admittedly within the privileged world of MIT, this was a radical meritocracy – ruthless, perhaps, in who it excluded as well as generous in who it included. Skill alone was valuable, because it was only skill that could make computers do new and interesting things.[6]

The barriers and walls that the old world put between them and mastery of the computer were also things that hackers sought to undermine. John and Richard led me over to one of the walls of the TMRC, to a key-box, containing strange, long circular keys. 'Many of us were lock hackers too,' said John. When they needed something, the TMRC would form the Midnight Requisitions Committee. In the dead of night, they'd creep out and pick locks, cabinets, safes – whatever they needed to get the components or parts they needed. They were racing to build a new life for themselves; inspired by, close to, and constantly improving the computer at the centre of all of their lives. They weren't just using the computer to change the world. The computer was also changing them.

The TMRC is quiet now. 'We only have four members,' said John, sadly. 'People don't really play with trains any more.' But whilst the club is empty, the Hacker Ethos has grown and grown,

6 Steven Levy wrote his own, brilliant synopsis of the Hacker Ethic in *Hackers*, and I am deeply indebted to it in the description I give here.

playing out on grander and grander stages. The people in this club, people like Richard and John, opened the door to a grand new universe. It's a universe that generation after generation has willingly stepped into. They have been driven by the same impulse and moral code, a philosophy that is at once sharing and open, anti-authoritarian and rebellious. The members of a train club in MIT became the first to taste the power of mastering computers, but only later did it become a power that we would all in some way feel.

Defcon

'Hi Carl,' the message read. 'A friend who prefers to remain anonymous offers you some advice. I highly advise you to take this very seriously . . . Get a burner phone, keep bluetooth off and don't bring any electronic gear with you. Also, get cash before you go. Do not use cash machines in Vegas this week.'

The vast neoclassical edifice of Caesar's Palace sits right in the middle of the Las Vegas strip. Inside, it is all pink and white marble; glitz and vice. And whatever yours is – Texas Hold'em, Omaha Hi/Lo, fixed-limit Badugi, Seven-Card Stud Eight-or-Better, Blackjack, roulette, slots – it's all laid out in endless abundance, stretching as far as you can see across a timeless hall of flashing lights.

Outside, women in bikinis and men in shorts play in the fountains and pick at food from Snackus Maximus. But threading in among them are people that look out of place in the baking dry desert heat of Nevada. Black jeans, black T-shirts, pirate bandannas, blue mohawks, Japanese anime tattoos. Some are wearing full face masks, others steampunk goggles. 'BORN TO HUNT' one T-shirt reads. Many others feature skull and crossbones. A very different crowd has just arrived, here to play a different kind of game.

These are some of the descendants of the TMRC hackers. While once the games and dreams of hackers played out on a model railway, now their presence alone causes the world to change around them. The electronic bus timetable is now only a blue screen of errors. The digital menus have disappeared. The UPS store has shut. Some stores have stopped accepting credit cards. My phone is off and all my electronics are packed away. These are the people who have carried on the mission that Richard and his friends started. They have kept on pulling things apart, refusing to let technology become the black box that it is to everyone else. For a few days in July every year, Las Vegas becomes the site of the single most important annual gathering of hackers in the world.

Early DEFCON was truly underground. 'Twenty years ago, we had to book undercover,' a veteran hacker told me. 'We'd change hotel every year. The first time they knew DEFCON was in the house was the opening ceremonies.' His name was Major Malfunction, and DEFCON is today hosted by a man called the Dark Tangent. Other DEFCON regulars are known as Jericho, Shaggy, Suggy, Cybersulu, Crypt. You go by your hacker handle at DEFCON. You don't tell anyone your real name, and no one wants to know it. 'For ten years, no one knew my real name,' Major explained. He is dressed in the red T-shirt of a DEFCON goon (staff member): long camouflage shorts, a dark hoodie and access-all-areas lanyards. 'DEFCON wasn't considered a force for good. Everyone thought we were crazy evil hackers.'

'I've been involved in hacking when it wasn't illegal,' Major continues. 'The concept of the computer hacker didn't exist. It was assumed that if you could connect to another computer, you should do it. I was exploring this strange world out there and I'd never know what I'd find.' I felt, for the first and only time, a pang of sympathy for the casinos. Back in DEFCON 13,[7] Major hacked his hotel television using an infrared remote control. To a laughing crowd, he showed how he could reset his minibar bill, log into his neighbour's television and watched them surf the internet, set their wake-up call for 5.30 a.m. and check them out.[8] 'We know from leaks that one year the police had a Las Vegas SWAT team waiting around the corner from one of the conferences, waiting to go in,' he chuckled. 'Good times.'[9]

DEFCON, now much bigger than its early days, doesn't stay underground any more. For its tens of thousands of guests, it is a party and shopping mall, a conference and technical play park all happening at the same time. There is a trade fair, where thronging crowds press five-deep in around vendors to buy all manner of cheerfully branded hacking hardware 'for research purposes'.[10] In the 'villages', hackers are granted the opportunity to get their hands dirty. There are large, open rooms, full of people soldering circuitboards, mangling gadgets, peering at code. In the 'car hacking village', hackers learn how to send specific commands to electrical components, and fool braking systems. At the IoT (Internet of Things) village is an array of hacked children's toys, routers, thermostats – almost anything that can be connected to the internet. 'Like all hackers, we are looking

---

7 In 2005. DEFCON 25 took place in 2017.
8 www.youtube.com/watch?v=mgNZnH2UGFM
9 www.youtube.com/watch?v=MfecapOHkoM
10 Yeah . . . right.

to subvert the dominant paradigm . . . of life itself,' says the Biohacking Village, where hackers play around with weird strains of yeast to try to control what they do. There are villages for social engineering, WiFi, cryptography, reconnaissance, lock picking. As I arrive, two hackers battle to free themselves from a pair of handcuffs. One edges ahead, opens a locked box, and – sealing the win – shoots the other with the Nerf gun stored inside.

There is a tangible sense of competition everywhere you turn: the need to be recognised and respected by the other people who *get it*. To thumping music, teams from around the world spend three days locked in a competition called Capture the Flag.[11] They make thrusting attacks at their opponents' servers (flags), while parrying attempts at their own. The team that emerges victorious becomes, in DEFCON lingo, 'inhuman', winning a Black Badge granting them free access to DEFCON for the rest of their lives.

From the monastic, insular world of the TMRC, hacking has now gone global. It's now about superstars, big money, sky-high stakes and tragic falls. From the TMRC hackers to today, computers have remained a portal into a new reality for its devotees. But as computers and technology have spread all over the world, hacking has changed how the world can be shaped.

Lessons in Power

On DEFCON's biggest stages, the year's most cunning and sensational hacks were revealed. Each was a revelation of tech-

---

11 Typical playlist: CTRL/rsm, Dual Core, YTCracker and Zebbler Encanti.

nical prowess, of 'ownage'. To the whoops and cheers of ten thousand assembled hackers, each was a proof of arcane and technical mastery: a new route through some defence or the identification of a new vulnerability. But each was a revelation of another kind too. Every crescendo on these DEFCON stages meant one thing: power. Each hack let them cause things to happen, stop things happening, to learn things or to hide them. Each was proof that they could make different parts of digital life act according to their command. Each was a demonstration of the coercive kind of power these hackers hold over technology, and so all of us.[12]

'OK chaps, so we're only manipulating a byte at a time, so it will explore "inc [0x0000000c]", "inc [0x0000a100]", "inc [0x00040000]", and "inc [0x08000000]", but it will never search "inc [0x0804a10c]".' Sleepily contemplating a twenty-foot-high screen, I was letting the technical stuff wash over me (or, really, over my head). The screen was now displaying 'mov eax, [ecx + 8 * edx], of{1a-1f}xx'. Then I suddenly started awake. Everyone was on their feet, cheering. The person next to me had pulled open a frothing can of beer in celebration. The hack had been an intricate one. They had built something called a tunnelling algorithm to comb (hacker lingo: to fuzz) an Intel microprocessor. Baked on the chip itself were instructions that allows the microprocessor to work. And the hacker was now revealing what he found: hidden instructions that weren't in the manual and for which there is no explanation. Flaws? Bugs? Or worse, secrets

12 Hackers fight on both the defensive and offensive sides of cybersecurity, so also demonstrated was their capacity to protect us. The very fact that these hackers were making their discoveries public implied, usually, that they were more the latter than the former – but you never know.

and backdoors! On the screen, the hacker demonstrated how one of these hidden instructions locked the microprocessor and any computer using it.

'What about computers not connect to the internet?' another hacker asked. Many of the most secure systems are deliberately cut off from the internet – air-gapped – to keep them out of the clutches of attackers. But hackers don't need the internet. The man had another idea – light! Hack with light. In a dour monotone, he showed the audience how to send instructions through the air using light, and into the ambient light sensors of the computer, the things that adjust the screen to different light conditions. The huge screens around the room cut to a live video on the stage. A laptop and a bulb, connected to a small circuitboard by a few wires, stood in front of a normal laptop, not connected to the internet. The bulb started to flash, an impossibly fast Morse code. Then – to rising applause – the laptop, not connected to the internet, opened the calculator program. In hacker lingo, this is called 'popping calc', and it's the hacker demonstration of ownage. It means that the hacker has achieved the Holy Grail: remotely programmable code. If you can get it to open the calculator, you can get it to open anything. The laptop, through the bulb, responded to his commands. He could make it run things, drag data out of it, do whatever he wanted.[13]

I watched hackers show how they could seize control of the huge turbines of wind farms and cause one to stop-start-stop-start-stop-start until it would shudder to the ground or burst

13 The same hacker then exploited this principle to hack the laptop with light you cannot see, and then with sound, and then with sound you cannot hear.

into flames. One hacker group called the Exploiteers seized control of cameras, printers, routers and doorbells. Another – a shadowy Chinese group – could receive calls meant for your mobile phone, and send calls as if you'd made them. I watched hackers bury a malicious payload into Microsoft Word. I watched them turn an innocent computer mouse into an attack vector, opening it up and injecting their own code into its micro-processor. DeepHack was an artificial intelligence that had learned how to hack into websites itself, and steal any data that was there.

But for me, the most alarming hack wasn't a set-piece revela-tion during one of the big talks, but happened almost casually in one of the hands-on villages. The village was small, by the scale of DEFCON, and when I walked in there were around fifty people milling around. Some were sitting in front of laptops full of code. Some were hunched over circuitboards, and some were grouped around the twenty tall, grey machines that were spread over the room. For the first time, DEFCON was hacking voting machines.

The room opened at 10 a.m. By 11.30 a WINVote machine had been wirelessly hacked. After that, they all started falling. Punch-card voting machines. Optical scan paper ballot systems. Direct recording electronic systems. All were quickly owned in one way or another. Some needed direct, physical contact. Others could be hacked remotely. Hackers found how to change the vote logs, lock access to the device, stop people voting and completely cover their tracks. I was terrified, but the hackers seemed almost bored. 'People probably stayed away', one hacker told me, 'because hacking voting machines is technically too trivial to waste their time on.'

Hacking the World

Hacking didn't matter much in the 1960s. To most people, mastery of a tiny number of incredibly expensive computers was a complete irrelevance. And although the early hackers were pioneers, visionaries, indeed even artists – the power they earned over the computer stopped the second they left the room.

Today, of course, nothing could be further from the truth. Computers are everywhere. We trust our lives to them. Everyone relies upon technology, but hardly any of us understand it. It just works – we don't need to understand how. Hackers have made it their business, their identity, to never stop asking how technology works and why. They do not accept, nor do they trust locked doors, black boxes, hidden code or anything else that might be used to control them, and they go to extraordinary lengths to break them open. To them, the technologies that surround us actually make sense. They are open; chips understandably arranged on circuitboards, obeying programmatic instructions that they can interpret, and throwing out data, wifi, radio frequencies or whatever, according to rules and laws that they have studied.

The people at DEFCON have a completely different relationship to the world around them. Because hackers understand how technology works, they understand how the world works. And because they know how the world works, they can use this understanding to shape it, and influence it. Reality has become a sort of playground that, with enough talent, skill and and in many cases bloody-minded obsession, will answer to their commands.

Classes within societies have often been divided by their relationship to the fundamental resources of the age. The primary source of wealth in agrarian societies came from cultivating crops and farmland. Land was its fundamental resource, and when it was organised – as often it was – into a small number of large estates owned and protected by a small number of powerful families, they sat atop that society's economic and social pyramid. They were a group who spoke a different language, maintained different customs, and whose rank, honour and privileges directly related to how much land they controlled. Within industrial society, there was a new class that, through not only land, but also capital, owned the mills, factories and mines, the means of production that now produced wealth. Owning a fundamental resource makes you different; it puts you at the very centre of how your society works and what it does.

In hacker lingo, to own, or 'pwn', doesn't mean you have formal property rights over it. But you don't need to legally own digital resources to control and exploit them. Hackers pwn a device when they get something to do what they want and that it wasn't originally intended to do. Pick a lock; you've owned it. Similarly, you've owned a website if you take it offline, or get data out of it. Hack a server so it thinks you're an administrator – pwnage! Computers are the fundamental resource of our age. And it is the hackers who pwn it on their own terms. They are not the only ones; others too own the digital world in different ways. But they, or certainly the most capable and successful of their number, are a strange new kind of ruling class.

It isn't a class based on family lineage or wealth. As with the TMRC hackers, being a hacker is defined by skill, knowledge and mindset alone. At DEFCON I saw a twelve-year-old American boy excitedly coding with a Japanese couple in their mid-sixties. A group of executives from an arms company traded coder in-jokes with a man covered in My Little Pony tattoos.[14] A man who worked for a large British auditor was teaching three American cyberpunks how to pick locks.

It also isn't a class that is coordinated or consistent. Hackers aren't motivated by any one kind of politics or ideology. Their views differ on many different issues and political conflicts. The Syrian Electronic Army is a pro-Assad hacker group. They have hacked the BBC and other prominent news websites, and flooded the internet with pro-regime propaganda. Anonymous, an amorphous hacker collective, has launched #Op Syria, and scrawled digital graffiti across the Syrian Ministry of Defence's website. There are neo-Nazi hackers, anarchist hackers, hippy hackers. A large slice of hackers, I suspect, think that politics is generally for losers. And, as we'll see in the next chapter, they also work on both sides of the law. 'White hat' hackers spend all their time defending computer systems against attacks by 'black hats'. At DEFCON, as in hacking in general, cybersecurity specialists and cybercriminals hone very similar skills and interests, sometimes together.

While I was at DEFCON, I managed a single hack: I picked a lock. You slide a tension tool into a lock, and insert a thin metal bar. The aim is to tickle each of the tumblers up, just enough. If the tumblers are too high or low, the lock won't open. But get all of them to the right level, and the lock – stupid lock! – thinks you're a key, and clicks open. For a beginner, it's frustrating and delicate work and for an hour I failed again and again. Finally, with my fingers aching, the final tumbler fell into place and the lock snapped open. Somebody whooped and threw a peace sign.

14 For instance, if you're a hacker, someone googling 'what is 127.0.0.1' is genuinely funny.

In some small way, I understood what the hackers get from this. You learn how something works. You notice the imperfections in that device. You use a method to turn that imperfection into a vulnerability and then exploit it. The device isn't doing what the maker designed it to do. It's doing what you wanted it to do. You, through a mixture of knowledge, skill, perseverance – you've owned the device! You have reached out and changed the world.

The TMRC-ers had been the people to feel it first. It had been an intoxicating, consuming realisation. Power was right there, at their fingertips. At first power over the computer was for its own sake – to make it do what you wanted because you could. But generation after generation of hackers have come after Richard and his friends. And they have seen their power over computers become power over wind-turbines, a power over doorbells, pace-makers, yeast and micro-chips. Power over computers meant power over the world. The hackers are not the only ones who have found new forms of power in the digital age. Nor do they agree with each other about how this power should be used and to what ends. But a new power elite has quietly, first underground and now stepping into centerstage, gaining in number every year, and joined – and defined – by a body of ideas formed some decades ago in a small room in a far corner of Cambridge Massachusetts, where a model railway now sits idle, gathering dust.

2

Crime

Subject: iCloud
USER: 23:44:05: Alright man, got an icloud, don't know how
long it'll last email@provider.com: password
SUSPECT: 23:57:45: on it
USER: 00:04:44: Nice one. She looks like one of those ones that
looks innocent but she is a slut, let's hope that shows in the
backup.
SUSPECT: 00:17:26: download, nothing good. She used to use
the password xxxxxxxxxx it seems.
USER: 00:19:59: ah fuck! I've got this one as well if you want
a bash. email2@provider.com: password2
SUSPECT: 00:31:41: will give it a go
SUSPECT: 01:04:43: some win there. <LINK> but just under-
wear. Give it half hour or so to upload, 13 pics.
USER: 22:35:58: Ah bastard, seen those 2 before, was hoping
she had more. Cheers again bud.

Operation Field-day

'This is the third phase of Operation Field-day. This phase relates to a person by the name of . . . He lives at 1 . . . Road, with a postcode of . . . Our aim is to operate a warrant under Section 8 of PACE. The suspect will also be arrested. His arrest is necessary to protect vulnerable persons and property.'

A photo of the suspect is silently passed around. He's in his thirties, but looks many years younger. A thin beard, short, downy hair, unblemished skin and at a glance soft, even kind, eyes.

A sweltering July day was just beginning to draw into dusk. I was in a building in the middle of an anonymous, featureless industrial park. Neatly trimmed bushes, empty pavements, glass and brick; it could have been anywhere. It was a precisely, deliberately average building in a precisely, deliberately average place: walk through it and I doubt you would remember a single detail. But if you tapped one of the rotting wooden bollards that surround the building, you'd notice a difference – they are actually metal, and would probably stand up to a tank. The front door of the building was blast-proof and, inside, a small sign said that the awareness level was 'heightened'. Framed portraits – one after the other – neatly lined the wall. An Uzi sub-machine gun. A yacht. Thirty bin bags full of drugs. A fleet of Range Rovers. Photographs of goods seized from criminals. I was in a covert police headquarters.

Following the briefing, six police officers gathered equipment: stab vests, utility belts, CS spray, batons, mobile phones. Two huge black rucksacks were being filled with specialist electronic equipment, in case the squad needed to take copies of computer hard drives, crack into mobile phones, or scan devices to find specific information at speed.

I was here in this secret and nondescript place because I knew I had to get to a new kind of frontline. Power, of course, is often a question of conflict; the power of one group is determined by its strength or weakness in relation to another. Across the social landscape, balances of power are changing, finding new equilibriums, striking new settlements. I was here to learn about one of the oldest and most important conflicts of all: between those who enforce the law and those who break it. This conflict, I felt, had to be changing too, but what I didn't know was how. In the digital age, who is coming out on top? Is more power falling into the hands of criminals, or the people who sought to catch them?

The light now fading, we pulled out of the building in a small convoy. Three unmarked police cars quietly snaked through evening traffic, past emptying parks and filling restaurants. A radio squawked from the boot, but otherwise the car was silent. The sergeant turned to me: 'It's going to be an uncomfortable situation. There's a wife and a child there. They're going to wonder what he's done.' To really understand what was going on, to really understand criminal power, I had gone to the frontline of cyber-criminality. The third phase of Operation Field-day had begun.

Flawed by Design

'If you gentlemen could come forward. We are . . . ah . . . joined today by the seven members of the Lopht . . . ah hacker, ah, think tank, from Cambridge Massachusetts.'

It was 19 May 1998 and a hearing of the Governmental Affairs Committee of the US Senate was just getting underway. Seven young men in suits sat in front of US senators to give evidence. It was just like any other hearing, with one small difference. The witnesses were called Mudge, Weld Pond, Brian Oblivion, Kingpin, Space Rogue, Tan and Stefan von Neumann. 'I hope my grandkids don't ask me who my witnesses were here today,' said the chairman, smiling. The camera panned onto Space Rogue and Kingpin, quietly organising their notes.

They were from Lopht Heavy Industries, a hacker collective that operated out of Boston Massachusetts, not far from the TMRC. As seven of the most famous hackers and computer security specialists in the world, they had been invited to testify in front of the Senate Committee on Governmental Affairs. But there was nothing routine about their appearance in front of the Senate that day, nor in the evidence that they gave. They were there to deliver an extraordinary warning:

'If you're looking for computer security,' said Mudge, their spokesman, 'then the internet is not the place to be. If you think you're the exception to the norm you're probably mistaken.'

They all looked awkward, sitting there in front of the senators. Mudge had hair flowing down well past his shoulders, and he was in a suit he looked like he'd never worn before. But there was also a self-assurance to this owlish young man. 'How can one be expected to protect a system on a network where any of the seven individuals seated before you can tear down the network the system was built upon?' he asked.

Emerging in the late 1960s, inter-networking was designed to reliably and efficiently move information between the small number of computers that then existed in universities and the US military. Although funded by the US Defense Department's Advanced Research Projects Agency, the early internet was a project that was largely academic in character; a way for to move researchers to share data and, and to remotely access the research supercomputers that many of them needed. The way it was designed reflected the like-minded, collegial group of peer-academics who too part: a network with no central authority, that would allow anyone to join, and would obligingly shuffle whatever data you wanted to wherever you wanted it to go. 'It's not that we didn't think about security,' one of its inventors, David Clark, said in an interview to the *Washington Post* some years later. 'We knew that there were untrustworthy people out there, and we thought we could exclude them.'[1]

'I think they [the inventors of the internet and its early pioneers] succeeded fantastically,' continued Mudge. 'It grew up, it flourished, it struck everyone by surprise.' Throughout the 1980s, the internet had spread, but only within a closed, tight-knit world of people almost exclusively within academic and government research organisations. It was a raucous but communal space, full of technically-minded fellow travellers, 'a bunch of geeks who didn't have any intention of destroying the network', as another of its inventors, Vint Cerf, fondly recalled. Few outsiders had heard of it, but, for those on the inside, it was almost entirely free of crime.

The 1990s saw the first dot-com boom. It saw the first slew of companies with the mass consumer in their sights. Millions joined, and then millions more. 'Now big business is saying let's jump

1   www.washingtonpost.com/sf/business/2015/05/30/net-of-insecurity-part-1/?utm_term=.29f3199e1075

on board and make some money off of this,' said Mudge. From the online geek-commune of the 1980s, the internet was main-streaming. Opened up to everyone, virtual life was fast becoming part of normal life. Its inventors couldn't keep untrustworthy people away from the internet forever.

Now Lopht was warning about a new danger. 'While the technology still works, it's being asked to perform tasks it was never intended to,' said Mudge. While the uses of the internet had changed enormously, the basic technology, the protocols and plumbing that made the internet work, remained unchanged. The same architectural principles that had worked for a network of researchers were now used by banks, retailers, normal people and, of course, criminals too.

If you let this happen, the hackers were saying on that portentous day in 1998, if you let a Cold War academic information exchange system become everybody's bank, their shopping mall and their private diary, there will be terrible consequences.

Of course, the senators didn't listen.

One morning in 2015, a 28-year-old woman called Susan from the east of England woke up and discovered she couldn't log onto her Facebook or Twitter accounts.[2] She couldn't control them because somebody else was. They were sharing a stream of photographs to all of her contacts, including her family, friends and colleagues. Horrified, she watched as image after image appeared. They were all sexually explicit, private pictures of her.

Susan had been the victim of a horrific, violating – misogynistic – kind of robbery while she slept. Her Twitter and Facebook

2 Details, including the names of the victims have been changed

accounts had been stolen, but also her Apple iCloud account, and with it every picture, every text, every call, every WhatsApp message that had passed through her iPhone. A mysterious attacker had captured both her public and private digital life, and had turned both against her. She complained to the police, but nothing happened. There wasn't much, she was told, that they could do. I couldn't begin to imagine how powerless she must have felt.

Eventually, the images stopped. But then, in 2016, the same nightmare happened again. Again, her iCloud account was seized. Again, sexual images of her were shared on the internet, but this time even more widely. She found herself on shaming sites, amateur porn sites, often with her full name and contact details. She was flooded with calls and messages from nameless, faceless men all over the world, propositioning her, offering to help her, or simply gloating.

'The victim had all sorts of anxiety and stress issues, as you can imagine.' Brandon[3] is a detective constable in the police force that covered the area where Susan lived. After the second time it happened, the victim went to the police again for help, but this time the case reached Brandon, just after he'd joined his new team.

Deep within the police headquarters is a room without any window to the outside world, and full of power computers, all, I learned, seized from paedophiles. The six officers here specialise in 'cyber-dependent' crime; crime only possible due to the internet.[4] Formally, this is the office of the police force's Serious

---

3 Not his real name
4 Technically, there are eight different categories of cyber-dependent crime used by the UK Home Office. Computer Virus/Malware/Spyware; Denial of Service Attack; Denial of Service Attack Extortion; Hacking – Server; Hacking – Personal; Hacking – Social Media and Email; Hacking – PBX/Dial Through; Hacking Extortion.

Crime Directorate, Cyber Crime Unit. But everyone calls it the 'Batcave'. And it is Brandon's office.

'I'm a geek,' Brandon said, grinning, as he introduced himself. 'I experiment with stuff. I keep up to date with the newest vulnerabilities – I write in C, Python, Java. I do a lot of digital design.' He mixed policing with a joy for pulling technology apart, for building things, for trying stuff out to see if he could do it. Brandon wasn't only a police officer; he was also a hacker, in the true meaning of that word. After two years, the case had finally reached someone who could actually investigate it properly.

'We got Apple data for a month, looking at who was logging into her iCloud during the time of the attacks,' said Brandon. But rather than one attempt to gain access over this time, or perhaps a few, they found dozens. Some, of course, were the victim herself in those horrible hours after the attacks, desperately trying to regain control. But many of the computers that were accessing her iCloud account were faceless, ictimizat, made deliberately untraceable by the people doing it. Of all these incursions, Brandon found a single lead: one that wasn't from the victim, and that also hadn't been ictimizat. 'It traced back to a company that provided software for downloading iCloud backups.' The attackers had used a service to download the iCloud of the victim, and this was the crucial clue. From that company, they could find the person that had downloaded the victim's iCloud.

'What I found was astonishing,' said Brandon. 'This person hadn't just accessed one iCloud. They had accessed 272 other ones too.' A serial iCloud hacker! But as Brandon's investigation moved from one victim to 273 victims, he found something else that was

odd. He'd been expecting the victims to be scattered around globally – perhaps the victims of some previous leak of personal
information. But they weren't. They were all clustered around
specific towns. There weren't only lots of attacks. They also
seemed targeted.

Like any other detective, Brandon went from lead to lead,
following a meandering online trail that this serial iCloud hacker
had left behind. Methodically, he worked to turn possibilities into
likelihoods. Sometimes the trail vanished, sometimes it led him
into dead ends, but eventually it brought him to a small website
dedicated to the sharing of amateur sexual images. 'It's a British
community. It's all UK,' Brandon explained. 'It's all about people
looking for images of women living close to them – women that
they might know. That's their thrill.'

As well as the public face of the website, Brandon found a
private area. Restricted only to an inner circle of users who
had paid money, or shared images, to get in, this was where
special 'wins', as they called them, were shared. Here, naked
images of women were used as a currency, especially those not
seen before, and not in public circulation. Within the restricted
area there was a forum and it was here that Brandon made the
major breakthrough of the case. The reason the trail had led
him here was that, on the forum, there was a large, flourishing
community of people working with each other to steal iCloud
accounts.

'Online tonight from 11ish if people want some doing. Can do
iOS 9 and done quite a few recently for people with good results'
  'iOS 9, the lot, incognito'
  'Free if needed'

It was also here that Brandon found the suspect that we were now heading to confront. The messages that he and others left were deliberately vague, but everyone on the website knew what they meant. iCloud accounts, like most accounts online, have password reset questions, in case you've locked yourself out and there's no other way of getting in. Knowing the name of your first pet, your mother's maiden name, or where you first went to school is often enough to convince Apple you are who you say you are.

People would enter the forum with a specific iCloud account to crack. They would often know the victim and, hidden away on internet, would try to guess their password, or find all the information they needed from the target's public social media. The reason they came here was to find the people with the technical skills to actually make the hack happen. That was the deal: login information from one party, technical nous from the other, and they'd both get to keep the photos from iCloud itself.

The iCloud 'rip' would typically happen in the early hours of the morning. The attacker would use the information they'd been given to reset the password, gain access, and download the entire iCloud backup. By morning, the attacker would be gone.

Brandon had found a thriving community of men, waltzing into women's online private lives and stealing whatever they wanted. There were 3,000 users registered on the website, and the 'Official iCloud thread' had 19,312 views. Operation Field-day had gone from a single victim to 273, and from one suspect to hundreds, possibly thousands. But Operation Field-day was just a single glimpse into what has happened as we move very valuable and very private things onto a network never built to handle it.

The Rise and Rise of Cybercrime

Every year since 1981, the UK's Office of National Statistics has conducted the Crime Survey of England and Wales. It asks ten of thousands of people about their experience of crime over the last year, whether they reported it to the police or not. It has become the key barometer of how much and what kind of crime happens, and in 2015 the survey was showing the lowest amount of crime since it began. Fewer than 7 million crimes, the survey estimated, had been carried out in the UK over the last year, a whopping 64 per cent below its peak in 1995. When the results came out, the then UK Home Secretary, Theresa May, was able to confidently declare that 'crime has never been lower – meaning families are safer and more secure'.[5]

But then, in 2016, the Crime Survey was given a tweak. Two questions were added – one asking respondents if they had been the victim of fraud, and another of computer misuse offences. The response was staggering. John Flattley, the statistician responsible for the survey, summed up the results: 'This is the first time we have published official estimates of fraud and computer misuse from our victimisation survey . . . Together, these offences are similar in magnitude to the existing headline figures covering all other Crime Survey offences.'[6] In other words, these two questions had unearthed around as much crime as all the others combined.

5 www.theguardian.com/uk-news/2015/apr/23/crime-rate-ons-lowest-level-england-wales-police
6 www.ons.gov.uk/peoplepopulationandcommunity/crimeandjustice/bulletins/crimeinenglandandwales/yearendingmar2017

The survey estimated that 3.9 million cybercrimes had been committed over the previous year. Over half of fraud (1.9 million incidents) were cyber-related, and there had been another 2 million computer misuse offences. Two thirds of these involved a computer virus, and one third 'unauthorised access', like those that Operation Field-day was investigating.[7] This was pure 'cyber-dependent' cybercrime (as measured by the survey); crimes that could not be done without computers.[8]

When they started asking the right questions, the survey uncovered an enormous and hitherto unmeasured aspect of criminality. More than 40 per cent of crimes that people living in the UK actually experienced, it estimated, were committed through the internet, and these numbers only covered, of course, crimes people *knew* had happened to them.[9] Almost one in three adults had recently experienced some sort of negative incident online, more than all the adults surveyed who had been a victim of offline crime.[10] They had added just two questions, and their estimate of how much crime happened had doubled.

They weren't crimes you could see on the streets, but behind closed doors, cybercrime had been growing and growing. Online fraud had become the most common crime in the country. You were twenty times more likely to be robbed at your computer than mugged in the street. Your social media accounts were as likely

---

7 www.ons.gov.uk/peoplepopulationandcommunity/crimeandjustice/bulletins/
   crimeinenglandandwales/yearendingmar2016#new-estimate-of-58-million-csew-fraud-
   and-computer-misuse-offences
8 A much broader span of crime is what the police call cyber-enabled: crimes like scams
   or harassment that are possible without a computer, but increase in their scale or reach
   with the use of one.
9 4.9 million cybercrimes out of a total 11.8 million crimes are estimated to have been
   committed in 2016: www.ft.com/content/03e8674e-de47-11e6-9d7c-be108f1c1dce
10 Ollie Gower, speech to the Police Superintendents Conference, 6 September 2017.

to be burgled as your house. You were more likely to be targeted by a computer virus than all forms of violent crime put together.[11] Operation Field-day was part of something much bigger. Only in 2016 did we get the first picture of how profoundly crime was transferring from offline venues onto online ones. Crime hadn't really been falling at all; it had been migrating.

The global estimates on how much money cybercrime is actually worth differ, but it is doubtless an enormous industry. A 2014 report by the Saïd Business School in Oxford estimated that cybercrime costs the global economy $400 billion a year.[12] In 2015, researchers estimated its value to be somewhere between $500 million and $3 trillion, but for it to potentially exceed $6 trillion by 2021.[13]

In 2017, new government statistics revealed that nearly seven in ten large UK companies had suffered a cyber breach, with the cost of each breach averaging £20,000 to the company. The median cost of a cybercrime for a US business rose by 200 per cent between 2005 and 2015.[14] A multinational cybercrime gang called Carbanak has stolen as much as $1 billion from as many as a hundred financial institutions.[15]

If these estimates are right, cybercrime is worth more than the global drugs trade. The global energy industry is believed to be worth only slightly more, at around $7 trillion.[16] IBM's CEO, Ginni

11 www.reuters.com/article/us-cybersecurity-banks-idUSKBN0LJ02E20150215

12 www.eulerhermes.com/economic-research/blog/EconomicPublications/energy-global-sector-report-feb17.pdf

13 www.telegraph.co.uk/news/2016/07/21/one-in-people-now-victims-of-cyber-crime/

14 www.sbs.ox.ac.uk/cybersecurity-capacity/system/files/McAfee%20and%20CSIS%20-%20Econ%20Cybercrime.pdf

15 www.idtheftcenter.org/Press-Releases/2016databreachespressrelease.html); cybersecurityventures.com/hackerpocalypse-cybercrime-report-2016/

16 www.hamiltonplacestrategies.com/wp-content/uploads/2016/09/HPS%20Cybercrime2_0.pdf

Rometty, has called cybercrime 'the greatest threat to every profession, every industry, every company in the world'.[17] The former head of the National Security Agency, Keith Alexander, has called cybercrime 'the greatest transfer of wealth in history'.[18]

The human cost of cybercrime is harder to count. The UN has estimated that 431 million adults have fallen victim to cybercrime across the world at some point.[19] Another report has estimated that, in 2016, cybercriminals had stolen over 2 billion individual personal records across the world.[20] Around a quarter of victims of 'cyber-dependent' crime are vulnerable, the UK police believe, and are most likely to be aged between forty and forty-nine, live in a big city, and describe it as having had a 'severe' or 'significant' impact on their health or financial wellbeing.[21]

'Facebook and Ebay are the most common places for cyber-enabled crime,' Brandon said. 'Facebook is usually harassment – it's a lot of domestics,' he sighed. 'We have a domestic abuse team, and a good chunk of their work will be social media-type stalking and harassment, or threats to kill.' A couple breaks up – but the former spouse can log into their partner's Facebook account on their iPad. 'If we split up, I may be able to look at your Facebook. You're moving on with your life – I'm able to monitor, see what you're doing. It's coercion and control. I can send messages from your account. Take over your life.' Breach of court orders is another big one for Brandon's team. 'You can create

---

17 www.ibm.com/blogs/nordic-msp/ibms-ceo-on-hackers-cyber-crime-is-the-greatest-threat-to-every-company-in-the-world/
18 www.zdnet.com/article/nsa-cybercrime-is-the-greatest-transfer-of-wealth-in-history/
19 www.unis.unvienna.org/unis/en/events/2015/crime_congress_cybercrime.html
20 Hiscox Cyber Readiness Report, 2017: www.hiscox.co.uk/cyber-readiness-report/
21 www.cityoflondon.police.uk/news-and-appeals/Documents/Victimology%20Analysis-latest.pdf

a fake profile in order to send messages to a complainant telling them to drop the case, that you're sorry. That you didn't really mean it.'. Perpetrators use fake accounts to be a fictitious third party, intimidating witnesses in court cases, , antagonists in a dispute as well, former partners or anyone else they, by law, shouldn't be talking to. 'It's useful to divide cybercriminality into tiers,' Jamie Saunders told me. He's the director of cyber crime at the National Crime Agency. I had met him to understand the span of cybercrime, from simple hacks to national shutdowns, and from crude to terrifyingly sophisticated. 'The bottom are the "have-a-go" hackers. The middle are more capable and organised.' But then there's the top-tier cybercriminals. 'There's absolutely no doubt', said Jamie, 'that some of the high-end criminals have become outrageously rich on the back of this – in ways that it would be quite impossible to imagine anyone achieving through offline crime.'

But what about the people who do it? 'We haven't seen conventional criminal outfits so much adopting cybercriminal activity,' Jamie Saunders told me. Old-school gangs, it seems, have been caught as flat-footed as everyone else by the shift of crime onto online spaces. 'We've seen entirely new kinds of criminal outfit formed,' Jamie concluded. And new kinds of criminal as well.

The Unhardened Criminal

It was evening by the time the convoy quietly pulled up to our destination. With the car idling, the officers scanned a large, red-bricked house with a white stucco front. It sat in the middle of a new suburban estate; an affluent, quiet commuter dormitory. Neatly planted flowerbeds ringed the outside of the house, and the curtains of the neighbours had started twitching. An officer turned to me, his thumbs hooked into his stab vest. 'It's amazing how everyone's windows suddenly need cleaning when we turn up.'

We sat in tense silence, watching the house, looking for movement, checking the cars that sat in the drive. 'OK,' the sergeant said. 'Let's go.' He and Brandon knocked on the door, it opened and they disappeared into the house. Minutes ticked by until, finally, the silence was broken. Above the hiss of radio, I heard that it had been the suspect's wife at the door. He wasn't home. Away in a conference in London, he was only expected back later that evening. Entering the house, we had around an hour before he came home. All of the different parts of his digital life had to be seized.

Wearing blue sterile gloves, the officers methodically moved from room to room, working only to the rustle of evidence bags being opened, and electronics – projectors, USB sticks, a PS4, lots of SIM cards, and the computer itself – being stuffed in. Upstairs was the cybercriminal's lair: a comfortable, domestic computer room. There were *Iron Man* and *Thor* posters on the wall, next to Captain America's shield. The couple's marriage certificate was perched on top of a stack of paper, and two doors down from the computer room, their child was quietly sleeping. But among the domesticity, the police became more and more suspicious. The suspect had a large box crammed with SIM cards for different mobile phones, and around a dozen different hard drives pushed into a corner. 'A normal person just doesn't have all this stuff,' one of the officers muttered as she crammed bag after bag with carefully catalogued evidence.

Then, there was a ripple of motion. The man's car had pulled up outside the house, and was sitting there, unmoving. Worried scenarios ran through my head. What if something went wrong? What if the suspect pulled a knife? Or tried to escape?

The door opened, and he stepped into his house. The suspect looked even younger than his photograph, pale and blinking hard in disbelief, looking around his house full of evidence bags and police officers. I'd read the private messages he'd sent on the forum: his obsession with the 'win', the naked photos, the advice he'd offer to new members, allusions he'd made to a mysterious collection he'd been archiving and cataloguing, and all the discussions he'd had about how to avoid getting caught by the police. He had felt invulnerable, invading the lives of others whilst remaining unknown, untouchable himself.

But his mask of anonymity was now ripped off, and all of that chatroom bravado had drained away. He was so shocked he could barely talk. He could barely even stand. Brandon stepped forward: 'I'm arresting you on suspicion of hacking iCloud accounts between June 2016 and June 2017. You do not have to say anything, but it may harm your defence . . .' The suspect's prominent Adam's apple kept wobbling as he vainly tried to swallow, again and again. Supported by the officers almost as much as led by them, he went out to their car without uttering a word. There was no resistance whatsoever. There had barely been a raised voice.

His wife sat stricken on the sofa. Sobbing, she spoke to somebody on the phone: 'He's done something awful. I don't know what he's done, but he's done something. I can feel it. Something to do with the internet . . . I don't know! . . . During the first year of our son's life . . .' A large aquarium sent out bubbling noises across the now-silent room. An officer accidentally stepped on a child's toy, and carefully put it aside, still wearing his sterile, blue gloves. This wasn't Hollywood. The raid wasn't remotely exciting. It was just tragic and sad. A family was in pieces.

A New Route to Power

Online offenders were, I was told, often like this suspect: not hardened criminals, but shy, stammering and awkward. 'You can't just profile the rough kids living on the council estate now as the ones that will turn to a life of crime. It isn't like that any more,' the police had told me. 'They're often kids that don't venture outside of the house. They're stuck in their room. You can be a different person online than you are in the real world. And no one else can see that.'

The suspect 'coughed' – confessed in police lingo – during the interview the night he was arrested. All the images that had been stolen were of women, and all were sexual. It was a gendered, horrible crime but it wasn't, he insisted, really about sex. He'd started breaking into iCloud accounts, he said, and kept going back for more. 'It was like a crack addiction,' he said during his interview. 'I don't know how I'm going to stop.'[22] He was glad, he said, that he had been caught.

22 He was not, it turned out, involved in the hacking of the original victim, but he was one of the most active members within the community Brandon had uncovered.

'They always want the best collection,' said Brandon. 'They want new and exciting things. After you've seen a picture a few times, it doesn't have the same appeal. If they've got good results from an account, they will literally keep visiting it multiple times to see if there are any updates.'

I wasn't convinced it wasn't about sex. The forum where he operated was exclusively male, their victims exclusively female, and their 'wins' exclusively sexual. It was undoubtedly about sex, but it was also about power. He had begun to feel a kind of control that he'd never had before. He could invade people's intimate lives without them even knowing. He had found a new opportunity to exert a form of dominance over women. And new kinds of people seemed to be drawn to the new kinds of power that cybercrime offered. There was something about the nature of this crime that had made it singularly attractive and available to him. It wasn't only new kinds of crime being committed. It was also new kinds of criminal committing them.

I met Mustafa Al-Bassam in Bloomsbury, central London. He was born in Baghdad, and still remembers the long and dangerous journey to the UK when he was five. From Iraq to Yemen, Yemen to Turkey, then to Albania. They took a small electric boat from the coast of the Adriatic, and after some time in a detention centre, arrived in Germany, then the UK.

Mustafa was quiet and thoughtful and, given the amount of chaos that he has caused, surprisingly shy. 'My computer was my primary form of entertainment,' he said. From the age of seven, he started learning how to code, sharing Flash games with his friends. As he reached his early teens, Mustafa made good money doing freelance work, writing scripts and creating websites. 'I'd spend most of my time online,' he said, all the time getting better at coding, learning more about how the internet worked.

'And then,' Mustafa said, a smile spreading across his face, 'I became a criminal. A very serious cybercriminal.' During this time, most people wouldn't have known him as Mustafa. They would only have known him as tFlow.

Mustafa's life on the internet was as much social as it was technical, and in 2010 he spent more and more time on a forum called 4chan. Started in 2003 by a teenager called Chris Poole, 4chan was a simple set-up: just a collection of boards where you could upload a message, an image or some video. It has since become more notorious, but back in 2010 it was still a remote, underground, largely anonymous pocket of the internet, and on it new feelings of identity and collectivity began to set its inhabitants apart from the mainstream. It grew quickly and soon millions, then billions of posts flowed through the site, all of them impenetrable to anyone not steeped in the thickly woven layers of lore, slang, inter-board trolling, in-jokes and running feuds that each of the different boards on 4chan quickly developed.

Something that many of 4chan's regulars could agree on was a hatred of the guardians and supporters of copyright law. 'Copyright has become a content control mechanism for corporations who sit on large swathes of intellectual property rights, rather than its original purpose of motivating creativees' said Mustafa. 'And it stops under-privileged people having access to software and books that could really improve their lives. To us that was unacceptable.'

Hanging out in Internet Relay Chats (IRCs), tFlow and his friends from 4chan began to realise that all the corruption and injustice they believed was happening wasn't something they needed to passively accept. 'Pirate Bay[23] was inspiring to me; they were encouraging illegal activities, but they were proud of what they were doing. They were breaking the law for a social and political purpose, and they'd do it in a humorous way.' They didn't need to accept the world as they found it. The internet had created opportunities for tFlow and his friends to take on organisations far bigger and richer than them.

For the next year, tFlow would join a number of internet collectives that aimed to use the internet against their ideological enemies. One was called Internet Feds, another Anti-Sec. The aim was, in Mustafa's eyes, 'not preventing crime, but doing crime to stop bad things happening. We were kind of like vigilantes. To me, crime was a kind of art form.'

One of their earliest weapons was called a DDoS (a Distributed Denial of Service) attack. They would flood the target website with requests for information and, overwhelmed, the website would become unavailable to everyone. DDoSing (although illegal) is seen by activists as an internet sit-in, and they are very easy to organise. It was used against the Motion Picture Association of America, then against a notorious law firm – ACS Law. 'They made a lot of false accusationsto people who were illegally torrenting [distributing] porn,' said Mustafa, but 'they targeted lots of innocents, and it was essentially a blackmailing operation. 'They were DDoSed and then the company accidently leaked their own emails showing they were operating a blackmail operation, causing their head lawyer to lose his license. I wasn't personally involved in the DDoS'.

---

23 The Pirate Bay is an anti-copyright online platform that contains digital content – audio, video, games, porn etc – which can be downloaded via peer-to-peer networks.

By December 2010, thousands of people were flooding into IRC channels associated with these hacktivist groups, mobilising against new apparent injustices. Then, under American political pressure, many of the world's largest payment providers froze the accounts of the whistleblower website WikiLeaks and announced they wouldn't process any more donations. The movement decided to launch a DDoS attack against Mastercard and PayPal, trying to knock their sites offline for all their customers. And as the Arab Spring started, there was another explosion of operations. But for tFlow and his comrades, knocking websites offline could only get them so far. 'I realised we had to move away from DDoS attacks and get into actual hacking,' says Mustafa.

tFlow hacked into the official website of the Prime Minister of Tunisia. 'Some of the Tunisians we worked with were arrested, perhaps tortured,' said Mustafa. He and his friends realised that the Tunisian government was infiltrating the Tunisian Revolutionary Movement's social media presence. The Tunisian government was injecting malicious code into webpages, trying to throttle the information reaching the revolutionaries. Fighting back, he created a browser plug-in to protect activists against this threat.

In May 2011, Mustafa and six others founded LulzSec, a group intended to be half political project, and half comedy. 'We realised that comedy and justice are intricately linked. People laugh when bad things happen to bad people. That's what happens in sitcoms. They get what they deserve.' Now they were targeting 'anyone who deserved it, basically', said Mustafa. For the next month, they went on an online rampage.

They got the transaction records of 3,000 ATMs in the UK. They hacked the American TV distributor Public Broadcasting Service (PBS) and posted a media story that Tupac Shakur and

Biggie Smalls had been found alive in New Zealand. They hacked Sony six or seven times. They hacked into an FBI affiliate – called InfoGuard – and obtained the usernames and passwords of FBI agents. They hacked games studios, porn websites, IT security companies, and sprayed tens of thousands of login credentials into public domains. Their final hack was a faked story in the *Sun* announcing that Rupert Murdoch had been found dead in his garden: melted after being exposed to a radioactive poison, 'palladium'. It was a querulous, heady, breathless whirlwind of cybercrime.

The 'fifty days of lulz' was brought to an end in June 2011. 'For the past fifty days,' the group's communique read, 'we've been disrupting and exposing corporations, governments, often the general population itself . . . just because we could.' But this bravado hid a growing fear and fatigue. 'We were getting tired,' said Mustafa. 'There were so many people trolling us, trying to discover our identities . . . I thought being arrested was possible, but I didn't think it was likely.' But one day in July 2011, he was. Hector Monsegur, 'Sabu', one of the core members of LulzSec, had become an FBI informant and helped to unmask the other members of the group. Mustafa was sixteen when he was arrested.

On 16 May 2013 at Southwark Crown Court, alongside Ryan Cleary (aka ViraL), Ryan Ackroyd (aka Kayla) and Jake Davis (aka Topiary), Mustafa stood to answer a long charge sheet. The group's charges included using online DDoS attacks to crash the websites of the United States Airforce, the CIA, the FBI, the Serious Organised Crime Agency, Sony and Nintendo. It was alleged they stole personal data belonging to millions of people, and put also put private information – including credit card details – online, causing damages estimated in the millions of pounds. All four defendants pleaded guilty, and Mustafa, then eighteen, was sentenced to twenty months in prison, suspended for two years, and 500 hours of unpaid community work.

Mustafa maintains that the chaos he caused was driven, in the end, by good intentions and political beliefs. But it was also clear that for Mustafa, as for the suspect in Operation Field-day, there was an attraction to cybercrime that went beyond the crime itself. There was a feeling of power and agency, a dark thrill at what could be done just by sitting behind a computer. 'I was a fifteen-year-old schoolboy in my bedroom,' Mustafa told me, 'but I realised that I could have a massive positive impact on the world through hacktivism, and revealing certain truths about corporations and governments.'

'Hacking is fun. It's great when you manage to get into the system, it boosts ego,' said Mustafa Digital crime can clearly give people an enormous, addictive sense of control over the world that they otherwise can't have.

Whether someone is stealing intimate photos or shutting down the CIA's website, cybercrime is a dark new route to power. LulzSec's 'lulz' had caused all kinds of damage and hurt, and aside from the large corporates and governments that they targeted, plenty of normal people had been caught in the cross-fire. Services they needed had been blocked; the personal details, emails and passwords of tens of thousands of people had been leaked online.

Did Mustafa hesitate? Did he ever think twice about what he was doing? 'You're very detached from the real world consequences. You're just typing commands into the computer,' he said, shaking his head. Sitting behind the computer, the criminal isn't confronted by the victim. They don't have to see them bleed.[24] As a way of feeling powerful there is, perhaps, little difference between cybercrime and many other kinds of conventional crimes. And in the impact to victims, crimes through computers, have no doubt, can be just as devastating. The real difference between offline and online crime isn't, really, why it is being done; or what it does to the people that it is done to. It is in how easy it is to do and the likelihood of getting caught.

Point-and-Click Cybercrime

The stereotype of the cybercriminal is the teenage savant pouring over binary code, and Mustafa, perhaps, lived up to that. But the reality, I learned, was far different. Committing cybercrime barely needed any skill, knowledge, time or money at all. In reality, it was so simple, so straightforward, that anyone could do it. Even me.

In terms of sheer numbers, the most common complaint that Brandon and his colleagues have to deal with is something called ransomware. It is a form of cybercrime where the victim's computer is locked by an attacker, usually until some form of ransom is paid for it to be released. Businesses have been quietly hit by ransomware attacks regularly, and global ransomware damage costs were expected to exceed $5 billion in 2017, up from

---

24 Humans generally tend to be ruder, more critical, even ruthless when they interact with each other separated by computers. This is a general effect called 'online disinhibition'.

$325 million in 2015.[25] In 2017, the phenomenon appeared on front pages across the world, as a particularly virulent form hit 150 countries. Called the 'WannaCry' ransomware attack after the type of cryptoworm that it used, it crippled Renault factories in France, telecoms giants in Spain, a Russian mobile phone operator and, most damaging of all, large swathes of Britain's NHS.[26] Thousands of appointments and operations were cancelled, and it even forced a small number of accident and emergency departments to close.[27]

With a hacker friend, I set out to commit a (mock) ransomware attack. To do so, I did not need to code. I didn't need even to think. All I needed was a new kind of product, one of many that are aggressively marketed in online gaming forums and on other online communities. The software was called Stampado, and was written by Rainmaker Labs, a hacking team that sells malware from a dark net market called AlphaBay. For the reasonable price of $39, I could simply buy a program that would make ransomware as easy as possible.

Stampado smoothly opened into a command and control centre from which I would manage my ransomware campaign. As a hacker sits down to begin a day of capturing victims' computers, they do not see a screen full of binary code, or forbidding, intimidating computerspeak. They see, instead, a list of options that run down the left side of a grey window: 'build new campaign', 'new proof', 'new unlock', 'settings'. Like any other piece of

25 https://cybersecurityventures.com/ransomware-damage-report-2017–5-billion/;
    https://enterprise.microsoft.com/en-us/articles/blog/microsoft-in-business/health-care-beware-the-rise-of-ransomware/
26 www.telegraph.co.uk/news/2017/06/15/wannacry-ransomware-north-korea-say-uk-us/
27 www.nao.org.uk/report/investigation-wannacry-cyber-attack-and-the-nhs/

software, there are even 'support', 'help' and 'about' buttons in case you get stuck.

Click: I'd started a new campaign. I set how long I wanted the campaign to go on for, and the message I wanted my victims to receive. Click click. 'Email for your victims to contact you' is a box that needs to be filled in, so I do. Click. The campaign is ready, and we have a file to save, just like any other piece of software. The only difference is that the file we're saving isn't a Word document or a spreadsheet. It's a payload. 'We wish you huge income!' says the software, helpful as ever.

The options for the criminal on how to deliver this payload are depressingly broad. You can load the file onto the internet and get people to click the link. You can camouflage the file as something else, and send it over email. You can put it on USB sticks with the word 'secret' on, and scatter them around car parks.[28] Normally hackers will send out a payload as a phishing exercise: an email saying you're locked out of your Uber account, your gym membership has expired or your season tickets at Arsenal are about to be reassigned. The possibilities are endless – anything that gets the target to click the link.

For the victim, the software is much less friendly. When the payload is delivered, a message appears on the victim's screen. 'All Your Files Are Encrypted. The encryption was done using a secret key that is now on our servers.' When encrypted, nothing on the computer can be opened; nothing can be accessed or saved. It is held to ransom, in other words, by the attacker. 'To decrypt your files you will need to buy the secret key from us,' the message

---

28 This seriously happens. And half of people who find one plug it in: www.theregister. co.uk/2016/04/11/half_plug_in_found_drives/

continues. 'We are the only on [sic] the world who can provide this for you.'

And now . . . the clock starts ticking. On the screen, six hours start to count down before a random file is deleted. Russian Roulette file deletion, it's called, a fun game where your files are whittled away one by one until, four days later, the whole computer will be deleted. The victim now has only two options: lose the files (or restore them from a backup), or pay up and hope. With the ransom paid, the attacker can send the code over to the victim and everything is unlocked.[29] Or not. It's entirely up to the attacker.

Stampado makes it easy for an attacker to run thousands of these attacks during a campaign, helping the user keep track of payments, unlock keys, and all the back office administration involved in running a criminal enterprise at scale. But I knew Stampado wasn't even the best ransomware available, or even the best from Rainmaker Labs. Running across the top of the screen was advertising for the latest product in their series, deluxe ransomware called Philadelphia. For $400 I could upgrade to something that had an 'easy-to-use headquarters', 'fully customisable builds (text, colors . . .)', and many other exciting new features.

This is off-the-shelf, point-and-click, drop-down-menu, on-demand cybercrime. Cybercrime with banner advertising. Cybercrime with a help button. Stampado and Philadelphia are just two of a whole market of services and software for the cybercriminal, competing on price and quality just like any

---

29 In this case, the victim would have breathed a huge sigh of relief when the unlock key, B87A4B28737A1FF1F7F12B3E8624FC1F, restored all the files. The average ransom demanded by hackers is also growing, reaching $679 per data breach in 2016, up from $294 in 2015: www.symantec.com/content/en/us/enterprise/media/security_response/whitepapers/ISTR2016_Ransomware_and_Businesses.pdf

product. Ransomware, droppers, downloaders, keyloggers, cryptors, joiners and crackers are all different kinds of crimeware that allow cybercriminals to break in, hide, take or control data or software. Criminal information is also easy to get. The details of someone's Visa Classic or Mastercard, with the number, expiry date and name of cardholder, costs around £28 to buy in the UK on the dark net. Cards with the same data, but a higher credit limit (Visa Premiums), will set you back slightly more, at around £40. Email accounts and social media profiles are more expensive, costing around £90 for login credentials. Corporate emails will set you back £350.[30] Then there's also cybercrime infrastructure. A robot network, or botnet, is a network of infected computers under the remote control of a cybercriminal. They are often used for crime – for distributing malware, or bombarding a website with information, and they can be rented online. You can also outsource hacking entirely. In one service, you simply submit the name and email address of the victim, place an 'order', and receive their password.[31]

Cybercriminals don't need skills or knowledge. They don't need to travel to a crime scene, or to confront the victims of their crimes. They just need money, and not very much of that either. Safe, convenient, comfortable and with rock-bottom barriers to entry, it's easy to see why new kinds of people have turned to cybercrime as a new route to profit, control and power. People who otherwise probably wouldn't break the law.[32]

---

30 www.equifax.co.uk/resources/dark-web-infographic.html
31 www.mcafee.com/uk/resources/white-papers/wp-cybercrime-exposed.pdf
32 The National Crime Agency say: 'We have high confidence in our assessment that a number of UK teenagers who would not otherwise be involved in "traditional" crime are becoming involved in cybercrime. This is due to extensive experienced officer feedback and lack of previous convictions or records amongst UK cyber offenders.'

The Big Problem

It was early in the morning by the time we returned from the raid. Lightning rolled across the sky, and rain silently tumbled onto the thick, blast-proof windows of the covert police station. Under harsh white neon light, the police officers sipped coffee and started eating a mound of chips. I watched as they began to seize each of the suspect's online identities; his email addresses, his social media accounts, his messaging apps. Message after message, file after file, they began to build a window into the suspect's life, as intimate and detailed as the ones he had stolen from his victims.

As the dawn began to lighten, I thought about the whole span of Operation Field-day; from the first complaint in 2015, to Brandon finding the forum, to the blanched, scared face of the suspect a few hours before, to this exhausted rain-swept morning in the police headquarters. It's true. Police, as well as criminals, have never been able to collect information on this scale before. Seizing a suspect's phone is often the best source of evidence there is. But that didn't seem to me to be the most important way that the balance between crime and law enforcement is changing.

There was much about Operation Field-day that wasn't surprising at all. That the crime existed wasn't surprising, nor, even, the size of the community that Brandon's investigation had uncovered. Lopht's warning had come true; cybercrime has become common. The perpetrator wasn't a surprise either. He was one of a new kind of criminal. So far, Operation Field-day was true to type – a single example of a much bigger problem.

There was, however, one thing about Op Field-day that really did set it apart. The suspect had been caught largely because he had been unlucky. Simply unlucky. Digital technology might be one of the best things ever to happen to law enforcement, but it is one of the worst things ever to happen too. The most unusual thing about Op Field-day was that it had actually led to an arrest, that it had been successful; indeed, that it existed at all.

Another operation had run in parallel to Field-day. It had two female victims, both of whom had joined different online dating sites. They had been contacted there, and exchanged letters, cards and heartfelt messages, connecting, they thought, with another lonely heart. Five months later they both believed they were in a relationship. 'It starts out with "an invoice hasn't been paid yet, I need a short-term loan",' said the investigating officer. Their new boyfriend said he was the owner of a manufacturing company. There was a website, paperwork; everything seemed legitimate. Then the boyfriend needed an operation, but the hospital wouldn't go through with it because there was a problem with his insurance. Then he was kidnapped by business competitors, and held to ransom. Between the two victims, they had sent over £1million to bail out their boyfriend. They had taken out loans, and borrowed from friends and family. Only the boyfriend didn't exist. He was a character invented by a gang of romance scammers. The police only learned about the fraud when one of the victims reported her fiancé missing when he didn't arrive at Heathrow airport. She thought he'd been kidnapped again. 'One of the victims comes from a very traditional Chinese family,' the officer said. 'She hasn't admitted to her family what she's done with all the money they've given her. She's lost a lot of weight; she suffers from depression.'

Unlike Field-day, it hadn't succeeded in finding the perpetrators. As she tried to pursue them, the investigating officer had run into a huge problem, one that most operations came up against: geography. The boyfriends' accounts were traced to Nevada, but that information might be false. The victims themselves lived in Macau, although one was a British citizen. The money launderers lived in the UK and the scammers themselves were probably Nigerian. 'If all these people were in the UK,' the officer concluded, angrily, 'I could have solved it in a couple of months. I've been working on it for almost a year now.' Of the £1 million paid over to the scammers, she had managed to recover £3,000, and she didn't think she'd be able to recover any more.

'Almost every single investigation', an officer told me, 'hits this same basic wall. You can't reach the victims; you can't reach suspects. When it leaves the UK, we can't get involved. We can't chase them. It doesn't matter if they're in China, Russia, Germany; we can't do anything about it, at our level.'

A scam, a piece of malware, an extortion, child abuse images – they all flash across the world in an instant. Criminals never need to meet their victims, nor be in the same country. Evidence of online crime is overwhelmingly held by online service providers, and the criminals themselves do not need to be in the same country as the services they access, where the evidence is held. 'If they use any service, any server based out of the UK, you're in trouble.'

Even trivial, obviously local incidents, often have an international dimension. The police told me about a school nearby that had got DDoSed (one of Lulzsec's favourite tactics), but the school used a service offered by Amazon, an American company, to host their website. 'And Amazon won't give that information out,' the police officer investigating the case told me. 'I need to formally go to the Crown Prosecution Service to go to Amazon – and that can take over a year.'

In this case, the trail of digital evidence led to a cooperative jurisdiction – the US – and here it can be only time-consuming and expensive to get the information. The UK has Mutual Legal Assistance Treaties – MLATs – with around a dozen countries, as well as the European Union, and these allow police, eventually, to gather evidence and contact people abroad. 'The process is so, so ridiculously long,' said Brandon. 'A lot of the information we rely on is IP data and that only lasts for twelve months. By the time we get that information through the massive loop that is the MLAT process, any follow-on information we need is lost.' MLATs are often costly to execute, which means fewer low-level crimes are investigated because the cost in doing so can't be justified.

Police investigations, however, often lead to jurisdictions that won't cooperate, and then there is almost nothing the police can do about it. 'People from non-cooperative jurisdictions can pretty much act with impunity,' one officer said. 'It's incredibly frustrating for us. Until we sort out international policing, the risk of doing crime is basically nil.'

A ransomware attack, so easy to carry out, is also an example of a cybercrime that is incredibly difficult to police. 'We get at least one a week, and not a single one has been successfully investigated while this unit has existed,' one officer told me. A person in Cambridge has their life savings stolen, and the trail disappears into Russia. Investigation over. A criminal's phone is seized in Essex and there are indications that a scam has targeted people in India. Investigation over. Victims, suspects and the evidence that linked them together are scattered all over the world. Crime on the internet – like anything on the internet – flows across borders with incredible ease. The only thing that doesn't is law enforcement.

The problem of international policing is partly to do with borders and countries. But it is also due to the whole way that law enforcement is organised. A tiny layer of only the most serious crimes are investigated by Britain's intelligence agencies and national bodies like the National Crime Agency. These agencies are truly international, working in and with countries across the world. Underneath them, there are regional organisations – like the Regional Organised Crime Units and Counterterrorism Units – that deal with crimes that are serious but reasonably small in number.

Below this, on the ground layer, over 90 per cent of police officers work across forty-three local police forces. It is here where the vast majority of crimes are investigated, and where victims are given support. Each is organised around a local patch, with its own leadership, budgets, policies – often even their own computer systems and equipment. Some of these constabularies are large, but many are small. Cleveland Police cover an area in north-east England with around half a million people living in it, and have around 2,000 staff. Lincolnshire Police employ around 1,000 people; Warwickshire Police 900.

Ever since Britain has had a professional police force, this is how it has been structured. 'Peelers' first appeared on the streets of London on 29 September 1829. Sir Robert Peel, the home secretary, had built a police force around nine 'Peelian' principles, handed out to every police officer as they joined. 'The police are the public and the public are the police,' said Peel. He wanted to describe a new contract between the public and the law that was based on cooperation, consent and voluntary observance of the law. The police's power, he thought, came from the support of the public that they were themselves drawn from. The police was a uniformed citizenry policing themselves, and local policing was at the heart of it.

Peel's model is still enormously important to the police today, but it is hard to imagine a more terrible organisational principle for investigating cybercrime. How could you expect observance of British law from people all over the world? It is not just people living in the UK who are asked to cooperate with the police. It is also giant technology companies in Silicon Valley and foreign governments. Most police simply cannot do what most cybercrime requires: operate across borders. In some constabularies – like the one where Brandon works – they do not contact people outside of the UK at all. Peel's model had worked for almost 200 years, but now – thanks to cybercrime – it is coming apart.

A Crisis of Law Enforcement

'Stephen, are we living through a crisis of law enforcement?'

Stephen Kavanagh is chief constable of Essex Police, the chair of the Digital Policing Board at the National Chief Police Council, and the national policing lead on Digital Investigations and Intelligence. The UK's 'top digital cop', as the newspapers call him.

There was a pause. 'Unless we start moving at pace, it could become a crisis. We need to transform at pace. Four years ago, I heard a chief constable say they didn't have a digital crime problem. I don't think there's a chief constable in the country now who doesn't recognise the scale of the issue.'

Speaking to Stephen and others at the top of the police, it was clear none of this was being ignored. If anything, the police are frustrated with how long it is taking *us*, the public, to wake up to how big a problem digital crime now is. 'There's a real risk', Stephen continued, 'that this is seen as being all down to the police. But we, the police, can't do it alone, based on the scale of cybercrime that we've now seen.' One of Stephen's colleagues, Commander Steve Head, said something similar in 2015: 'Because there is this hidden element to cybercrime we are not having a sensible debate about it because we do not understand what a huge threat it is. My view is that cybercrime is more of a threat to this country than drugs. This is not a problem that policing can solve. We cannot investigate our way out of this issue; we have to look at it in a different way.'[33] Again and again, the police had started to say that it couldn't just be them that took responsibility for law and order in the online world.

'Take the jurisdictional problem,' I continued. This problem, of all of them, had stayed with me. 'If a criminal is in Russia, and the Russian authorities are not going to cooperate with British law enforcement, the criminal basically can't be caught'.

'I think it's a brilliant challenge. The policing model is very reactive. It is not set up to deal with a spotty teenager from the Ukraine hitting 40 million IP addresses. How do we get on the front foot? Will we get into that country and secure that custodial sentence? Probably not. But are there other means of securing justice for that victim? If we know you've been defrauded and

33 www.standard.co.uk/news/crime/cyber-crime-is-a-bigger-threat-than-drugs-says-exfraud-police-chief-a2955716.html

where the money is, we should be able to hack the account – freeze the funding – and shut that account down.'

'Like mini-GCHQs?'

'They only deal with the top end of criminality. Most cybercrime will still need to be dealt with by local policing arrangements. There needs to be ways for some of the top-end skills that people like GCHQ have to be passed on to local police, of course with public support and the right legislative safeguards.'

It's clear that the police are contemplating some very big changes in what law enforcement looks like in digital spaces. Penalties for cybercriminals and justice for victims are likely to end up very different from their offline equivalents. Equally clear, however, is that the problem is too big for the police to handle themselves.

They have been saying, increasingly loudly, that a new contract needs to be forged; perhaps a new kind of agreement that refreshes Peel's for the digital age. This agreement can't just include the general public; it must also include the technology companies whose platforms and products are often the new frontline in the fight against cybercrime. 'I do not think the likes of Facebook and others are taking responsibility at the moment,' said Stephen. 'These are multi-billion dollar organisations, but are they delivering public safety? It's not being evidenced at the moment. They need to start stepping up. We've tried to be patient. There are moments of brilliance, but that's not good enough for victims.' But they are also looking more broadly to the public to help too. 'I can't be optimistic', said Stephen, 'until I see us working across government departments – from the Ministry of Justice to the Department for Communities and the Home Office. This is not just a law enforcement problem, this is a social problem.

'This is the most profound shift the police have experienced since Peel,' Stephen continued. 'We *will* adapt in a way more fundamental than anything since Peel's reforms.' Yet while everyone accepts that change at a profound level is needed, it wasn't what I saw happening. For all of the efforts of people like Stephen, Brandon and his colleagues in the Batcave, the reaction hasn't been anywhere near as great as the change in crime itself had been.

Fewer than a quarter of forces have, like Brandon's, a dedicated cybercrime unit.[34] The situation has probably got better in recent years, but in 2014 a report by HM Criminal Justice Inspectorate found that only three of the forty-three UK police forces had developed comprehensive plans to tackle cybercrime, and that only 2 per cent of police staff had been trained in how to investigate it. Just fifteen UK police forces even acknowledged cybercrime threats within their Strategic Threat and Risk Assessments. The report also identified 'a generally held mistaken view among those we interviewed that the responsibility for responding to a large-scale cyber incident was one for regional or national policing units and not for forces'. The average spend on cybercrimes across nine UK police forces (which responded to requests for budgetary breakdowns) was just 1 per cent of their budget.[35] One 2017 estimate by law firm RPC put the number of UK police officers specialising in cybercrime at just 250.[36] And this, lets remember, for a kind of crime that in volume is around half of the total that happens to people in the UK.

34 National Crime Agency: Gower's speech to the Superintendant's Conference.
35 https://inews.co.uk/essentials/news/uk/investigation-90-per-cent-increase-cyber-crimes-reveals-tidal-wave-computer-offences-sweeping-britain/
36 www.rpc.co.uk/press-and-media/cybercrime-prosecutions-fall-as-under-resourced-police-struggle-with-increasingly-complex-threat

The reason that the police are not reforming anything like as quickly or as profoundly as they need to is, partly , down to money. We have recently lived through a dangerous political fiction: that cutting police budgets was accompanied by a decline in crime. At the moment when crime began to migrate online, everyone thought crime figures were falling. And because everyone thought they were falling, revenue for the police began to be taken away too. In 2014, before the scale of cybercrime was known, Theresa May declared: 'Police reform is working and crime is falling . . . we have achieved something no modern government has achieved before. We have proved that, through reform, it is possible to do more with less.'[37] Overall, funding for police has dropped by around a fifth between 2011 and 2016, and in 2016 there were 21,000 fewer police officers than in 2010. So the period when the police force needed to begin to reshape itself in a fundamental way to respond to cybercrime was exactly the time when its budget was being slashed.[38] Indeed, it looks like some police forces are actually *decreasing* spending on digital infrastructure.[39]

'This is one of the fundamental issues,' said Stephen. 'What is the bandwidth of any local force at the moment – from dealing with anti-social behaviour on a council estate to homophobic abuse on Twitter? The bandwidth does not exist. My force is still trying to find savings after eight years of austerity and also finding

---

37 Theresa May, 'Lessons of Police Reform' (speech, 2014): www.reform.uk/wp-content/uploads/2014/08/Home-Secretary-Reform-speech-03-09-2014.pdf

38 To be fair to the government, they have recently set up something called the Police Transformation Fund.

39 Research by the Reform Foundation shows that local police 'forces are decreasing investment in digital infrastructure . . . Medium-term financial plans show reductions in IT investment in the coming years'.

resources for policing in the digital world . . . The infrastructure that underpins the transformation is missing.'

What we are seeing, he continued, is that victims and others 'are turning to other bodies to deal with their concerns'. What is at stake here is the basic relevance of police to cybercrime at all.

I came away from my time with the police depressed and worried. I had met plenty of officers, like Brandon and Stephen, who I genuinely admired, yet despite all their efforts we seem, I thought, to be living through an extraordinary moment. It is one that I don't think we've really admitted to ourselves, and I certainly don't think we're on the way to solving. Others, both within law enforcement and outside of it, might disagree, but there was only one way I could understand everything that I'd seen: it is a crisis of law enforcement. I don't think it is going to happen; I think it already has happened, and it will only get worse. For all the amazing benefits digital technologies have brought us, here is one terrible downside: crime is benefiting far more from these new developments than law enforcement. It is creating a rapidly growing body of crime that is almost impossible for the police to do anything about.

Crime has suddenly changed. Without most of us realising, almost as much crime now happens through the digital world as happens anywhere else. Some criminals have reacted quickly to all the new opportunities that have opened up for them. They have invented new ways to obtain power over people: whether it is breaking into people's private lives, scamming them out of their money, shaming them publicly, or taking on large companies and governments. They can move quickly because they are less weighed down by the ballast of offline life. They don't need

MLATs, or to argue for new budgets or to work within organisa-tional limits. Instead they have a constantly evolving set of tools that makes cybercrime convenient and unbelievably easy to do.

The police can't change nearly so quickly. They have been set up to enforce the law within the communities they are drawn from. Most are in local constabularies that aren't able to operate inter-nationally. And, in any case, we live in a world where international cooperation around law enforcement is reserved for only very serious kinds of crime, and certainly not the day-to-day variety.

A profound shift of power has happened. As cybercrime has risen, the police have become less relevant in actually policing it. Cybercrime is one of the most under-reported kinds of crime, because people simply don't turn to the police for help. There have been reports in the British press putting the level of reported cybercrime as low as 2 per cent, although it is notoriously difficult to know the exact figure.[40] Official estimates have stated that over 80 per cent of business fraud cases go unreported.[41]

This isn't just about the relative power of cops and criminals, however. At the heart of this are the victims: people like Susan who have watched, powerless, as their accounts have been hijacked and used against them. Or the many tens of thousands of people whose personal details LulzSec leaked online. The people who lost their life savings to a gang of romance scammers. Or the people turned away from NHS hospitals because WannaCry meant that they couldn't be treated. Millions of people are being defrauded, hacked, extorted, invaded and hijacked online. Between the police and the criminals are all of these, the people the law is

40 https://inews.co.uk/essentials/news/uk/investigation-90-per-cent-increase-cyber-crimes-reveals-tidal-wave-computer-offences-sweeping-britain/
41 National Audit Office, 'Online Fraud', 30 June 2017.

supposed to protect. As criminals become more powerful, their victims become more powerless.

This all is so serious, it undermines the relevance of the law itself. Because it can't be enforced, the law doesn't extend into online spaces the way it can on the streets. The power of political systems to pass laws to define some behaviours as unacceptable is being undermined. The power of the state itself to protect its own citizens is being undercut. As all of our lives become more digital, the law itself – the politicians who pass it, the judges who interpret it, and indeed the police who enforce it – are all sliding into a greater irrelevance.

The law is how we collectively control and civilise the most coercive forms of power – whether it is the power to take control over someone's life, to make the private public, to steal, to humiliate or control. It limits the kinds of power that we experience, and shields us – or should – from its bluntest, most damaging and abusive forms. This isn't just about a transfer of power; it is also about how power is controlled.

It was some months later, just as this book was going to print, that the first of the Operation Field-day trials went ahead. It was a great victory for the operation and for Brandon: a conviction and a heavy custodial sentence. Brandon himself was nominated for an award for the skills in digital investigation that he'd brought to this case and others.

That was, of course, entirely the problem: Brandon is an exception, not the rule, in policing, and so was Operation Field-day. This isn't how most stories about cybercrime end.

3

Business

'*We build products you can't live without*'

Larry Page, Google[1]

'*I've become an expert on how to increase economic inequality, and I've spent the past decade working hard to do it.*'

Paul Graham, YCombinator[2]

'*We believe that modern technology platforms, such as Google, Facebook, Amazon and Apple, are even more powerful than most people realise.*'

Eric Schmdit and Jared Cohen, *The New Digital Age: Reshaping the Future of People, Nations and Business*

1 www.businessinsider.com/larry-page-the-untold-story-2014–4
2 www.paulgraham.com/ineqold.html

The Valley

It was very early in the morning when my alarm went off. I got up immediately and stumbled bleary-eyed from my hotel room. Outside, the sun had barely risen over San Francisco, but warm sweat already trickled down my back.

I took the Caltrain – a double-storey, screeching silver monster of a commuter train – south out of the city, tracing the contour of the coast. The gridwork skyscrapers of San Francisco disappeared behind me, so too did the giant white cranes of Oakland's docks. I clattered through South San Francisco and Millbrae, Redwood City and Atherton. From my window I watched the neighbourhoods start to spread, suburban and balmy. Then I began to walk.

On my left, salt flats stretched out towards the horizon, a white expanse bright against the relentless blue of the sky. On my right, on a gently sloping verge of grass, was a billboard roughly twice my height. On it, four white fingers bunched into a first larger than my head, giant thumb pointing straight up, towards the sky. A few dozen people solemnly hovered around the sign, some taking photographs, others just silently staring. There, on a promontory jutting out into the bay, was a great crucible of power. The headquarters of the largest social network ever built.

The road to power can be winding and indirect, leading to places you'd never heard of, or imagined existed. But sometimes it isn't. Sometimes, power concentrates in a way that is impossible to miss. I had always known that sooner or later, I would end up here.

*

'The Valley', as it is almost always called by the people who live there, is more of a flat-bottomed basin. It hugs the southern shore of the long, thin, glittering inlet of the Pacific Ocean, called, invariably, 'the Bay'. Around the Bay and the Valley rises steep hillsides covered in redwood trees ('the Hills') that give the whole area its shape and boundary: you can see across it at its fattest point, and it takes little more than an hour to drive its length.

In 1848, San Francisco became a boomtown. Gold had been found in California and hundreds of thousands of people arrived to find more. They trekked overland, braved jungles and swamps, arrived in ships, from Latin America, Europe, China. It threw California into spasms of growth and change: new norms were created, ideas and beliefs, new ways of life explored. The new modernity was both brutal and exciting: fortunes were made and lost, legal rights were clarified and, later, gay cultures flourished in the tolerant society that grew up around the early adventurers. The world couldn't ignore the Gold Rush. It caused manufacturing and industry to boom, transportation and banking to prosper. It was a moment when the economy suddenly shifted, when new value was found in places where it wasn't thought to be, and when new opportunities opened up that that didn't exist before.

The Caltrain now traces another golden arc. In San Francisco there are the headquarters of Uber, AirBnB, the sky-high obelisk of Salesforce and Twitter's nerve centre, a huge building that looks a little like a Soviet department store. Menlo Park is the home of Facebook. Mountain View, Google. Cupertino, Apple. All just a few stops apart. This stretch of suburbs and skyscrapers, drenched in the Californian sun, is in the midst of another great gold rush. Another almighty pouring of wealth into this one small valley in

California. Another wave of migration and of new ideas and beliefs, another new modernity.

Until recently, the word 'business' would have conjured up images of people in suits, of boardrooms, spreadsheets and annual reports, of Wall Street and the Square Mile, of the FTSE and the Nasdaq, of mergers and acquisitions, and the giant, immovable corporate edifices of power. Or on a lesser scale, it would have perhaps meant transactions, customers, the accumulation of wealth, growth.

But today, although some of the key principles remain the same, business means something very different indeed. I had flown to San Francisco to visit the greatest concentration of financial power in the world, and there wasn't a suit in sight.

It's clear to everyone that the digital revolution has changed what business is, and how it is done. All over the world, industry after industry, market after market, has either been transformed by the Valley directly, or by the new models of business it represents. Companies here have become the world's most successful in almost every sphere: retail, advertising, recruitment, transport, telecoms, banking, film and television, fashion and information. But whatever the industry being turned over, it is being done by companies that – first and foremost – are technology companies.

They were the companies that built the platforms, apps, networks and devices are now the ways through which *we* increasingly buy things, find things, decide what to do and how to do our work.

These new companies have transformed the way business is done, and the way we spend our money. They have grown, and the larger they have become, the more power they get and even larger they grow. Data, networks and the capacity to turn both into money – these are king. Simply put, more users mean more data mean a better product mean more users. It is a 'cycle of dominance'.

I had arrived in the Valley to see what this new model of business looks like, but also to see what power it really controls. Inherent within the technology of this new economy is an operation of power that creates a single winner, creating giants that stand today as a challenge to the workings of capitalism. And possibly a challenge to democracy itself. The laws created to challenge monopolies, and protect free markets, rely on definitions that simply don't fit, and don't work, any more. Political power is increasingly incapable of breaking up the concentrations of economic power that dominate the world today.

Why has this happened and what kind of economic landscape are we stepping into? Will the wealth and control of markets fall to an increasingly small number of people? Will the decisions of a handful of companies have greater and greater say over all of our lives? Are these companies offering a world of ease, simplicity, efficiency and equality in business? Or a vision of hell?

Disruption

I sat on a bench a little way from the billboard, and tried to clear the fog of jet-lag. Sleepily, I looked up to see a small white delivery robot jauntily trundle past on six small wheels, followed by a bored-looking man carrying a clipboard. The robot continued ponderously down the sidewalk and paused at a crossing, in front of a wide black asphalt road. Eventually the lights changed, the traffic stopped, and the robot moved off. The man made a small check on some kind of form, and walked after it. A few minutes later, a small dog wearing what looked like experimental climbing boots walked past, its owner in tow. Shortly after, I was handed a leaflet advertising a new service in pet biometrics.

Silicon Valley was a strange place, but also one of contrasting weirdnesses. Twee mock-Victorian houses and cutting-edge tech. A place that thrived on openness, but required you to sign a non-disclosure agreement before you stepped into any office. It was a place with very few children, but also not grown up. A strange, Neverland kind of a place. It didn't have to deal with darkness, or the cold, or fear of war. There is world-class cycling in Marin. World-class skiing in Tahoe. It is a pleasant, relentlessly buoyant, optimistic place, at least on the surface. The Hills form a geographical boundary around the Valley that packs people in; it doesn't sprawl off into hundreds of miles of suburbia. You are either in the Valley, or you are not.

There was, I learned in the days that followed, a delicate ecosystem to the Valley. 'Founders' are the great dreamers. They start the companies, and are both the rock stars and wannabes A few become immortal. Everyone else fails. The venture capitalists are the lubricant of the Valley, the people who provide the money to take an idea off the ground and turn it into something real. Between San Francisco itself[3] and the sweeping Sand Hill Road next to Stanford University, a network of investors exists as the greatest concentration of venture capital in the world. More money chases ideas here than anywhere else. Tech workers are

3 Which is also a centre for finance as well as tech.

the middle-class multi-millionaires, the systems engineers, product designers, genetic technologists, user-experience specialists and machine-learning experts who worry about rising house prices and school fees. The two academic centres of gravity are hippy, counter-cultural Berkeley at the north-eastern tip of the Bay, and at the other end, smooth, expansive Stanford. But there are other centres. There are the invisible workers of the tech companies, for example – security guards, catering staff, drivers – who are struggling and angry.

The word that the Valley hums to is both their cliché and mantra: disruption. Disruption doesn't treasure tradition. Disruption doesn't tolerate the status quo. The kind of innovations that so many in the Valley are striving for are those that profoundly undermines the basic order of things. The Valley is a factory to think them up, finance them, build them, and scale disruptive offerings to the rest of the world.

Facebook's central plaza is known as Hacker Square. Clean white buildings are arranged around a broad central boulevard of springy asphalt. Underfoot are huge letters: H-A-C-K. Hundreds of people were milling around in this central space, some sitting at small clusters of tables in the shade of trees, some in small wooden gazebos and alcoves that are irregularly sprinkled throughout. A massive jumbotron screen showed what was happening on Facebook at that moment, far above our heads, as if from the heavens.

Unlike Disneyland, everything inside Facebook's giant campus is free. Around the outside of the central plaza is restaurant after restaurant: Magic Meats was serving barbecue; someone was cooking ramen noodles. There was an ice cream parlour. Stepping inside these headquarters was like a firm, warm, embrace. The software developers, artificial intelligence specialists, user-interface designers and others that work here have some of the most sought-after skills and talents in the world and there is a huge arms race between the tech giants to hire and keep them. Facebook, like many of these types of companies, does not have an office: it has a campus, an expansive patch of land supplying everything these workers needed. I stopped at one of the buildings and peered inside. It was an empty woodwork shop full of new, gleaming machines. Lathes, saws, a 3D printer, a 3D engraver. 'I'm making a bird table for my wife,' a Facebook employee said to me. A full, professional wood shop as a hobby. Free too, of course.

Across the road from Hack Square is Building 20. Designed by the world's most famous architect, Frank Gehry, it is the largest open-plan working environment in the world, its monstrous size genuinely hard to put into words.[4] It takes the form of a giant hangar, the roof around 30 feet above my head, holding beneath it a maze of silver piping and bundles of cables. At ground level, the common aesthetic is pink and wood. Within the vast internal space are islands, lines and squares of desks, variously broken up by small meeting pods of deeper mahogany, curved alcoves containing alcove kitchens with see-through columns of cereal and urns of coffee and juices. Soft, carpeted pits are sometimes sunk into the floor, where people sit and gather. Nothing feels regimented or repetitive. In any corner, there might be a wall made of blackboard scrawled in child's drawings, a single bike

---

4   Like with Facebook's address itself, there is strong tip of the hat to their MIT computing forefathers. Building 20 was the big wooden shed at the Massachusetts Institute of Technology where major advances were made in linguistics, nuclear science, acoustics and computing.

stuck vertically on a wall, a screen showing a live data feed, or a cluster of toadstool cushions. It is a vast sea of unique spaces that feels as much play-space as work environment. Black vending machines stand in regular intervals against walls, with the word HACK written in silver across the side. From them, you can vend batteries, a keyboard, a mini-projector, 16GB USB sticks, Mac chargers. All free.

The Gehry building stretches on and on, rolling into the far distance, impossible to see one end from the other. Peer, as I did, across this vast complex, and the only obstacles that break the sightline are balloons, dotted around, floating above desks, each with a number stencilled across the front. There's a 4, 1, 7, even a 10. Balloons are sent to celebrate 'faceversaries', the recipient's anniversary of joining the company.

The roof of this enormous building has been turned into a giant roof garden/nature reserve. I walked past wild forms of rugged green-brown grass tugged by the wind rolling in off the Bay. I climbed sculpted grass hills and passed cosy wooden gazebos surrounded by thicker, dark green hedge, passed fragrant rockeries and herb gardens snuggled next to juice bars. Footsore and tired, I reached the other end of the building and, standing on a bench, I squinted in the sun to once again look out over the salt flats on which Facebook's campus is built. Over on the other side of the road, thousands of amber lights blinked in the rapidly falling dusk. It was a huge construction site. Facebook was growing at a tremendous, ear-splitting rate. 'I've only been here seven months,' an employee told me, 'and I've been at Facebook longer than 38 per cent of the company. . .' I was looking at the construction of Building 21, and it was going to be 20 per cent bigger than Building 20.

The Rise of the New Gods

Both Andrew Carnegie and John Rockefeller were born into a society that was changing fast. In the middle of the nineteenth century, as California boomed, as gold started flowing out of those valleys, America was in the midst of a huge economic change. Both men were born poor, but both bore names that would become synonymous with their age, the industrial revolution.

John Rockefeller was born in 1839, in upstate New York. He became a book-keeper and started a food business, but in 1863 he entered the fledgling industry of oil. From his first investment in a refinery in Cleveland, Ohio, he made significant amounts of money, and continued to invest in industry. By1870, he was in a position to consolidate his growing basket of assets into a single company: Standard Oil.

Andrew Carnegie was born in Scotland in 1835. He arrived in America in 1840s Allegheny, Pennsylvania. Young Andrew worked in a textile factory, as a telegraph operator, and on the railroads. He noticed, like Rockefeller, that America hungered for the new basic materials on which the industrial revolution was based. But rather than oil, he concentrated on what the trains ran on, what the factories were built with. The essence of machines. So, in 1874, he built his first steel mill, for producing railway lines. Good, cheap steel hungrily consumed by a booming market. He and his associate bought other steel mills, and in 1892, he pulled them all into the Carnegie Steel Company.

Both companies were smart, competitively sharp, and grew fast. Standard Oil found ways to use gasoline that competitors actually dumped. Carnegie Steel found new uses for steel, and built better factories to make it. As they grew, they used their success to become ever more dominant. They bought up competitors ruthlessly, shutting down some and swallowing others. They cut rates to the ground where there were competitors, and in places where there weren't, they pushed rates up high. Carnegie especially 'vertically integrated' by buying and controlling companies up and down the supply chain, from iron ore fields and blast furnaces to steels works, coke works and rolling mills, and took out large shareholdings in competing companies. Carnegie Steel and Standard Oil, both huge and complex, were obviously different in lots of ways. But as they got bigger and bigger, both used their enormous heft to control the new markets the burgeoning new markets that they were in.

By 1890, Standard Oil controlled 88 per cent of the refined oil market in the US. By 1904, it controlled 91 per cent of production and 85 per cent of sales. By 1901, Carnegie had been rolled into an even bigger company, US Steel, that possessed a 60 per cent market share of steel production in the US, and an 80 per cent share for wire.[5] Both companies sat atop their industries. They didn't just sell oil and steel, they *were* oil and steel. They made and shaped the markets they were in.

What Standard Oil and Carnegie Steel actually did was a world away from the tech giants of today. But now there are, again, new drivers of growth and change, of shifting economic patterns and ideas of value. As there were during the industrial revolution there are new markets, new ways of selling and buying things and new patterns in consumer behaviour. And new companies and people that become synonymous with them.

5   http://repository.cmu.edu/cgi/viewcontent.cgi?article=1062&context=shr

They started above shops and in dorm rooms, made by groups of shoestring visionaries trying to change the world. Google was incorporated on 7 September 1998, based in a garage in California. TheFacebook.com (as it was then called), went live on 4 February 2004, launched from a dorm room at Harvard University. Amazon.com was registered on 1 November 1994. Its first offices had desks made from old doors in order to save money.[6] Apple was founded decades earlier, in 1976, though its renaissance is normally linked to the return of Steve Jobs in 1997.

The origin story of each of these companies is different. Each is complicated, and more often than not, disputed. But each was a little like the rise of Rockefeller or Carnegie. Sometimes they began as the underdog, sometimes as the first mover, but each started early in their market, with a cloud of ravenous competitors around them. In some cases they simply were better; in others they were just lucky. Google had a better idea for how the internet could be searched, and didn't allow advertising to pollute their results, unlike their competitors. Facebook was established in 2002, a small player in a crowded field. It was a simple service, but it was initially blessed by circumstance. Its founder, Mark Zuckerberg, was a student at Harvard, and Facebook was rolled out to college campuses one at a time. It achieved a critical mass in each, as friends, friends-of-friends, friends-of-friends-of-friends all joined in a cascade of mini-cascades.

Like Carnegie and Rockefeller's, these companies, too, were smart, competitively sharp, and grew fast. They bought competitors,they found value in what other companies had simply

6   https://mashable.com/2011/07/22/facts-amazon-com/#keMyNuRi7qqs

ignored, and they also became sprawling commercial empires that emerged at a time when when new resources had appeared, when new processes, ideas and ambitions drastically changed what people did to make money.

Other companies rose with them, across a huge range of economic activities that digital technologies and data were beginning to transform. There were search engines, internet browsers, video sharing platforms, app stores, payment systems, social media networks. Other companies followed later that – like Uber and AirBnB – brought their own brands of disruption to new industries too. But four companies stood out. Four emerged from their garages and dorm rooms to became among the largest, smartest, most powerful companies that have ever existed, so universal that they got their own acronym: GAFA.[7] Google, Apple, Facebook, Amazon.[8]

The way that each became dominant was also different, but they had common themes: their networks became more valuable than anyone else's and they attracted the greatest talent in the world to monetise them. It is a remarkable new cycle of dominance. But this time it is driven by a new raw resource. Now the rush is for data: extracted, refined, valued, bought and sold.[9]

---

7 In October 2015, Google created a parent company, Alphabet, which brought together its many companies, including YouTube and Android. As the new name is still not as well known, I've opted to continue to refer to the company as Google, or a specific Alphabet Company by its specific name.

8 This, of course, is also disputed. Many have added a fifth western company to this list: Microsoft. It also doesn't cover the tech giants that have risen in China. Tencent, Alibaba and Baidu have risen to similarly dominant positions there but within a state capitalist system their story is quite different and it is one that, for sake of scope, I'm not going to attempt to cover here.

9 Announced, indeed, as the 'Fourth Industrial Revolution' by the World Economic Forum: www.weforum.org/agenda/2016/01/the-fourth-industrial-revolution-what-it-means-and-how-to-respond/

A New Cycle of Dominance

The whistleblower inserts a small authentication key into his laptop, and rotates it to face me. A message is written across the screen:

*****WARNING*****
This system is a restricted access system. All activity on this
system is monitored.
****

'They can't track this?' I say. 'Look, it says it's monitored.'

'Trust me,' the whistleblower says. 'It's fine. They won't notice.' The black screen is scrolling rapidly with white code, sometimes pausing for a moment, a cursor winking in the middle of a wall of numbers. Then, the text starts rolling again, moving through layer of after layer of authentication and checks. Then, suddenly, the screen empties. The warnings disappear. We're in.

'There's a non-trivial dollar value attached to this,' he says, still staring at the screen.

'What are you getting them to do?'

'I'm getting them to look for you.'

I didn't know this was the plan. Unbidden, my mind starts flashing with all the possible parts of my digital existence that would be embarrassing to be confronted with.

GAFA, each in their different ways, built a company around enormous, ridiculous, mind-boggling amounts of data. 'Once data about you hits our servers', the whistleblower tells me, 'it's gone. Thousands of different copies fly off in all directions. Once you're exposed to one bit of the operation, you're exposed to all bits of the operation.'

He keeps coding instructions into the computer. 'What I'm technically doing', he continues, 'is building a data cube about you. I'm using certain bits of information, pulling in more data using that data. Putting it all together.' The white screen keeps mechanically scrolling downwards, each line with a small <carlm-iller> buried in the machine-readable code. Data is so copious within this tech giant, so woven into its DNA, that he needed to task thousands of computers, spread across data farms and clusters all over the world, to actually find and pull together all the information that is held about me.

The black screen stopped scrolling downwards. It was done. It took, in the end, 9,000 computers five minutes to find all the different parts of me spread out in the data universe of a single company. My cube has been built.

'If this were, uh, an Excel spreadsheet,' (I risk the archaic comparison, and pretend not to see him wince) 'how big would it be?'

'Thousands of rows. Thousands and thousands. Every time you update something. Every time you touch one of our services, every opportunity that we have, we're collecting data.'[10]

I have heard all the stats for how much data we now produce, and am, in truth, a little bored by them. But sitting face-to-face with *my* life as data still shocked me. There was too much to read through, too much even to scan. A good slice of my life, sliced up into code, copied, enriched and linked, sent spinning

---

10 You can do a version of this yourself. It's not well publicised, but Google lets you do a data dump of all your data. Google 'My Activity', go on 'Other Google Activity' and click 'Create Archive'.

in more directions than I could imagine. This was just one person, one request.

These companies don't just produce raw data, they also build or bought the world's finest refineries of it. Like Rockefeller and Carnegie, they have invented new ways of wringing as much value as possible from what they have. When they started, they hoovered up what others thought was waste, used it to find value and invent products and competitive advantages that no one else had thought of. Each built enormous infrastructures for storing and computing it. Enormous, flat, grey, high-security factory hangars sprawled across obscure locations, they are hidden from most of us, but they *are* the new refineries. Loud, visceral places of electricity and heat.

Making data useful was a subtle challenge. Each of the tech giants brought together teams of extraordinary talent and skill to build the analytical craft to unlock the value that it held. A data science emerged that built tech techniques to spot patterns, establish links and discover the consistencies or anomalies or whatever it was within the seething chaos of raw data that would be useful.

The whistleblower scrolled through page after page of data that had been collected about me. 'There,' he said, stopping at a line, 'that is your fingerprint. It's been built by AdTech companies. We use it all the time.' Technology companies, and especially Google and Facebook, 'fingerprint' your movements around the web. Identifying devices is one way, 'cookies' or small files uploaded to your computer is another. Sometimes websites have automated logins, but there are hundreds and hundreds of increasingly exotic and obscure ways to do it.

The 'fingerprint' shown to me was an effort to identify me across all the different devices and internet connections that I used.

It was made by a constellation of things I rarely thought about – my browser, the model of my computer, its operating system, whether I had JavaScript enabled, the cookies I had accepted, the device pixel ratio of my screen. 'It isn't perfect,' he said, but 'it's a pretty good picture of you walking around the internet, regardless of your privacy settings of course.'

This was here because of the final piece of the puzzle: money. 'We don't need you to type at all. We know where you are. We know where you've been. We can more or less know what you're thinking about,' Eric Schmid, the CEO of Google said in an interview with *The Atlantic*. Fingerprinting is an entire industry. A 2016 technical paper estimated that over 80,000 different entities were using over 700 different, increasingly exotic techniques to track people across the web.[11] Each of the tech giants began to make money in different ways, but a great deal of what they were doing was trying to understand you.I noticed that a lot of the pieces of data about me weren't actually 'real' or primary things that I had done. There were inferences, conclusions, probabilistic guesses about what I might be like or what I might do next on the basis of what was already known about me. This was 'metadata', or data about the data. And that's something that you can never know about, until you're shown it.

The wellspring of all this data was a network. Each company, in a different way, built a network, and these networks benefited in a particular way from scale. People joined Facebook because their friends were on Facebook. They downloaded Skype

---

11 http://randomwalker.info/publications/OpenWPM_1_million_site_tracking_measurement.pdf

because someone wanted to call them using it. If everyone is on YouTube, that is where you post your video if you want it to get the most views. You buy on Amazon because everything is available there at a reasonable price. Apple's network effect was the linking of all their devices – iPod, iPhone, Mac and iPad – together with iTunes. Google Search learned each time someone used it, returning better searches the next time, which meant more people used it. The growth of each network made it more attractive, which caused it to grow even more.[12] Each of these was a network effect.

Jaron Lanier in his book, *Who Owns the Future?*, explained the idea of 'siren servers'. Power, Lanier argued, was increasingly coalescing around ultra-influential computers. In the past, Lanier wrote, 'power and influence were gained by controlling something that people needed ... Now to be powerful can mean having information superiority, as computed by the most effective computer on a network ... the biggest and most connected computer.' Some of these computers ran financial trading, some insurance companies, some elections, others giant online stores or search services. But each was the most powerful and central computer in a network. Concentrated information means concentrated wealth and power.

Each of these things fed from each other. Enormous amounts of data made the methods to analyse it more sophisticated, which in turn made the data itself more valuable. Many data scientists wanted to work in the places with biggest computers, not to

---

12 Originally for ethernet users, Robert Metcalfe formulated this as Metcalfe's Law, where the value of a telecommunications network is proportional to the square of the number of users connected to the system. As each network gets bigger, it becomes exponentially more valuable.

mention the largest salaries. As each network got bigger it produced more data. This data made the company smarter, more valuable and more lucrative, all of which fed back into a better service that more people used. It was a powerful, self-reinforcing cycle that turned an advantage into dominance.

Much like it was at the turn of the nineteenth century, this economic revolution too had the tendency not just to create new markets, but also to create a tiny number of huge winners within these new markets. It created not peers, but winner-take-all monarchs. By 2015, more than half of the world's global population use one of GAFA's services. Two billion people regularly use Facebook, 1.2 billion regularly use Google. YouTube (owned by Google) has over a billion users, and so does Android (Google's mobile phone operating platform). Eight hundred million people have an iTunes account, and in the first quarter of 2015 Apple was selling over 550 iPhones each minute.[13]

Google has a 90 per cent share of general search in most European countries, and five of the six billion-user web platforms – search, video, mobile, maps and browser. It is top in thirteen of the fourteen commercial functions of the internet.[14] Not only does Facebook control the largest social media network in the world with 2 billion users, but its empire now includes WhatsApp (1.5 billion), Messenger (1.3 billion) and Instagram (800 million).

13 Martin Moore, 'Tech Giants and Civic Power', p. 9: https://www.kcl.ac.uk/sspp/policy-institute/CMCP/Tech-Giants-and-Civic-Power.pdf

14 Martin Moore, 'Tech Giants and Civic Power', p. 13. Of relevance to this is something called the Herfindahl-Hirschman Index. It's a measure of market concentration – how many different companies are in any particular market, trying to out-compete each other with better products, undercutting prices, better customer service etc. It's calculated by squaring the market share of each firm competing in a given market and then adding the resulting numbers. An HHI in excess of 2,500 is considered to be highly concentrated. The HHI in internet search is 7,402.

Google and Apple together share 97 per cent of mobile phone operating systems.[15]

Actually knowing the size of the tech giants is difficult, and guaranteed to be out of date well before these words hit the page. Judged by a measure called 'market capitalisation' – the public's opinion of a company's total value – the tech giants are the most valuable traded companies in the world. In the fourth quarter of 2017, Apple was the largest, at over $868 billion. Alphabet second, at $727 billion, Microsoft third at $659 billion, Amazon fourth at $563 billion, and Facebook fifth at $512 billion.

The Cult of the Founder

'It's super-weird,' the whistleblower told me, 'the cultiness of it. There's this idea that the founders of the unicorns have this kind of preternatural gift.'[16] In the Valley, the founders are referred to by their first names. 'Mark', 'Jeff', 'Jack' and 'Larry' don't need surnames. 'They actually print their sayings in the offices,' he continued. 'CEOs elsewhere are respected, but they're not seen as philosophers.'

Back in the UK, I met with Izzy Kaminska, a technology journalist for the *Financial Times*. One of the most important and overlooked centres of power that she has seen is how the tech giants are actually run. 'Technostructures,' she said. 'If you look at the kinds of shares they have, the founders and

15 Martin Moore, 'Tech Giants and Civic Power', p. 13
16 A unicorn is a privately held start-up that surpasses a valuation of $1 billion. They, like their mythical counterparts, are extremely rare.

owner-executives within the tech companies have more power than the shareholders.'

In traditionally structured public organisations, the shareholders that own them have a great say in what the organisations actually do. Shareholders elect the board of directors and cast votes in annual and general meetings to approve any major shifts of policy. Activist shareholders who own major stakes can change the direction that companies take.

'Technostructure' was a term invented in the 1960s by the economist J. K. Galbraith. He saw that there was shift in power within some corporate organisations. A technostructure was an organisation where an executive layer – the managers, administrators, scientists, lawyers – had more power over what their organisations did than the shareholders. Shareholders, he argued, wanted to maximise profit, but influential employees want to maximise the size and power of the organisation rather than maximise its profits.

In 2012, the founders of Google wrote their first letter to shareholders. 'In transition to public ownership, we have set up a corporate structure that will make it harder for outside parties to take over and influence Google . . . New investors will fully share in Google's long-term economic future but will have little ability to influence its strategic decisions through their voting rights,' they said.

It differs from company to company. At Amazon, control is linked to share ownership, and Jeff Bezos's stake of both has fallen from 25 per cent in 2007 to 16 per cent in 2017. But other tech giants have used different classes of shares to mean that they keep control of the company even as their financial stake becomes more diluted. Larry Page and Sergey Brin have an 11 per cent stake in

Alphabet, but have kept 51 per cent of its voting rights. Mark Zuckerberg has a 14 per cent economic stake in Facebook, and he too has kept 51 per cent of voting rights.

Here, then, was the final concentration of power. The direction of the digital revolution had concentrated into a small valley in California. The direction of the Valley was driven by a small number of tech giants who held huge, expansive concentrations of power, political and cultural as much as financial and techno-logical. And finally, there were the owner-executives atop the whole pile, with huge control over the direction of the tech giants themselves. The digital revolution concentrated into just a few pairs of very human hands.

Software Eating the World

The cycle of dominance that swept the tech giants to such power and size is one of the most important economic logics that the digital revolution has unleashed. But perhaps unlike previous epochs when economic dominance relied on more tangible assets, today's dominance doesn't seem particularly durable.

Generations of tech giant past have also been huge, and they simply haven't persisted. The Digital Equipment Corporation was beloved of many of the early MIT hackers, and became briefly bigger than IBM. Sun Microsystems also had a sprawling campus in Silicon Valley and at its height shipped more computer servers than its next three biggest competitors combined. MySpace was once the most popular site in the US, and for years the most popular social media network in the world. America OnLine –

AOL – seemed an immovable feature of online life. Who remembers these companies any more? The competition, the tech giants
often say, is only one click away.

The ghosts of slain tech giants loom large in the peripheral
vision of the ones alive today. As strange as it sounds, the larger
they have become, the more vulnerable their founders must feel.
True to the ethos of Silicon Valley, they were companies born and
made rich by disrupting the status quo. Now, they have become
the status quo, and that is terrifying.

Each has desperately sought to hold onto the energy and hunger
of an early stage start-up. 'Hack!' say the vending machines in
Facebook. 'Move fast and break things' is their motto. In 2016,
Jeff Bezos, the CEO of Amazon, sent a letter to its shareholders.
'I've been reminding people', he wrote, 'that it's Day One for a
couple of decades . . . Day Two is stasis. Followed by irrelevance.
Followed by excruciating, painful decline. Followed by Death.
And that is why it is *always* Day One.' 'Day One thinking' is a
term of high praise, I was told by an Amazon engineer. But if
your boss thinks an idea is 'Day Two', well, that idea won't live
to see Day Three. From tech worker to tech worker, I heard this
basic belief again and again: you are either ruthlessly disrupting
the status quo, or you are dead in the water and sinking.

Sir Nigel Shadbolt is one of the UK's most eminent authorities
on computer science and artificial intelligence, in a career than
stretches back to the late 1970s. He is the principal of Jesus College
Oxford, and recently he served as an information advisor to the
UK government.

I met him at his office at the Open Data Institute, a non-profit
company that he cofounded to champion the use of data for the
public good. Advanced computing 'has been shifting the balance

of power for the last fifty years, but people are really noticing it in perhaps the last twenty, thirty years, with the internet and web,' he said, leaning back in his chair. 'I think what advanced computing has done is provide the means for the production and control of power in an extraordinarily pervasive way.'

The power the tech giants have crosses geographic borders, markets and industries, disciplines and professions. Everything, it seems, now comes down to software. Amazon, the world's largest bookseller, is a software company. Today's dominant media companies – Spotify and iTunes – are software companies, and so are the world's largest advertising (Google, Facebook), telecoms (Skype), recruiting (LinkedIn), taxi (Uber) and payments (Paypal) companies.Advanced disruptive computing (something we often just call artificial intelligence)is being deployed across a vast range of different industries. Now the tech giants are among a tiny group of the world's leading centres of advanced computing and artificial intelligence, they are not really bound by any particular market.[17] Their capacities built in one area are readily applicable in another. Andrew Ng, the founder of Google Brain, an artificial intelligence team, said in a January 2017 speech at Stanford University: 'At large companies, we often launch products not for the revenue but for the data . . . and we monetise the data through a different product.'[18]

These companies are poised to take over large swathes of the economy, invading and, of course, disrupting one industry after

17 An idea I owe to the writer Evgeny Morozov, who has made a convincing argument that five companies control most of the world's data for AI, and that their use of it will expand into more and more areas: www.theguardian.com/commentisfree/2016/dec/04/data-populists-must-seize-information-for-benefit-of-all-evgeny-morozov

18 When he was then head of Baidu: www.theguardian.com/technology/2018/jan/28/morozov-artificial-intelligence-data-technology-online

the next. Google is now a partner of some NHS Trusts to process NHS patient records. Google made more than 170 acquisitions between 1998 and 2015, from 3D modelling software to social gaming, robotics to satellites. Amazon is a retailer, but it's now also a marketing platform, a delivery and logistics network, a payment service, a credit lender, an auction house, a major book publisher, a producer of television and films, a fashion designer and a hardware manufacturer.[19] Amazon Web Services, its cloud computing division, is three times as profitable as its retail arm.[20] In all of these companies, there isn't a desire to do one thing. There is a desire to do everything.

Software is eating the world.

Power and Monopoly

It was a predictably bright morning when I walked between the skyscrapers of Sansome Street. In the middle of the financial district, the street runs through the north-eastern quarter of San Francisco, and the stiff breeze from the Bay gusts down the long, straight streets. I went into one of the elevators, and stepped out on the second floor into a wood-panelled room with a long, gleaming boardroom table. In the middle of the table, surrounded by a sea of polished wood, was a small pot. In it were badges, sitting like battle honours from previous military campaigns. On the top of the pile, a large white button had L-B-J written in

19 https://papers.ssrn.com/sol3/Papers.cfm?abstract_id=2911742
20 www.usatoday.com/story/money/markets/2017/07/22/a-foolish-take-how-amazoncom-makes-money/103769610/

blue across it: Lyndon Baines Johnson, the thirty-sixth President of the United States.

Sean Clegg sat across the table from me. He had neatly parted, greying hair and, unlike anyone else that I'd spoken to in over a week, was wearing a suit. He'd worked on the senate staff of Joe Biden, and in 1992 moved into political campaigns, both national but especially in California. He was now a partner in SCL partners, a political campaigns consultancy.

Sean explained to me a little of what life was like as a political insider and campaigner in the state of big tech. 'Politics follows wealth,' Sean sighed. 'You worry about it on a lot of different levels . . . We're not priests here, but we're cause-driven.' There was another sigh. 'The concerns are many.'

The tech giants are the single greatest concentrations of power that the digital revolution has produced. They exploded to the top of the economy as remarkable centres of data, advanced computing, artificial intelligence, the owners of huge platforms and networks. But as they grew in size, these new forms of power began to take more conventional forms too, including political clout. Older and newer forms of power, I learned, began to feed from each other.

In part, there has been a longstanding reluctance, Sean said, for tech companies to have much to do with politics; it was a kind of oil and water relationship. They didn't seem to *get* politics. 'There was something deep-rooted in the brain chemistry of people who rise to positions to power in tech companies – an engineering brain – that prefers perfect systems and not the messy compromises that go with politics. There is view that we're above it, that we're sullied by it, and I think that still holds true as a mainline, old-school tech view of the world.'

Yet this ambivalence towards politics hadn't stopped the tech companies becoming more and more powerful within the political milieu. A new generation of large, muscular tech companies had arrived after GAFA, he told me, that were much more politically confrontational. Uber had challenged taxi regimes around the world and AirBnB had done the same for hotels.

'What you've seen,' he continued, 'and I know some of these people and I think they're wonderful professionals, is the top practitioners have left the Obama administration and migrated out here to California as fixers, to do this sort of street fighting that you need to do if your business model involves contravening local and state regulation.' Chris Lehane, 'the master of disaster', had moved from his successful crisis management and PR practice to AirBnB. 'He's over there, south of Market, running a multi-state, multi-city campaign on a full-time basis. Every city they go into, it's a street fight for them,' said Sean. The top Republican consultant in California, Aaron McLear, closed up shop last year to work in policy and communications for Uber. David Plouffe, Barack Obama's 2008 campaign manager, had a stint in Uber and then moved to Facebook. The names Sean rattled off went on and on.

Citizens United was a crucial decision by the US Supreme Court that found that the Election Commission couldn't limit the expenditure by groups to pay for their political advertising and communications. 'That basically eliminated federal regulation of campaign contributions. Not to sound like Bernie [Sanders],' Sean said, chuckling, 'but it's a system written for millionaires and billionaires. It's the Wild West of big money influencing political races, coming from the tech sector. Nobody's blowing a whistle on it.' It wasn't only that big money could attract big political talent. The rules were changing to make big money itself more politically powerful.

Corporate lobbying in the United States is typically dominated by defence companies, and also the telecom and energy sectors. But in 2017, for the first time, a tech company outspent any other company to influence Washington. The company was Google, and it spent $18 million, lobbying politicians on immigration, tax reform and anti-trust in Washington. Facebook, Amazon and Apple all broke their own company records for political expenditure.[21]

As Carnegie Steel and Rockefeller's Standard Oil grew bigger and bigger, public opinion began to swing against them. In 1903, the journalist Ida Tarbell published the first of a series of pioneering investigations into Standard Oil. Story after story emerged, as Tarbell, the mother of investigative journalism, laid out the 'bribery, fraud, criminal underselling and intimidation' of Standard Oil to an astonished readership. She documented what happened when a corporation eliminated its competition.

These monopolies became known by one of the new legal arrangements that they created. Rockefeller consolidated his control over the sprawling empire of companies that Standard Oil owned by creating a 'trust agreement', where the owners of each company pooled their ownership centrally. Rockefeller held 41 per cent of the shares in this new trust, which itself owned fourteen corporations and exercised majority control over twenty-six others.

---

21 www.washingtonpost.com/news/the-switch/wp/2018/01/23/google-outspent-every-other-company-on-federal-lobbying-in-2017/?utm_term=.b3e9bb6a20d7

Theodore Roosevelt came into power as the tide was turning. 'The great corporations', he said in a speech on Rhode Island in 1902, 'which we have grown to speak of rather loosely as trusts are the creatures of the state, and the state not only has the right to control them, but it is duty bound to control them wherever the need of such control is shown.'

The first anti-trust laws passed by Congress were those that targeted Carnegie and Rockefeller. They were the Sherman Act of 1890 and the Clayton Act of 1914. Both laws, in essence, were about keeping an open, level playing field for economic competition. The problem with Rockefeller and Carnegie wasn't that they had simply out-competed rivals. It was that they had out-competed rivals and then rigged the market to mean further rivals couldn't compete.[22] And beyond it, they had become powers so great that they became a source of domination and control. During the passing of the original law, Senator John Sherman said: 'If we will not endure a king as a political power, we should not endure a king's power over the production, transportation, and sale of any of the necessities of life.' Economic concentrations of power were confronted by a politics that sought to break it up.

Yet, from the 1960s, the broad set of concerns that had animated US anti-trust law narrowed. It has become concentrated on a single concern: consumer welfare. It isn't, now, about competition. It is now mainly about price.

Yet in many cases, the areas the tech giants have dominated aren't what American law considers a 'transaction'. They aren't selling a service for money. They are relationships where services

---

22 For a very good look at US anti-monopoly law, see the *Financial Times*: https://ftalphaville.ft.com/2017/09/01/2193133/podcast-does-amazon-present-an-anti-trust-problem/

are given for free, in exchange for data, attention and clicks. The 'consumer' isn't losing out, because the consumer isn't paying for the service at all. They are benefiting from it. Indeed, Google responded to anti-trust charges levied by the European Commission by pointing out, 'Search is provided for free . . . A finding of abuse of dominance requires a "trading relationship" as confirmed by consistent case law. No trading relationship exists between Google and its users.'[23]

For sure, there are some conventional markets where the tech giants are unusually powerful. Apple and Google together make three times more from app sales than all third-party stores combined. And unless you're in the tiny group of criminal bibliophiles who have stolen this book (which would break my heart), chances are you bought this book on Amazon, which accounts for 65 per cent of all new book sales (not just digital).[24] As we saw in the chapter on the media, Facebook and Google together take almost all the new money spent on online advertising.

In a world where the quality of your product in part depends on the scale of data you have and how many people already use it, barriers to enter the markets where the tech giants operate are incredibly high. They have more and fresher data to quickly detect competitive threats, and simply buy them out, in their hundreds. The multi-billion-dollar depths of the pockets of the tech giants mean that many start-ups angle to be bought out rather than compete.

That has meant that, by and large, in the US the tech giants have not suffered the same fate as Carnegie and Rockefeller. As

23 Martin Moore, 'Tech Giant and Civic Power', p. 19.
24 Jonathan Taplin, *Move Fast and Break Things*, p. 6.

Robert Reich, a former US Secretary of Labor under Clinton wrote in the *New York Times,* 'Big Tech has been almost immune to serious anti-trust scrutiny, even though the largest tech companies have more market power than ever. Maybe that's because they've accumulated so much political power.'[25]

Economic revolutions are not only about new technologies; they also deeply challenge the way that power is controlled. The tech giants have brought with them new business models and ideas of what is valuable and they have confounded conventional anti-trust assumptions.[26]

Sí, Se Puede

It was morning when I climbed up the stairs from the underground, and emerged in the middle of San Francisco at a station called UN Central Plaza. A work crew swung a high-pressure hose in long, sweeping arcs across the wide pavement, and on the other side another was throwing bags of rubbish into an open-topped truck. A man, right by the station, was wrapped in a grey shawl,

---

25 https://www.nytimes.com/2015/09/20/opinion/is-big-tech-too-powerful-ask-google.html

26 The only political institution that is really taking on the tech giants is the European Union. It has generally taken a dimmer view of Big Tech than its US counterparts, and over the last few years has launched a series of actions over its anti-competitive practices. Margarethe Vestager, the European Union anti-trust chief, has fined Google $2.7 billion for favouring its own services in its search rankings, has raised concerns over Facebook's dominance in the data it holds and ordered Amazon to pay billions in unpaid fines. French regulators have fined Facebook too, and the Federal Cartel Office in Germany has opened a case on how Facebook collects data. It's significant that they're doing it, but the action has been nowhere near significant enough – yet – to threaten any of the Big Tech positions in the markets that they dominate.

slumped against the wall, a needle sunk, openly, into his arm. Two others leaned against a metal trolley, smoking crack cocaine. Another ran in between the lanes of rolling traffic, gently pressing his open palm against the windows of the swerving cars.

It was as striking as the shining campuses of the tech giants. Ground zero of the digital revolution was creative, optimistic but also horribly unequal. A few stops away from those piles of wealth was a world of chaos and suffering. Silicon Valley wasn't just about concentrations of power, but also concentrations of powerlessness.

I spent that day weaving through the streets of San Francisco, through the Mission District, and by evening, after the light had fallen, I walked down one of the city's long, sweeping hills. I passed a tent city nestled under a giant flyover, booming cars flying overhead, and entered through two thick doors into a large building on the corner, the Multi-Service Centre, or MSC. Inside, a large yellow central hall had the words 'compassion', 'strength' and 'esteem' stencilled up on the wall. In a giant room above, there were maybe 500 men in a huge dormitory, some chatting, most just sitting on row after row of metal military cots, each spaced a few feet apart. Every dozen beds or so, a fan vainly fought against the Californian summer.

I was there with a man from San Francisco's local government, volunteering to help a technology company called Miracle Message. It was an app where homeless people recorded a message, and volunteers would try to track down that person's family and give it to them, if they wanted it. As soon as we began, Cornell (bed 64) came up: 'I need my son in my life.'

The people in that room had been granted a ninety-day tenancy on a cot in the MSC. There was also a long line of people snaking around the ground floor, waiting, sometimes for days, for a cot to become free.

The next day, far on the other side of the Bay, I walked through the low-rise, predominantly Latino neighbourhood of San Antonio East Street, San Jose. ' One of the first spot the Mexicans headed to was East of San Jose,' Maria Fernandez told me. ' At the front of a restaurant, we sat with Maria's colleague, Gabe Cardenas. Sipping a kind of thick, milky, cinnamon sweet drink full of ice cubes, Maria and Gabe told me how they are now part of a new generation of community organisers. They are members of a campaign, an important one, called Silicon Valley Rising.

'This area used to be called Sal Si Puedes – "get out if you can" said Maria. I wanted to bring you here, because right down there', Maria motioned down one of the streets, 'is Our Lady of Guadalupe Church. That was a gathering place, where Cesar Chavez starting organising.

On 31 March, California celebrates Cesar Chavez Day. Originally a farm worker, Chavez became one of the most important labour organisers of the twentieth century. He led strikes and protests, and through long decades of work forged a union to represent farm workers, winning legal victories and better conditions. He became an icon for the empowerment of labour, the original voice that said, 'Sí, se puede' – 'Yes, we can.'

Silicon Valley Rising was launched in 2016 for the forgotten and invisible tech workers of the Valley. The security officers, shuttle bus drivers, cafeteria workers and all the other people that might work on the tech campuses but that live in places like San Antonio East Street. For every job in technology, four others are created in the local economy. The problem is that, amidst the skyrocketing rents and cost of living that the new gold rush has brought with it, these four additional jobs often simply cannot support a decent life.

'We don't want the tech industry to go somewhere else. We want the jobs here. But we want to be part of those good jobs too,' said Maria. 'These are not little islands that these companies are on. They are – literally – in our neighbourhoods, in our backyards. In some cases, displacing teachers, public servants. It's up to us to push the idea that they are in relationship with our communities.'

Under my arm was a Spanish-language magazine from one of many small shops nearby. At the back of the newspaper, properties were advertised for rent. But they weren't entire buildings, or even entire rooms. The listings were dominated by quarters of individual rooms, and single couches, for rent.

'If you knock on any single door,' said Gabe, 'you talk to any worker here, they will likely say they cannot afford to pay their rent. They're likely renting out a couch. Or they have curtains or screens set up, and they're sharing their room with four other families.'

'Other families?'

'On *any* door,' said Gabe.

He was born and raised in East San Jose, 'about a half mile up,' he said. His mother had been a hotel housekeeper, his father a line cook. 'But yeah, man, this is home.'

Gabe had been a manufacturing worker in San Jose, making printed circuitboards for fourteen bucks an hour. 'They cut our wages, and at the time, I was like, "I need to find another job."' Google had just launched a same-day delivery service, a competitor to Amazon Prime, called Google Express. 'I was like "Oh my

God",' Gabe said, flailing his arms in mock excitement, 'one of the biggest companies in the frickin' world. So I ended up getting a job in one of their warehouses.' He shook his head at his naivety. 'I had the Google emblem on my shirt and everything.'

'We're unloading trucks, day in, day out. For low pay, and piss-poor health benefits as well. We had a lack of ventilation, we had to share back braces. Some guy passed out from heat exhaustion.' The warehouse Gabe was working in used to be an old meat-packing factory. 'They got it super-cheap. They didn't do much renovation to it.'

Gabe had a difficult, physical job, but not that different to ones he had done before. This time, however, he became angrier and angrier. The warehouse was across from the actual Google campus – the GooglePlex – right on the border of Palo Alto and Mountain View. As people passed out in his warehouse, there, on the other side of the road, people were playing hackey-sack on the GooglePlex's sunlit lawn or resting under the sign of their corporate motto, 'Don't Be Evil'.

'For me it was the big picture. We were living in one of the richest areas of the world. It's the inequality. That's what pulled me into community organising.' The warehouse wasn't unionised and Gabe spoke to some community organisers that he knew. 'It was underground, yeah, just a few folks that I trusted.' After he'd laid the groundwork, they broke cover and started collecting pledge cards. Under Californian law, 70 per cent of the workforce needs to petition for a union election. One hundred and twenty of the 150 workers in the warehouse came forward to support Gabe's call.

It wasn't actually Google who had employed him, but another company that worked on a contract for Google, called Adecco. It acted, Gabe thought, kind of like a firewall between Google and himself and the other people that worked in the warehouse. Adecco, Gabe says, tried desperately to stop the unionisation happening. 'We went through an anti-union campaign, where they pulled people into captive audience meetings, hours on end, talking to them about why it wouldn't be a good idea to join the union.' Relations between workforce and management got worse and worse, and Gabe was candid about himself during this time. 'I'm not gonna sit here and pretend I'm an angel.'

The end of his story wasn't a happy one. Google changed their entire business model, and did away with the warehouse altogether. Gabe and his colleagues all found themselves out of a job. But despite that, I left Gabe and Maria with a sense of optimism and hope. They were angry, but they were also hopeful. They knew that they had power. They were fighting against the most powerful companies in the world . . . and they were winning. 'There are workers', said Maria, 'that manage to make it into the middle class because of the organising. That's real. I speak to those workers every day.'

The campaign has had significant wins. They've pushed up the minimum wage, pushed through new policies on affordable housing, and unionised over 1,000 workers across Apple, eBay, Yahoo and others. 'With Silicon Valley Rising, we're definitely demonstrating that when we demand certain things, we have the power to make it happen.'

For all their power, the tech giants have a weak spot, an Achilles' heel: their own workers. 'We made all sorts of noise,' Maria said. 'Brand sensitivity is a big piece . . . I think our power comes, somewhat, from how much we can threaten their image.' These aren't faceless holding companies that nobody has heard of with no reputation to protect. From the way they build their offices, to how they speak about themselves, their brand and mottos, the big technology companies have spent a fortune to not appear like large unfeeling corporates, and it is enormously damaging and embarrassing to them when their own workers say they are. Silicon Valley Rising was using old-school labour organisation tactics, face-to-face conversations in a warehouse, the power of solidarity and collective action to inspire the tech industry to do better. 'It's that basic,' said Maria, 'believing you can do something.'

Progress or not, however, both Maria and Gabe think it's reaching a crisis point. 'From me, my perspective,' said Gabe, looking at me from under the rim of his cap, 'I'm angry every single man. Yeah, I just don't show it. We know we can burn this motherfucker down . . . I'm not saying that's something we'll do.'

Decentralisation

The Valley and the tech giants represent the clearest concentration of power of the digital revolution. But maybe things are changing again. That concentration of power is starting to be disputed and opposed – not by monopoly law, but by technology itself. A new wave of technology is bringing with it new possibilities for businesses, finance and work, many of which reject concentrations of power. Now there are new shoestring visionaries, feverishly making tech,seeking to usher in a different kind of world, a disruption of a different kind. This time the vision is for 'decentralisation'.

Eugen Rothko is a softly spoken 24-year-old German, and immaculately polite. 'Thanks for interviewing me,' he said as he came onto the line. He goes by the online handle Gargron.

Eugen had loved Twitter, but he didn't like how the service was run. He didn't like that there was one rule for everyone, set by a central authority. He didn't like that it was an American company that followed laws that, where speech is concerned, are often different from Germany's. 'It really ought to be a public utility,' he said.

Eugen decided to experiment. He began to build a piece of software that was open source. Anyone could download the code for free and see exactly what it is, and likewise anyone could suggest improvements or build their own entirely new versions of it. A few volunteers joined and together they worked to build a new social media network that looked like Twitter, felt like Twitter but was set up in a completely different way. He called his new platform Mastodon.

I brought Mastodon up on my screen. Its default colour was black, and in front of me was a long list of posts. Like Twitter, Mastodon is a 'micro-blogging site', where users post short messages that others can interact with. There was a list where I could see the posts of all the people I followed, and another where I could see if anyone was mentioning me in their posts. Very similar, in fact hardly different at all, from Twitter.

Eugen designed Mastodon, however, so that neither he, nor anyone else, would be in charge or control of it. Mastodon was a protocol, not a commercial service. It has no central server, and Eugen hadn't started a company to run it. Anyone could set up their own Mastodon server and effectively become a mini-Twitter.

After Mastodon went live, it did what hardly ever happens to new social networks. People actually started to use it. Other things had come before that were similar to Mastodon, but they were fiddly and difficult to use. Functional, not fun. Mastodon, in comparison, was sleek and accessible. 'I like pretty things. I want this to be useable for everybody,' he said.

At first mainly technical users got interested, and then small communities began to migrate to it. 'Queer people joined,' said Eugen, 'And Furries.[27] It comes in waves. There comes in a huge wave. Then it falls down as users go back to the commercial platforms. But it never falls back as far.'

In 2017, Mastodon passed a million users. But rather than all connecting to a central sever, they were spread across 2,000 different ones. Equestria.social ran Mastodon 'for all pony fans'. Scifi.fyi was for the sci-fi community. Bookwitty.social was for discovering books. One server was dedicated to Catalan users, another for computer fairies: 'as queer, friendly and furry as possible'. One Mastodon server sprung up for the G20; another, writing.exchange, was for poets, writers and bloggers. Mastodon.friendlydads.net celebrated 'the friendliest dads on the net'. Socialists, anarchists, Marxists, ecologists, greens, vegans, anti-racists and social democrats all had dedicated spaces.

Each of these servers is like a little self-governing island that sets it own rules, its own way of choosing the people who enforce the rules, or have no rules or authority figures at all. You're free

27 Reasonably hard to define, to be a furry is to belong to an umbrella group of different subcultures dedicated to animal characters with human features and characters. A furry might wear a fursuit, go to furry conventions, write furry fanfiction or draw fanart. For some it is a social thing, for others predominantly a sexual predilection.

to join almost all of the servers that exist, and if you don't like any that are offered, you can start your own. In Twitter, there is one set of rules for everyone, but in Mastodon, each island looks after itself. Each server also decides how to pay for itself. It can generate revenue from advertising, by using its users' data, by a straight-up fee. Eugen's server, Mastodon.social, is kept going mainly by donations.

They are islands apart, but not islands alone. The point of Mastodon is to connect each self-governing island up into something called the 'fediverse'. People who are on one server can follow and talk to people on another. When people connect to people in the rest of the network, they bring in content to populate their timelines. This has always been the dream of the internet – to create self-governing communities, for which people will vote with their feet.

Mastodon is still a tiny, insignificant speck compared to the major commercial platforms. But it is part of a wider backlash against the kind of centralised networks and systems that the tech giants have created. To many more people than Eugen, the emergence of the tech giants was never how the internet was supposed to be. And to many more, a simmering discontent has set in with the tech giants.Far from free, in their eyes we are now digital serfs, labouring on the enormous digital estates the tech giants have built. We are vassals in the new data economy, bound in a new kind of servitude to a new kind of feudal master. They know that it doesn't need to be this way, and in the past it hasn't been this way. And of all the technologies appearing on the horizon bringing their own kinds of disruption, there is another that is mounting an even more fundamental challenge than Mastodon to the centralised status quo.

*

It was 1992, and every day, from his home in Oakland, California, Eric Hughes waded through a stream of emails from 'The List'. Eric was a mathematician and he'd set up an electronic mailing list to keep the conversation going between himself a small group of academics, computer scientists, technologists and hackers.[28] He and his fellow travellers were gripped by a question they thought the greatest of the age: who would win the digital revolution?

The digital revolution, as they saw it, was poised on a knife-edge. Would the spread of technology usher forth a new world of autonomy? Or would it bring in an age of surveillance? Would the internet allow individuals to become truly free? Or would it be captured by the world of states, hierarchies and corporations?

They argued, debated, criticised and denounced each other, but within all the disagreements on the List, a fractious, pugnacious, confrontational new movement formed, focused on developing and applying a technology that members thought would be the clincher in the battle. It was called cryptography: the art and science of keeping secrets and identities safe. Those on the List called themselves cypherpunks.

Much like a number of other groups, communities and subcultures that formed around the same time, they didn't want the digital revolution to centralise power. They saw it as an opportunity to break apart old concentrations of power, not create new ones. The old world pitted against the new. Old concentrations of power versus new ways of dispersing it.

Decentralised systems, The List broadly thought, were less likely to fail accidentally. They are more expensive and difficult to attack, destroy and manipulate, because there are no vulnerable

28 See the chapter on the cypherpunks in Jamie Bartlett's book, *The Dark Net*.

central points that you can target to seize control of the much wider system. But the desire for decentralisation went deeper than this. Changing the structure of technology was about changing the structure of society. Decentralised technology would create a similarly decentralised society, one without the concentrations of data, control and yes, power, that centralised systems inevitably produced.

The ideologies that flourished on places like the List were various, but they could all find something to like about decentralisation. For the communitarians, it meant a world with hierarchy. For libertarians, a world without authority. For the left, a world without large corporates and banks. For the right, a world without states.

The cypherpunks knew that the future wouldn't be decided in a courtroom or at the ballot box. There was only one way that the digital revolution would be decided: through technology itself. Hughes sat down to write something that looked like their manifesto:

Cypherpunks don't care if you don't like the software they write.
Cypherpunks know that software can't be destroyed.
Cypherpunks know that a widely dispersed system can't be shut down.[29]

For almost a decade, the List was the centre of the crypto world. Hundreds of people joined, drawn to its strange mix of ciphers and radical politics, part technical to-and-fro and informal peer review, part learning guide, and part rhetorical sandpit. It shut down in 2001, but new versions quickly appeared. The most

29 www.activism.net/cypherpunk/manifesto.html

notable was called the Cryptography List, which was where many of the original cypherpunks migrated.

In 2008, it was on this list that a new poster sent a message. 'I've been working on a new electronic cash system that's fully peer-to-peer, with no trusted third party,' it began. It briefly laid out how the idea worked, and linked to a longer technical paper. The poster's name was Satoshi Nakamoto.

The reception was icy at first, but the community quickly warmed to it. The cypherpunks had long tried to create a system of 'e-cash' (that was also what Satoshi called it). Bit gold had been one attempt, as had RPOW and b-money, but none of them had quite cracked it. We are defending our privacy with cryptography, with anonymous mail forwarding systems, with digital signatures,' Eric Hughes wrote, 'and with electronic money.' In the eyes of many of the cypherpunks, money was a key battleground in the broader struggle for freedom. Old money suffered from a fatal flaw: it was 'fiat'. Governments and banks issued the currency – by fiat – and so had control over it. They could enrich themselves by manipulating it. They could spy on people using it. To the cypherpunks, banks and states weren't the guardians of the financial system, they were the corruptors of it.

Like Eugen's Mastodon, 'bitcoin' – as Satoshi's 'e-cash' was called – was a protocol that was published as an open source project. It was, really, just a set of rules that you had to follow if you wanted to spend, send, hold or generate bitcoin. The thing so striking about Satoshi's idea was that it had struck the technical Holy Grail of decentralisation. The method was arcane and complex, but the result was clear for anyone to understand. He had found a way for a network of peers to enforce the rules of bitcoin without central control. The idea at the heart of bitcoin was called blockchain. It was a complex but elegant idea. Satoshi proposed that 'miners' would act as bitcoin's auditors, doing the work of verifying each bitcoin transaction. As new transactions are made, miners check back through all the previous transactions to make sure they are legitimate. Miners verify blocks of transactions at a time, and, when they are done, add them to a chain of previous and verified blocks. This is called a blockchain – a ledger of all of bitcoin's transactions, visible to everyone and immutable. It meant that nobody could claim to give a bitcoin they didn't have, and nobody could claim to have received a bitcoin they hadn't actually been sent. The rules could be enforced without putting anyone in charge. No more centralised, capricious bureaucracies full of scheming, ambitious humans. This new currency would be enforced by the cold, hard impartiality of protocols without centre or core. It created consensus without trust. And it was only the beginning.

In the wake of bitcoin, a whole new world opened up, fizzling with new ideas about how to use blockchain to usher in – finally – an age of decentralisation. One of the most prominent was called Ethrium, and it was led by a university drop-out called Vitalik Buterin.

'So far, the "bitcoin" as a currency unit has taken up the bulk of the public attention,' Vitalik wrote in a paper to launch his new idea.[30] 'However, there is also another, equally important, part to Satoshi's grand experiment: the concept of a proof of work-based blockchain to allow for public agreement on the order of transactions.' It was blockchain that was important, and 'now', he

---

30 'A Next Generation Smart Contract and Decentralized Application Platform': https:// github.com/ethereum/wiki/wiki/White-Paper

continued, 'attention is rapidly starting to shift toward this second part of bitcoin's technology.'

The idea of Ethereum was to use the blockchain concept for far more than just currency. Vitalik saw that basically any transaction could be enforced by blockchain. It didn't have to be an exchange of value; it could be a mortgage, a loan, a job offer. You didn't need to write contracts in English that were secured by courts or executed by administrators. They could be secured by cryptography, and executed by an open network of computers that updated a public ledger, the blockchain. The point of Ethereum was to provide the technology to write new 'smart' contracts that would do what was agreed when pre-agreed conditions were fulfilled.[31] Once deployed, that script will exist, permanently and publicly, on the Ethereum blockchain.

Sarah Meiklejohn is an associate professor in Cryptography and Security at University College London. I had been told many stories about power for the book, and many strange ones. But what Sarah told me was the strangest, the most downright weird of all of them. She had been watching the emergence of Ethereum from its birth and, in May 2016, she had seen a new announcement. The Ethereum community, led by Vitalik, were pushing it one step further. The tech giants might be the largest companies ever to exist. But their astonishing vision was towards a world without companies at all.

---

31 For example, we both bet money that XXX is going to win the Swedish national handball championship. The stake for each of us is $50. We both load $50-worth of crypto-currency 'in escrow' into the smart contract. When the website YYY (which we both agree is an authoritative, fair source of Swedish League handball results) posts the result, the smart contract will read the result from there and give the full $100 to whomever of us is right. If it's a draw, well, we can code what happens then into the smart contract too.

The announcement was for the launch of 'The DAO': The Digital Autonomous Organisation. It was an investment fund that aimed to pool the money of its investors, and where the investors themselves would make decisions on what the DAO would invest in. But unlike any other investment fund, indeed any other kind of organisation, it didn't have a CEO, a board of directors or any employees at all. The announcement was that a completely new kind of organisation had been created, a new experiment in how humans could cooperate and coordinate with one another.

The rules were agreed in advance, and it had a constitution. In exchange for the money you put in, you got 'DAO tokens' that, a bit like company shares, gave you voting rights and a share of the profits. The plan was for stakeholders to write proposals for what the money should be invested in, and everyone else would vote on the proposals with a weight equal to the amount of money they put in. The terms of The DAO read: 'The DAO's code controls and sets forth all terms of The DAO Creation.' The bylaws, like everything else to do with The DAO, existed exclusively as code, enforced by the blockchain. It was an organisation controlled by software. If the world of business administration had astronauts, these were it, pushing the far frontiers (of business administration).

'It went crazy,' said Sarah. 'I mean hugely, insanely popular.' Money flooded in as people began to invest. 'It freaked out the founders and the longstanding members of the Ethereum community.' They had tried to raise $500,000, but within a few weeks, 23,000 people had put a total of $168 million into the DAO.[32] It became, at the time, the largest crowdfunded project in history.

---

32 Although by law firm Allen & Overy's estimates, half of the money came from just seventy addresses: 'Decentralized Autonomous Organizations', 11 July 2016.

The DAO was about to spring into action. The money was sitting there, ready to flow in any direction that The DAO decided. But before it did anything, disaster struck. The fateful day was 16 June 2016. 'I was on the DAO slack,'[33] Sarah said. 'It went into meltdown.' The DAO's investors watched as money began to drain out of it. The DAO's smart contracts were so complicated that they hadn't been able to make it watertight. An attacker had found a bug, a 'recursive send exploit', and it allowed them to drain the contents of the DAO without a vote, and without any project being agreed.

Technically, the attacker hadn't broken the rules of the DAO, they'd actually followed them to the letter. A day later, 'The Attacker' wrote an open letter. 'I have carefully examined the code of the DAO,' they said, and found a feature in it. 'I have made use of this feature and have rightfully claimed 3,641,694 ether, and would like to thank the DAO for this reward . . . I am disappointed by those who are characterising the use of this intentional feature as "theft" . . . I hope this event becomes a valuable learning experience for the Ethereum community and wish you all the best of luck.' The value of ether fluctuates wildly, but based on its value as I write this, the attacker had stolen over $3 billion-worth of ether.

Things then got even stranger. Under the rules of the DAO, the money hadn't actually disappeared. When the attacker had tried to take it, the money had drained into a last line of defence designed into the DAO. It had been put into another 'child DAO' where it would be held for forty days before the attacker could withdraw it. Time was ticking.

33 An online collaborative messaging and co-working system

'The DAO investors weren't willing to take this lying down,' said Sarah. They had a number of options: they could do nothing; they could change the currency so all the Ethereum that the attacker stole would be tainted, next to worthless. Or they could do something called a 'fork'. A fork was an actual departure from the code that would let them rewind time, reverse all the transactions that had happened on the blockchain after the DAO was hacked.

It was a terrible dilemma. Once the transaction is on the block-chain, there should be nothing you can do to reverse it. 'It was pretty sketchy,' said Sarah. 'There was a vote, there was a strong consensus to hard fork – to reverse it all, and restore the money.' And that, eventually, was what they did.

The strangest, weirdest, most confusing new kind of business in history had just suffered the strangest, weirdest, most confusing robbery. It was called a 'fork' because while the investors had created a reality where the robbery hadn't happened, it didn't extinguish the reality where it did. Both realities existed side by side, on different blockchains at the same time. Not everybody gave up on the fork where the robbery had happened. They called it 'Ethereum Classic' and it survived, even flourished.[34] A robbery that happened and didn't happen at the same time. Even weirder, you could spend across the forks.

The DAO was a grand new experiment in human cooperation. A failure, yes, but also a beginning rather than an end. Blockchain had begun to be used to make things possible to do in decentral-ised way that previously needed a central authority. There are

34 It is much smaller than Ethereum, but still has a market capitalisation of around $2 billion.

new ideas for blockchain communes. Blockchain is being applied towards decentralised file storage, computation, prediction markets, gambling. 'Initial Coin Offerings' create a currency that gives you a share in a venture, and there are ways for people to raise capital and also micro-invest in games, music, art – anything. Even social media platforms can function on the blockchain. Blockchain, in the eyes of many, is the single most important invention since the internet itself. It promises to remake how humans come together and cooperate.

The big difference to other more philanthropic, volunteer-led attempts to build decentralised services is that blockchain has attracted enormous amounts of money. In 2013, seventy-eight venture capital investments were made in blockchain companies, worth around $150 million. In 2014, 199 VC deals were made, worth just under $500 million, and by 2016, $663 million was invested.[35] IBM, Intel and others have backed the Linux Foundation's Hyperledger project, first announced in December 2015, to support open-source blockchain projects. The three largest crowdfunded projects in history have all been based on the blockchain.

However, just because a system is decentralised doesn't mean that power is decentralised. Decentralisation sometimes actually creates weird new concentrations of power. The great break-through of blockchain is to allow rules to be enforced in a decentralised way. As the DAO hack showed, the central Ethereum developers could decide to hard fork. So the governance of this decentralised infrastructure was in fact incredibly centralised. Sometimes small groups of developers can really call the shots on

35 PitchBook, *Fintech Analyst Note: Blockchain*, 2017

the direction that a decentralised service takes, and sometimes can actually reverse the blockchain when they feel they have to.[36]

'Developers are like politicians,' Joon Ian Wong, a crypto-currency journalist at *Quartz* said in an interview. Developers can change the rules, he explained, but they have to bring people along with them. They have to convince and cajole, and try to attain consensus. There is lobbying, there are factions, bitter infighting and bickering. And one of the key constituencies that developers have to win over is that of the miners – those who verify the record of transactions in blockchains.

SanShiangLiang industrial park sits on the flat grassy planes of Inner Mongolia. Nestled among abandoned, half-built coal mines are eight long, narrow hangars, sitting in a row. Each has a gently sloping roof, and the corrugated metal walls are painted blue and white. On the end of each hangar is the name of their owner: Bitmain.

Fifty staff work and often live at its sprawling complex. There is a dormitory, a canteen and a repair centre. Inside the hangars are rack after rack of winking, blinking machines – 25,000 in total – all built for only one purpose: mining crypto-currencies. At the end of each aisle, huge fans with blades over a foot long wash the machines with cooling air.

Probably ten or fifteen companies now have the vast majority of what is called 'hash power', the raw computational resources used to solve Nakamoto's puzzles in order to verify all of bitcoin's transactions and claim the rewards. The people who control mining

---

36 As for bitcoin, twelve people have held something called 'commit access'. These are the Bitcoin Core Developers. Only they can make any change to the basic rules of bitcoin. Only they hold the keys to turn a suggestion into reality. This is 'commit power', and it's a power that is handed from one of this inner circle to the next. A great and overlooked kind of power.

companies like Bitmain are enormously powerful. From second to second, they turn transactions into reality. If enough miners together decide to take their hash power away from bitcoin, it might set off a death chain spiral: transactions wouldn't be mined, they wouldn't be added to the blockchain, nothing would work. Bitcoin would become paralysed.

Sort of like . . . banks. OK, not completely. But what today's Bitcoin mining has in common with banks is that there are a small number of powerful institutions that have invested the fortunes required for the vast infrastructure needed to make financial systems work. They are the financial lubricant that allows people to exchange value and make trades.

Cryptocurrencies – especially those like bitcoin and Ethereum – rocketed up in value after they were first launched, becoming a sort of digital gold that was hoarded. HODL, people called it: 'holding on for dear life'. The actual ownership of crypto-currencies is also vastly unequal. It is estimated that around 1,000 holders of bitcoin – known as 'whales' – own about 40 per cent of the total amount.[37] As far as we know, its main owners are billionaire venture capitalists. Alongside them, 120 hedge funds are focused on crypto-currencies, holding billions in assets.[38] Libertarians, certainly, have no problem with inequalities of wealth. But the problem is that, outside of any kind of rules governing the market, that concentration of wealth could become a concentration of power, and that concentration of power can be abused. Whales can move the market as they wish. 'Pump and dumps' have seen

37 www.bloomberg.com/news/articles/2017–12-08/the-bitcoin-whales-1–000-people-who-own-40-percent-of-the-market
38 www.cnbc.com/2017/10/27/there-are-now-more-than-120-hedge-funds-focused-solely-on-bitcoin.html

anonymous actors placing huge buy and sell orders to cause the price of bitcoin to bump upwards or slip lower. Whales, much like the top miners, know each other. Many were early adopters who stuck with bitcoin through thick and thin. Asked whether large holders could move in concert, Roger Ver, a well-known early bitcoin investor, told Bloomberg in late 2017: 'I suspect that is likely true, and people should be able to do whatever they want with their own money.'[39]

The Birth and Death of Gods

At the heart of the question of who is now powerful in business, there is another question, unfashionable and often overlooked. It is about systems. The future of the economic landscape itself rests in no small part on that question. Systems architecture – how the technology is put together, where the pipes of data point, who controls it, and what they can do with it – will be a central factor in deciding the future of business. The tech giants represented a centralised kind of system. Sitting at the heart of these networks, platforms and apps, a small number of companies control the layer of services that we act through in order to buy and find things. They have built the layer of technology through which we interact with the world and, as the most effective new middlemen, they have swept into commanding positions in the economy, capturing huge user-ships and huge slices of market

39 www.bloomberg.com/news/articles/2017–12-08/the-bitcoin-whales-1–000-people-who-own-40-percent-of-the-market

share and profits. Power in business has moved away from the *owners* of the means of production, and towards the owners of the platforms applications, websites and devices that have become the means of mediation.

It's a system that has caused control and power to rush inwards, towards the kinds of companies that Silicon Valley has produced, to create dramatic concentrations in the hands of a tiny number of companies, indeed a tiny number of people.

They have also built platforms that other companies can't compete with. As the tech giants have grown bigger and bigger, they are swept along by an enormously powerful, and new, cycle of dominance: network effects plus data, plus huge smarts and enormous amounts of money. One social network to connect everyone. One website to index the internet. One platform to look for jobs. One messaging service to communicate. One portal to buy everything you need. It makes sense that there is one world-beating service in each area. If consumers vote with their feet, the billions of clicks, uploads and likes every day is a constant, ringing endorsement. The tech giants create services we all use because they are so useful. I wrote this book on an Apple laptop, I found my way through strange unfamiliar cities using Google maps. I shop using Amazon precisely because its power has meant that it has squeezed suppliers and pushed prices to the floor. The irony is not lost on me: this chapter on the tech giants wouldn't have been possible without them.

The tech giants never stopped hacking, however. They have kept disrupting and maintaining that start-up culture even as they have become the biggest companies in the world. The owners of the most data, the biggest networks, and the best technologies and people to exploit it have a power that can move from one market to another with extraordinary ease. Advanced, disruptive computer science has allowed a power to concentrate that is extraordinarily pervasive. As data increasingly drives capitalism, the world-beating skill to harvest and analyse it cuts through the traditional boundaries of markets and geographies, professions and disciplines. Theirs is a power truly unconfined by the conventional divisions of economic markets and industries.

Organised societies have always sought to limit power, to put it under democratic control, and one example of that has been to break up monopolies. Yet the monopolies of today are different from the past, and they generally haven't been challenged by anti-monopoly laws. The tech giants are based on monopolies of data and control of dominant networks. They are Lanier's 'siren servers' – immense concentrations of informational and computational power. This is an example of power sliding outside of the cages – in this case monopoly law – that had been built for a former age.

This pooling of power may eventually meet political challenge, in which democratic and state power will reassert itself, as it did with Carnegie and Rockefeller, and break up the organisations so large that they threaten to usurp it. But at the moment, the greatest decentralisation of power may come from new technology rather than law or politics. A new technology animated by a different kind of system.

A new wave of technologies is again beginning to change the kinds of services, opportunities and businesses that are available. Huge money is pouring into blockchain, an area fizzing with excitement and new ideas, re-architecting the digital world to be one without a central core. Social media platforms – like Mastodon – can be created without any company at their heart. Currencies don't need to have a central bank or state in order to work. The DAO was a failure, but it showed that entirely new kinds organisations are possible. It is a vision of a different economic landscape, based on technology that is plumbed to have no centre.

The use of blockchain to decentralise power is – like many new technologies – still only open to those with the technical nous to understand and use it. A handful of industrial-scale miners keep the whole system going, and its ownership is vastly unequal. It isn't a system that has, yet, democratised wealth and control in the way that its originators hoped.

But it has created a new opportunity: the plumbing of the networks and services that created wealth can be decentralised. The pipes don't all need to point to a central place. Blockchain could democratise access to capital, opening up new opportunities for investment for people beyond hedge funds and traders. It also poses a profound challenge to services that are centralised by providing an alternative vision.

Centralisation versus decentralisation. Giant companies versus no companies. Dominant middlemen versus no middlemen. So much rests on the architecture of the technology that will only become more and more important to our daily economic activity. Who we will work for, how we will find jobs, how we'll set up new companies and the kinds of markets any company will operate within. The tech giants represent one vision: of a world where the logic of digital technology pulls more and more control and power into a tiny number of companies. The blockchain innovators – visionaries like Eugen – represent a radically different future, where those mediators will themselves crumble.

Systems will be a central factor in deciding the future of our economic landscape. And on that question the cypherpunks were right: the vital battleground of the digital revolution will be technology itself. And that battle is still being fought.

4

Media

It was the end of 2012, and Eliot Higgins had just been made redundant. He'd worked for a charity helping asylum seekers, but they'd lost their government funding, and after a few frenzied months of transferring the work over to another charity, the employer had to let him go. A new father, and needing to support his young family, Eliot went straight into another job, a temporary administration assistant for a lingerie manufacturing company based in Leicester.

Four years later I met Eliot in the huge courtyard of Somerset House in central London. Fountains splashed onto the cobbles, and the air was crisp, clean, sharply cold. He sat down next to me on a small, wrought-iron table. Mid-thirties, bespectacled, in a pressed shirt and smart green trousers, Eliot's life over those four years had spectacularly transformed. From his living room in Leicester, Eliot had jumped into the middle of seismic world events. He'd uncovered the first plot to smuggle arms to Syrian rebels.

He proved that cluster bombs were dropped in the suburbs of Damascus. He'd tracked down the culprits of a mass murder and, on the front pages of the world's press, found himself at the heart of a desperate geo-political struggle for control of the truth. Conspiracy theories now hung around him in a thick online shroud. He's a CIA operative. A propagandist for MI5, MI6 or an agent of the Bilderberg Group – or the vassal of a group so shadowy and powerful, they didn't even have a name.

Eliot cleared his throat and pushed his glasses further up his nose. 'I had some time on my hands . . .' he began.

'Tongue in the Nation'

'He is new, I say; he has hardly lasted above a century in the world yet . . . He, with his copy-rights and copy-wrongs, in his squalid garrett, in his rusty coat; ruling (for that is what he does) from his grave, after death . . .' It was 1840, and the satirist and essayist Thomas Carlyle was writing about a new source of power that had recently emerged. His readers would have been familiar with three existing 'estates' of power: those who made laws (legislature), interpreted them (judiciary) and executed them (executive). 'But', wrote Carlyle, 'in the Reporters' Gallery yonder, there sat a Fourth Estate more important far than they all.'[1]

By the time Carlyle was writing, hundreds of newspapers had been founded, turning out millions of copies a day of thundering

---

1 Strictly speaking, Edmund Burke coined the term 'Fourth Estate', and Carlyle was quoting him. But Carlyle did it in a funnier way.

political commentary, commercial news and advertising, to an increasingly reading, increasingly voting public. Newspapers had become a window into the wider world, and Carlyle was pointing to the scribblers and hacks, editors, sketch-writers and interviewers who daily created it. 'Whoever can speak, speaking now to the whole nation, becomes a power ... It matters not what rank he has, what revenues or garnitures: the requisite thing is, that he have a tongue which others will listen to; this and nothing more is requisite. The nation is governed by all that has tongue in the nation.'[2]

A new class of press barons had emerged, grown fabulously wealthy from the money they made from the business of speaking to the nation. There was political power too, as Carlyle pointed out, in the hands of those whose 'tongue in the nation' mixed opinion with reportage, interpretation with straight news. Mass franchise created the idea of a 'public' opinion and the press had become the formers and shapers of it.

The power held by this Fourth Estate, however, was more important than either money or politics. As the profession of journalism developed, hacks and muckrakers began to dig, expose and pursue truths that were hidden. They spotlighted wrongdoing, embarrassed the mendacious and pursued the corrupt. This ability, to 'speak to the nation', was particularly able at holding power itself to account. In its most courageous moments, the Fourth Estate became not only a source and centre of power itself, but also a critic, opponent and investigator of it. It spoke the truth, not only to power, but also about it.

2   Lecture V, Thomas Carlyle: www.gutenberg.org/files/20585/20585-h/20585-h.htm

As I listened to Eliot's story, I realised that nothing seemed to be changing as quickly as the power of those who held 'tongue in the nation'. His journey was a story of how the Fourth Estate itself had transformed. The diggers and muckrakers weren't necessarily where you expected them to be any more. Journalism seemed to be living through a singular time of both great power and weakness, celebration and sorrow. Carlyle's world of press barons and hacks was being both destroyed and reborn.

The Mainstream Begins to Change

The entrance to Broadcasting House is at the end of a sweeping arcade that seems to cut into the buildings on either side of it. It is a building that mixes both new and old, friendly and imposing. Grand, blank faces of old Portland stone meet with new greenish-glass at the smooth convex entrance. Above it are those three letters, famous across the world: BBC.

Mukul Devichand rushed out of the building, apologising for being held back by a story. 'I studied law, actually, at the LSE – a good Indian boy,' he tells me, chuckling, as we stroll away from his office. In his late thirties, Mukul speaks in a soft Welsh accent and is a little nervous. I've asked him to do something that makes any good journalist uncomfortable. Mukul had been on the inside of the industry as journalism had begun to undertake a huge shift in how it did its work. I'd asked him now to become the story.

'My early days of journalism took place in a very different era,' Mukul begins. When he joined the BBC, his career began doing the kind of journalism broadly recognisable to generations of journalists who had gone before him. He became a researcher for *Panorama*, the world's longest-running current affairs programme, and then started to make documentary-length current affairs programmes on BBC Radio 4 and BBC World Service. It was typical shoe-leather journalism for venerable, traditional outlets: lengthy investigations, face-to-face interviews, building the characters and the detail that got to the heart of story. 'I'm actually quite old-fashioned,' he says. 'I'm more likely to know the names of US senators who deal with economic issues than the names of the members of One Direction.' But in the eyes of many of his colleagues, Mukul was about to take journalism in a very unconventional direction.

'I began to notice that, especially in authoritarian countries, the internet was a big shaker-up of things,' he says. He grew more animated, caught now in the pivotal realisation that went on to define so much of his career since. 'The conversation online, which a lot of people dismissed as being essentially shallow, was an interesting indicator of where things were going in society.' Within the BBC, there was already a growing sense that social media was changing how stories could be shared and promoted. But Mukul's insight was that the digital world was, itself, a place that should be reported *on*, as well as *through*. It was where stories happened, as well as where they should be told. And that needed its own journalists, its own reporting techniques, and its own rules. The BBC, he thought, needed a form of journalism to report on the internet, and he wanted to do it.

The idea was that surges of online activity were often meaningful in themselves. 'I thought if you site a team of reporters on the conversations that happen on the internet, that will make for actual stories, insights that other kinds of reporting don't have,' he says. Within the BBC, Mukul and a group of colleagues fought for a budget, for broadcast time and for the resources they needed to grasp this new opportunity, and slowly they won the commissioners around. They got eight minutes of broadcast time on BBC World Service each week and received support from the BBC's digital team. And slowly, the germ of a new kind of journalism began to grow. The team was called BBC Trending.

We are sitting now in the sun, and Mukul grins as he remembers some of the stories that watching the internet allowed them to break. 'We were able to notice things that hadn't really landed yet,' he tells me. 'Stories we reported on would weirdly become news stories a month or two after we reported on it.' BBC Trending had watched the online campaign to rescue the 276 female students who were kidnapped from a secondary school in Nigeria by Boko Haram for months before #bringbackourgirls exploded into a global campaign. They had seen the 2013 Gezi Park protests build in Turkey faster than the traditional news machine too, and were there, filing stories alongside the BBC's traditional correspondents and country experts.

'As a journalist, what you dream of is a ringside seat to history,' Mukul says. But he had found a new kind of seat; a new way of witnessing the stories breaking around him. BBC Trending itself grew, but its example grew larger, and other digital journalism hubs began to open up in and around the BBC. BBC Stories focused on domestic, young, under-served audiences by creating content specifically designed to be spread across social media. World Hacks was started to find and feature stories about making the world a better place. And beyond them, mainstream journalists – not digital specialists – began to report on digital trends as they would any other in society.

*

As Mukul and his colleagues were changing how the mainstream press reported on the internet, Eliot Higgins's own journalism humbly began at the bottom of other stories by other journalists. 'I started arguing on *Guardian* comment threads,' Eliot told me. It was the end of 2011, and Libya was in upheaval. Amidst a bewildering background of shifting factions and international involvements, Eliot followed story after story as journalists desperately tried to keep up with what was happening. He would get in to work at 7.30 every morning, and do a sweep of all the latest reports, and then post on the comments. 'I was bored, really. And I thought the journalists were often getting it wrong.'

Eliot – like Mukul – turned to sources that most journalists at that time neglected and overlooked. From shaky YouTube videos panning across across dusty, arid landscapes, pockmarked with shells, to fighters posting grinning selfies on Twitter, the war was being chronicled online. Eliot saw that this new information often wasn't making it into mainstream journalism. It wasn't forming part of the journalistic picture of the war that most people were seeing. 'It was an amazing new source of information,' Eliot said. 'I wanted to look at it in a systematic way. I got a reputation among the people on comment threads of being the first person to post every day with a list of links and other details I had gathered together.' Underneath the main piece, Eliot shared all the information he was finding, checking the facts about the war that appeared in the article itself. He had begun to do something that had started to spread across journalism more broadly, both professional and amateur.

It was a humble beginning. But it wasn't just Broadcasting House where journalism was embracing the new sources of information and ways of telling stories that had emerged. Perhaps more significant was that it was happening in Eliot's house too. Amateurs as well as professionals were building both stories and reputations doing it, and that signalled the first great change to the Fourth Estate: the walls around it were getting lower. More and more people were joining the profession, and its definition was becoming murkier. They weren't all sitting in the Reporters' Gallery any more.

The Old Gatekeepers

It was at the very end of 2012 that Eliot had his first break. He'd begun to follow the YouTube channels used by the Syrian opposition and each day he checked the new videos that appeared. He was an obsessive and regular observer, and started to notice that some of the things featured in the videos seemed strange and surprising. 'One', Eliot said, 'was a video of cluster bombs.' The Syrian government was denying that it was using cluster bombs in the conflict, and Eliot's finding was first written about by human rights organisations and then the mainstream press. 'They didn't mention it had come from me in the first place,' said Eliot, 'which didn't go unnoticed by some of my more vocal supporters.' From arguing in the comments threads, Eliot had begun to break his own stories. His reputation was growing.

Still combing through hours and hours of YouTube footage in the new year of 2013, Eliot found another surprise. In some of the videos, Syrian rebels seemed to be carrying weapons that looked different from any other that he'd seen being used in the country. 'I'd been watching videos from Syria every day and trying to ID new and interesting weapons and some stood out like a sore thumb,' he said. He collected them on a spreadsheet, looking for more videos from the same sources and taken from the area where the new weapons had appeared. 'Hundreds of them, but only four types of weapons, something that was unusual enough – but extra unusual because all four weapons had never been seen in the conflict prior to the last week of 2012.'

Again, Eliot wrote about the story on his blog, but now mainstream journalists were paying attention. The *New York Times* contacted him, and he agreed to write it up as a blog for them. But a week later Eliot received a call; it was C. J. Chivers, a Pulitzer Prize-winner, and one of the *New York Times*' most famous journalists covering the conflict. They had been following up what Eliot had found, and realised it was a huge story. The weapons were Croatian, and officials had admitted to the *NYT* that they were part of a smuggling operation. It was the first real evidence of a foreign nation arming the Syrian rebels. 'I had different film crews visiting my home on different days to film stuff about me. It was a bit crazy,' said Eliot. Rather than running on the blog, on 25 February 2013, the *New York Times* ran Eliot's discovery, acknowledged to him, on their front page.[3]

The press's role as gatekeeper to public life has been one of their longest-standing powers. With Eliot, the *NYT* had taken a big discovery and turned it into a huge story, and from Carlyle's scribbling hacks onwards, they have made these kinds of decisions over what the public sees and what it does not. This has been their

3   www.nytimes.com/2013/02/26/world/middleeast/in-shift-saudis-are-said-to-arm-rebels-in-syria.html

singular power of 'tongue in the nation' – and the clearest example of it doesn't exist in any newspaper or TV studio. It exists in the British Ministry of Defence.

The front entrance of the MOD building on Whitehall is as imposingly Soviet Realist as anything you'd find in Moscow. Giant statues sit on either side of a looming portico, opening out to an interior of echoing marble. When I had passed through the bomb-proof airlock, I was warmly greeted by a trim, upright man with a firm handshake and spotless, gleamingly polished shoes that made a rhythmic tapping as he strode down the marble corridor, leading me into the giant building.

Brigadier G. C. W. Dodds has spent thirty-six years in the British Army. A Royal Engineer, he ended up as the commander of the Joint Air-Land Organisation.[4] After he retired, he became the secretary of a peculiarly British institution, one that recognised the huge power that the Fourth Estate had as the filters of information that entered public life. Before the First World War, the Fourth Estate threatened to clash with the other three. The government wished to keep its wartime plans secret; the media wanted to report on everything and anything it could see. Different countries tried different ways to see off this clash and 'the British way', Geoffrey Dodds explained to me, was the creation of the Defence and Science Media Advisory Committee – or the DSMA-notice Committee.

Twice a year, always at six o'clock, five senior members of government file into an historic, panelled room within the Ministry of Defence. Already awaiting them are seventeen members of the

---

4 This is an organisation within the British military that, like many, has a purpose that sounds both important and totally opaque to anyone not in the British military.

UK media. There's the associate editor of the *Daily Mail*, the deputy editor of the *Guardian*, the executive director of the Society of Editors, the director of editorial policy at the BBC. Each is a media heavyweight, and there they talk, presumably argue, and eventually decide on the kinds of stories to be published and the kinds of things that won't make it into their papers, television channels or books. You won't find information on Britain's nuclear equipment, precise details on their counter-terrorism operations, the naming of British spies, and so on, because of what is agreed in that room.

The astonishing thing about the committee is that it has, itself, absolutely no hard power at all. 'Advisory only,' said Geoffrey. 'There's no sanction, no penalty; editors are quite within their rights to ignore my advice.' The British way to keep a free press and to avoid damaging national security is compromise through discussion. 'Good men wanting to do good things,' said Geoffrey.[5] 'That is at the heart of it.' The D-notice committee is a 105-year old gentleman's agreement.

The only way that something like the D-notice Committee can work is because the people on both sides of the table are actually more similar than they are different. The government doesn't want to censor the press. The press doesn't (usually) want to cause serious harm to national security. Spanning the press and the government are common values, and the consensus only works because of this common ground. It was, I realised, not only a committee but also a community. We have an annual dinner afterwards and an annual reception at Admiralty House

5 At the time of writing, of the twenty-three people listed as members of the committee, two were women: Sarah Whitehead, head of home news at Sky News, and Geetha Kanagarajah, personal assistant to Geoffrey himself.

and social events after Committee meetings – absolutely essential' said Geoffrey.

The D-notice Committee wasn't really about the power of the government over the press, but the power of the editors over public life. For over a hundred years, they have stood as gatekeepers choosing what goes into the newspapers, on the television and into books, and what doesn't. They were people not only with enormous power but, listening to Geoffrey, also a broadly similar set of values and loyalties.

Doubtless, the people sitting around that Committee table today still hold considerable power. Doubtless theirs are still important routes to speak to the nation. Members of the Fourth Estate are powerful and popular voices in the digital world, but now they aren't alone. Easily the most visible change is the one that so many of us have already taken part in. Millions of new, often tiny entrances to public life have opened. Eliot Higgins had joined countless others to use the internet to bypass the bottlenecks of professional publishing and talk directly to anyone who would listen. Eliot didn't need to be in control of an industrial process to put his stories into the public domain. He'd just started a blog.

Eliot's blog was called Brown Moses. 'It was the name of a Frank Zappa song I had been listening to. I didn't think anyone would actually read my blog, so I just used that.' While Eliot needed the traditional gatekeepers for publicity, he didn't need them to actually make his findings public. As Eliot began to break his own stories about the war, he didn't need to only court mainstream journalists, cosy up to an editor, or toe the line of a press baron to publish his stories. Suddenly the possibility of joining the Fourth Estate, and finding the power of 'tongue in the nation', had been placed directly into his – and, by extension, all of our – pockets.[6]

There was an obvious empowerment in how the internet allowed him and so many others to find their own voices. But speaking, Eliot was learning, wasn't the same as being heard. In one way 'speaking to the nation' was as distant to most people as it always has been. But what was changing was how some content managed to fight its way to the surface. In the face of infinite content, a new and more inscrutable kind of gatekeeper had arrived.

The New Gatekeepers

'When I was growing up,' said Ben Gomes, 'I lived in an information desert. I could take out four books a month from the local library.' I had met Ben at Google's UK headquarters. Nearby, the streets around King's Cross were full, thronging with travellers and commuters pouring in and out of the area's busy station. But Google's offices exuded an inviting, expensive serenity. A small river gurgled outside, next to a glade of bright green grass. Inside, it was all exposed wood and cork tables, industrial piping and pink angular carpets. Like many tech companies, Google avoids the kind of marble power dressing loved by banks and other corporations. But somehow that makes it feel even more corporate.

Ben was born in Tanzania, and grew up in Bangalore, India. He now speaks with a distinctive Californian twang. One of its

---

6   Indeed, the BBC Academy is now teaching their journalists to turn their smartphones into a broadcast-quality 'mobile newsroom': www.bbc.co.uk/academy/journalism/article/art20130702112133395

first fifty employees, Ben joined Google when everyone still worked under one roof. They had no business model, and weren't making any money, but they knew what problem they had all come together to find a solution to. The drought of information had turned into a deluge; what people needed was probably out there, somewhere, on the internet, 'but all this information wouldn't mean anything', he explained, 'if you couldn't find the information that was relevant to you'.

By the time that Eliot launched his blog, the online world had become deafeningly loud. As millions published their own content, they did so on a scale that might have literally outpaced the size of the audience they were trying to reach. By 2005, there were probably more blogs than readers of blogs.[7] Most of the content thrown into the furious churning melee of social media was simply ignored.[8] People's voices were out there, but most of it was unlinked, unshared, unloved simply unheard.

Alongside the spiralling volumes of content, Ben and his colleagues created a new kind of player in the media ecosystem: the mediator. His creation was the Great White Box. It became one of the most important of all of our windows into the universe, easily the most popular website in the world. Ben is the vice president of core search at Google.

Google trawls through 20 billion sites a day and maintains an index of 30 trillion URLS to allow 3 billion searches a day to flow through it. Google's crawlers scuttle from page to page, desperately trying to keep pace with an internet that is growing

---

7   Tim Wu's book, *The Attention Merchants*, states that in 2005, Nielsen estimated that at least 35 million people were reading blogs. Yet also in 2005, there was estimated to be 50 million blogs.

8   https://moz.com/blog/content-shares-and-links-insights-from-analyzing-1-million-articles

by millions of pages every minute. As they go they scrape, bringing the internet inside Google, allowing their vast array of data centres and supercomputers to build an index of the web, sorting pages by the words they contain. And so Google organises the vast universe of information for each of its users, turning it into a ranked, ordered response to your query in a fraction of a second.

There is a ferocious empiricism to Google's approach. 'It's like flying a plane', said Ben, 'that has got better by the time you land.' At any moment, Google is conducting over 100,000 tests to make its search system better, more relevant to you, and returning more authoritative, trustworthy pages. There are precision evaluations, side-by-side evaluations, 10,000 human testers. The holy grail, says Ben, is to create the 'knowledge graph', a kind scaffolding for the web that relates pieces of information together; the world's knowledge, embedded within Google's algorithms.

Alongside Google, Facebook brought a different philosophy for how to handle the vast amount of information that was being created. While Google tried to organise the web, Facebook reduced and organised content not on the basis of the information itself, but on the basis of who was creating and interacting with it. Your friends, your family, the things you and they shared, liked and did; Facebook turned its vast universe of information into an amount that was bearable and human-sized.

We couldn't cope with it by ourselves. Unfiltered and unsorted, the online world was far too large, far too daunting to cope with. So a shift has happened. Carlyle's Fourth Estate relied on an industrial process to produce content. Now we need an industrial process to cope with a world where content is unbelievably easy to create. Enormous servers, vast quantities of data and technologists who earn more than almost everyone else, are all now necessary to help us actually use and benefit from a trail of information that is stretching towards infinity.

Among all the voices that platforms like Google and Facebook have helped to organise and manage are the websites and social media profiles of the journalists, the Fourth Estate themselves, professional as well as amateur. And of all the content, there is also that crucial and precious category of information that paints for each of us a picture of what is happening in the world: news.

The digital world hasn't risen to the exclusion of all others. Plenty of people still watch television; it is still the main source of news for people over fifty-five. Some newspapers still have circulations in the millions, and even some books (can you believe it) find sizeable readerships. But the internet is now the main source of news for more people than any other; far, far greater than print newspapers. And for those that do use the internet to read news, most don't access their news directly.

'Tell me the news,' you might ask Alexa or Siri, digital assistants who organise and select the stories to show you. Yahoo! News is the most popular news website in the world – and it also categorises and organises content drawn from a huge number of different publishers. News apps on phones do a similar job.[9] Kakao Talk has become a key source of news in South Korea, and WeChat in China. In most news markets, a small number of platforms have risen to become key gateways to the work of the Fourth Estate. Google and Facebook, only two of these new

9 Snapchat has emerged has a new player for news.

mediators, between them account for 81 per cent of the traffic to online news sites in the UK.[10]

Almost by accident, almost without us noticing, mediators – a collection of search engines, aggregators, social media sites and voice-controlled digital assistants – have stepped between us and the Fourth Estate. Journalists are still speaking to the nation, but doing so less and less directly. Eclipsing editors, newspapers and the entire profession of journalism, are the technology platforms that mediate the information.

The power of speaking to the nation has changed. The power held by the members of the DSMA-notice Committee boils down to editorial decisions about what to publish. Now Eliot can publish too, and countless other amateurs alongside the professional journalists. Newspapers are no longer the bottlenecks, the gatekeepers over the news that people can see. As the power to speak has become democratised, a new power has arisen among the filters that serve us a tiny proportion of all the news in manageable streams, notifications or timelines.

The mediators have become a strange new kind of editor. Lurking somewhere in each of these differently engineered systems are choices about how to serve you up the information that the platform thinks you want. Rather than reading a publication, people have begun to consume news on a 'timeline' – the individual selections of lots of different editors, bundled together into a single stream. 'Tweets you are likely to care about most will show up first in your timeline,' says Twitter. 'We choose them based on accounts you interact with most, tweets you engage with,

10 See http://fortune.com/2015/08/18/facebook-google/. Globally it's less, around 50 per cent: https://reutersinstitute.politics.ox.ac.uk/sites/default/files/Digital%20 News%20Report%202017%20web_0.pdf

and much more.'[11] Instagram, too, orders your feed 'to show the moments we believe you will care about the most'. Facebook's news mixes together posts from family, friends, advertisers and media outlets. Fifty per cent of all Google's clicks go to the top two search results.[12] Around the world, more people access news through algorithms than editors.[13, 14] Over time, they learn your pleasure points and anxieties, and show you the stories that they think reflect them, whatever they are.

News isn't just ordered by algorithms, however; it's also often filtered through new bodies of rules that we can't see. I spoke to Olivia Solon, a *Guardian* journalist based in San Francisco who has doggedly covered the tech giants. She told me about a big story she and her colleagues worked on in 2017. 'We'd been sniffing around Facebook's moderator teams for a while. It was difficult to get anyone to talk, because they'd be sacked if they spoke to the press,' she told me.

Facebook employ thousands of 'content moderators'. They are based around the world, and review the millions of reports flagged to them by Facebook's users, deciding whether to delete the content, ignore the flag, or pass the content over the police. In a series dubbed 'The Facebook Files', Olivia and her colleagues exposed, for the first time, a leak of the secret rules and guidelines that advise these moderators. 'It was like they were trying to create a formula for decency,' said Olivia. 'They'd clearly put a huge amount of thought into it.' There are guidelines for what

11 https://support.twitter.com/articles/164083
12 www.weforum.org/agenda/2017/04/most-popular-websites-google-youtube-baidu/
13 https://reutersinstitute.politics.ox.ac.uk/sites/default/files/Digital%20News%20 Report%202017%20web_0.pdf
14 A serious and longstanding criticism of this new arrangement is that only the company knows how these algorithms actually work, and perhaps not even then – but that's for another chapter.

are credible threats to others and what aren't, what is allowable and non-allowable nudity, about the live-streaming of self-harm. 'There's a huge amount of documentation,' Olivia told me. It covers everything from child abuse and terrorism to cannibalism and match fixing. Videos of alleged police brutality and beatings, murders and infanticide have all been uploaded onto Facebook, and these documents determine which are allowed to spread, and which are systematically removed. Facebook's moderation guideline is one of the most significant editorial documents in history – across Facebook's 2 billion users, it is far more influential than the editorial decisions made by any particular newspaper or broadcaster.

Sometimes power can be desperately unwelcome. It isn't a power I think these digital mediators wanted, and they are probably alarmed that their wild success has meant that they have got it. But in effect, a tiny number of technology companies have taken over a significant part of the responsibilities of the free press. Their policies over what information to allow or remove are more significant than the guidelines of any news outlet, any publisher in the world.

This power has carried with it new burdens that the online mediators neither particularly acknowledge, nor welcome. 'A media company is about the stories that it tells,' Chris Cox, Facebook's chief product officer wrote in 2016. 'A technology company is about the tools that it builds.' They don't create the stories, they don't write them, they don't investigate them – they simply link you to them. They don't, in short, publish them. And whether there's a problem with defamation or a copyright infringement, they also don't take legal responsibility for what appears in the stories they serve up. If they were legally seen as publishers, even these enormous companies would quickly get sued into the ground.

These new kinds of decisions over what we see are also more inscrutable than they were before. There are often good reasons why tech giants do not release their policies, or reveal their algorithms, but nonetheless in the mediators the power of speaking to the nation hasn't only become more concentrated, it has become opaque. Why has your timeline been algorithmically curated in the way it has? Why has one Facebook page been taken down while another not? It's often hard to know. The rise of the mediator over the producer of content is one of the most important things ever to happen to journalism and caused a vastly important shift in media power.

Breaking the Business of Journalism

The business model of journalism has always been mixed. Some newspapers have always relied more on subscriptions than others. Some have relied on memberships, others on rich proprietors happy to make a loss. But just seven years before Thomas Carlyle memorably gestured at the political power of the Fourth Estate, the way most of them made money had begun to change. Early pioneers – for example, newspapers like the *New York Sun* – realised that the real money wasn't in selling access to what people wanted to see on the printed page. Far more lucrative would be to sell what newspapers collected so easily: attention. Newspapers realised that their readers were not their consumers; they were their product. As this new idea caught on, 'the lift generated by paid advertising exceeded the gravity of costs', wrote Tim Wu in his book, *The Attention Merchants*. 'And at that point ... the world was never really the same again.' Since then, the dominant source of revenue for most outlets, most of the time, has been advertising. Capture attention, and sell it on. That's been the way that news has paid for itself.

Matt Rogerson is the head of public policy for the Guardian Media Group. The first big change didn't come from Facebook or Google, he told me; it came from the smartphone. 'By 2008,' Matt said, 'digital advertising consisted of banners and skyscrapers on websites. 'Reader engagement meant youcould charge a relatively high fee for desktop advertising. The shift away from desktop to mobile immediately means that each ad is worth less, because it's smaller, and is perceived to have less impact.'

Ads were getting smaller, but there also were many more of them being sold. The appearance of Google and Facebook created a huge new source of advertising space. As billions started to use them, these services themselves were able to create 'inventory', advertising space in front of their audience that was vastly greater in scale than would ever be possible in a physical newspaper. 'They've increased the supply massively,' said Matt. 'And that oversupply of inventory advertising on Facebook's own site, again, brings down the price.'[15]

This isn't, however, the full story. 'Advertising', said Matt, 'used to be an artisan profession.' Experts would craft and design campaigns that wanted to buy access to an audience, and then work directly with publishers – like the *Guardian* – that wanted to sell it. 'Facebook and Google have been telling the story to agencies that they should be switching their spend out of mediums

15 Good for small businesses. Bad for newspapers.

like print and TV, and into programmatic advertising on Facebook and Google,' he said. Facebook and Google aren't just new sources of advertising space. They are also changing how advertising is done, not only on their own platforms but across the rest of the internet as well, including news outlets. In programmatic advertising, you do not buy space in a particular publication; you buy space in front of a particular kind of person, wherever they happen to go on the internet. It is a highly automated and technologically-driven arrangement, in which real-time ad exchanges allow advertisers to bid for advertising space, and cookies and other kinds of ad-tech track people as they travel around the internet. When a member of a target audience lands on a part of the internet where ads are being sold, the ad is bought and served up to them instantly. It makes no distinction where the actually is. 'This enables' said Matt, 'a situation where Mercedes Benz can end up buying ads on Breitbart. Premium inventory on the sites of high-quality publishers is being bundled together with low-grade inventory on long tail websites. Because of the lack of transparency in the market, brands are being sold premium sausages, that are actually full of rusk'.

Programmatic advertising is all about targeting, and targeting is all about data. The more data about an audience that an advertiser has, the narrower and more precisely they can slice the viewing public into their 'tribes', 'cohorts', 'segments', separating for advertisers more and more finely the kinds of people that they want their advertising to appear in front of, and the kinds of people that they don't. The companies who can give the most compelling offer to advertising agencies are those that know the most about who their audience is and what they might like to buy. 'The company that knows the most information about that person can target advertising to them in the most sophisticated way,' Matt explained to me. 'And that is not news organisations. Ultimately that is Facebook and Google.'

With far more data on their users than anyone else, it was Google's advertising products and Facebook's Ads and Audience Network that now sat between advertisers trying to buy an audience, and publishers like the Guardian trying to sell one. It was through these two companies that advertisers programmatically bought access to the targeted, sliced and profiled members of their desired audience. These were the new marketplaces. So Google and Facebook were not only the publishers' formidable new competitors, they also formed the markets that publishers like the *Guardian* had to now sell programmatic space through. To make money from its audience, 'you insert some script from Google or Facebook on your website' said Matt, 'and you get a cheque at the end of the month'. 'You're completely reliant on them to sell advertising, and then take a few pennies at the end of the month.' The tech companies weren't just new middlemen between the publishers and their readers; they had also become middlemen between them and advertisers.

Whether or not programmatic advertising is actually any more effective in reality, the story that Facebook and Google have told to advertisers has been spectacularly successful. So successful, in fact, that the entire online advertising industry is consolidating within these two companies. In 2016, Google and Facebook captured 64 per cent of the global advertising market.[16] Ninety per cent of all the new spending on digital ads goes to just those two companies. Some have even put it at 99 per cent.[17] At $1.2

16 World Press Trends 2017, WAN-IFRA: http://anp.cl/wp-content/uploads/2017/10/WAN-IFRA_WPT_2017.pdf
17 http://fortune.com/2017/01/04/google-facebook-ad-industry/

trillion, these two companies are now worth more, as far as I can make out, than every single newspaper and publisher in the world put together.

The real losers in programmatic advertising are publishers like the *Guardian*. It has been a painful commercial emasculation, as they've lost both control and desperate amounts of money. Not only do they now have to compete with Google and Facebook's own advertising space – websites that can harvest eyeballs at scales so vast that they actually push down the price of advertising for all other publishers as well. But as this new form of programmatic advertising has taken hold, publishers also have to sell their own advertising space to the very companies that they are competing against. Google, Facebook and a new chain of programmatic ad-tech middlemen – trading desks, data providers, demand-side platforms, ad exchanges and ad networks – capture 61 per cent of the advertiser's money. The publisher gets just 30 per cent.[18]

Talking to Matt was enormously concerning. Journalistically, the *Guardian* is one of the great success stories of digital publishing. The *Guardian* has never sold a great many print newspapers; in 2012 its print circulation was around 200,000, tenth of the eleven national dailies in the UK. But it was quick to embrace the internet. They began to publish on it from 1995, pioneering live-blogging, interactive data visualisations, citizen journalism, long reads. The *Guardian* is now basically a website that happens to print some of itself every day, and it has been fantastically successful in capturing new audiences around the

18 World Press Trends 2017, WAN-IFRA: http://anp.cl/wp-content/uploads/2017/10/WAN-IFRA_WPT_2017.pdf

world. From an unpopular British daily, it has become one of the most visited news websites in the world.

'We've never had more readers,' said Matt. 'But the commercials are challenging.' In 2016, the *Guardian* announced that it needed to cut 100 journalistic positions. In 2015–16 they lost £56m and in 2016–17 £37m The company is owned by the Scott Trust, a fund set up in 1936 to keep the Guardian independent. Without the £700 million that the Trust has in its kitty, the newspaper would have already folded and has is in the middle of a campaign to reduce its operating losses to zero in three years.

This isn't just a story of a lumbering dinosaur failing to react to new circumstances. The *Guardian* is living through a strange time of both triumph and crisis. Its great increase in readers has come at the same moment as the bust in its finances. Something seems terribly broken in the fact that it is succeeding as a newspaper, and failing as a business.

The experience of the *Guardian* is something that has been felt – in many cases much more acutely – across the whole of the industry and across much of the world.[19] US newspaper advertising revenue has fallen from $65.8 billion in 2000 to $23.6 billion in 2014. British newspaper ad spend went from $4.7 billion to $2.6 billion over roughly the same period.[20] *Le Monde* was suffering losses of €10 million (£7.92 million) a year and had to seek new investors in 2010 to keep the organisation out

19 It isn't all of journalism that has been hit this hard, or all of the world. Across Asia, Latin America, the Middle East and North Africa, the trends don't appear to be as sharp. Geography matters when it comes to how people decide to consume their news.
20 Jonathan Taplin, *Move Fast and Break Things: How Facebook, Google and Amazon Cornered Culture and Undermined Democracy.*

of bankruptcy. By 2013, it was estimated that more than 3,000 Australian journalists had lost their jobs in the previous five years. The number of journalists in the UK shrank by up to one third between 2001 and 2010; US newsrooms declined by a similar amount between 2006 and 2013.[21]

Global newspaper revenues are falling – down almost 8 per cent in the last five years.[22] Most media companies around the world are reporting falling revenues.[23] So far the revenue for broadcasters has held far firmer than for digital and print publishing. Their revenue tends only to be slowing in its growth, rather than actually falling.[24] But Matt advised caution. 'Facebook is coming for their dollars,' he said. 'This White Walker is moving towards them too.'

It's also true that the tech giants themselves have set up initiatives to redirect revenue back to the publishers. Facebook's flagship programme is called Instant Articles, which sends $1 million a day back to publishers. Google has the Digital News Initiative to fund new ideas for online journalism. And in China, WeChat has invested a lot of money in original journalism.

Despite these caveats, Matt's message was blunt: 'If you're in news business for profit, you're in the wrong business . . . On current trends, two businesses are going to own the advertising market and if you're relying on social media to fund high-quality journalism – that's never going to happen.'

21 www.theguardian.com/media/2016/jul/12/how-technology-disrupted-the-truth
22 World Press Trends 2017, WAN-IFRA: http://anp.cl/wp-content/uploads/2017/10/WAN-IFRA_WPT_2017.pdf
23 Yearly Survey, 'World News Publishers Outlook'.
24 www.accenture.com/t20170411T172611Z__w__/us-en/_acnmedia/Accenture/next-gen/pulse-of-media/pdf/Accenture_Future_of_Broadcast_V_POV.pdf

The Embittered Hack

We met in a pub in central London. He's a hack, a muckraker, who started in journalism covering gangs and crime on the streets of Glasgow. Now an editor at a UK tabloid paper, he's young enough to have half of his career still ahead of him, old enough to remember the journalism of a different age. On his first day 'and it was the same for everyone', he said, he was told to get out of the office. '"Go talk to cabbies, and don't come back until you've got a story." That's all I was told.' He was out for two freezing days. A rite of passage for all young journalists, he told me, was the 'death knock': knocking on the door of a family grieving for someone recently murdered. He even remembered how journalists, once in the house, might try to steal the picture of the victim from the mantelpiece. And they wouldn't always give it back. The kind of journalism he remembered didn't sound either pleasant or moral. But it was a world where journalists were on the streets, talking to people, chasing down hunches and rumours. He didn't want to be named because he wanted to speak honestly about how he had seen his profession change. 'Put me down as "embittered hack",' he said, dead-pan.

Online journalism earns money in one way: clicks. As the business of journalism came under pressure, it was inevitable that the practice of journalism would change too, in order to harvest as many clicks as possible for the lowest cost. 'There's a desperate race to fight above all the noise,' the embittered hack said. 'Journalists have to write an order of magnitude more stories than before. We're trapped in the office, in front of our computers, churning out stories.' And to do this they have to use tricks of the trade – things journalists regularly do, but rarely publicly discuss.

'There's all kinds of things we do to ramp up output,' he continued. Matt Drudge began to rise to prominence in the 1990s, with his news aggregation site Drudge Report. Living in Hollywood, Matt Drudge started to pick up celebrity gossip and opinion. He started to break bigger and bigger stories – the first media outlet to publish on the Monica Lewinsky scandal for instance, and by the early 2000s, he had one of the most visited news sites in the US. 'We literally write stories that we think he'll like,' the embittered hack said. The hope is that one of their articles will feature on his site, harvesting thousands of viewers a second. If he links you on his site, the traffic is totally ridiculous, more than from anywhere else. Everyone – it's not just us – is writing stories about sex robots at the moment because we've heard he's interested in that.'

He will 're-nose' stories – reproducing the same story with a new headline and photo, but essentially the same content. He will clone stories, wholesale, from other publications, and publish copy almost unaltered from the newswires that he receives. And the copy itself is changing. The editor told me how the search engine optimisation team ('an utterly depressing department') has meant that 'centuries of headline-writing skills have been replaced so we can learn to write stuff for Google'. It's as important to be as unoriginal as possible, he said. 'We'll do anything to experience the jag of a graph surging upwards.'

'That is churnalism,' said Martin More. From 2006, Martin was director of the Media Standards Trust, and he is now the director of the Centre for Media, Communication and Power at King's College London. A former journalist himself, in 2011 he set up a project to try to draw attention to churnalism. 'There is a significant and growing amount of "news" that is cut and pasted from a press release, wire copy, or other articles,' said Martin. 'Sometimes just a quote, sometimes paragraphs, sometimes the whole lot.'

There are more people trying to get stuff into the press (or keep stuff out), than there are people actually writing it. As journalists get sacked, many go over the road to PR companies, or any organisation that wants to get its message across to the media. Between 2013 and 2015, when there was a 6,000 drop in the number of UK journalists, there was also an 18,000 increase in public relations professionals.[25] The PR industry employs 83,000 people, journalism 64,000.[26] PRs use their journalistic skills to write releases in a style and format that can slot straight into news. This news-like (or news-lite) copy gets sent over to wire agencies, who combine it with other, real, news stories and send the feed over to journalists.[27] With the best intentions in the world, it's easy to see how time-pressured journalists would be thankful for this ready, easy supply of stories. 'It's a practice that has been going on for a long time,' said Martin, 'but I'm very anxious that it's been getting worse as journalists come under increasing pressure. There are some people in the industry whose entire job is to copy and paste.'

Newspapers under pressure will not only try to squeeze more out of their journalists, but also out of the advertising they run.

25 www.pressgazette.co.uk/6000-drop-number-uk-journalists-over-two-years-18000-more-prs-labour-force-survey-shows/
26 hwww.theguardian.com/media/greenslade/2016/jun/10/survey-finds-that-prs-outnumber-journalists-by-large-margin
27 Not PA, Reuters, etc, says Martin, but a 'sub-stratum' of wire services underneath it.

'Native advertising' is paid-for content that matches the style and design of the publication, has increased by 600 per cent between 2014 and 2017.[28] 'This is a huge change in the industry,' said Martin. 'It is more sophisticated, more camouflaged and more insidious.' The question now seems to be: 'How can we fool the reader into thinking this is actually news?'

Papers like the *Guardian* or the *New York Times* might have enough loyalty, enough exclusive content, enough brand power to survive. But underneath these famous names, smaller, more independent and local media has been massacred. According to the Press Gazette, there has been a net reduction of 181 local newspapers in the UK between 2005 and 2015.[29] Overall, the total number of daily newspapers published in the United States has declined steadily from 1,730 in 1981 to 1,480 in 2000 and 1,331 in 2014. This is a bloodbath, and it is highly concerning.[30]

News outlets aren't just businesses, they are also how we learn about the world. Crusading, investigating journalists have long been one of the ways that abusive uses of power have been confronted and checked. But churnalism, corporate puff pieces and sponsored content do not confront power; they are a reflection of it – of corporate muscle, PR savvy. The gutting of local journalism, and talented journalists chained to computers having to keep up a constant stream of clickbait material, merely adds to the problem.

28 https://venturebeat.com/2017/04/10/native-ad-spend-increased-600-in-3-years-but-early-adopters-are-bailing/
29 http://www.pressgazette.co.uk/some-47-regional-newspapers-have-closed-2012-39-have-launched/
30 www.mediapost.com/publications/article/294924/sign-of-times-more-local-newspapers-closing.html

What are most at threat are the local-issue stories, the nitty-gritty research, the expensive long investigations and the everyday reportage. It is the journalist sitting at the back of the courtroom, in the council meeting, digging up dirt on a dodgy planning permission decision and scribbling furiously during a local demonstration. It is the reporters who listen to communities and really understand what is going on in an area, who confront the daily abuses of power that most matter to people. As journalism's business model breaks, there has never be a better time to be a corrupt local official, a negligent councillor, or a profiteering supplier.

Fake News

The cloud of white dust began to settle around us as our car bumped up to the high curb outside Radio Café. I was in Pristina, the capital of Kosovo, and it felt more Mediterranean than central Europe: the temperature was in the high twenties and around me, the café was huge and full, hundreds of people sipping espressos in the shades of enormous canopies stretched over the vista of chairs and tables.

We waited in nervous silence. Bardha, who had organised the meeting, sent a quick text message: 'It would be an embarrassment to our country if you do not show up,' she texted, angrily. Bardha had spent days trying to convince this man to speak to me, and today he replied, simply, 'Noon'. Twenty minutes later, a man pulled up a chair to our table with a wary grin. He was young, with a neatly shaved head, grey, tight-fitting polo-neck shirt and red trousers. 'Do you work for Facebook?' he asked immediately, laughing but not joking.

His name was Burim. Twenty-four years old, Burim had graduated with a degree in computer science. He'd worked in IT for a private company in Pristina, and he'd worked in advertising. But his current occupation paid much better than either of them. Burim made his living from what we now call 'fake news'.

Like a proud vineyard owner, Burim took me on a tour of his digital estates. On his phone, he scrolled through all the Facebook pages that he owns. One seemed to be an evangelical group, with a big picture of Jesus Christ. 'I bought this one. This guy in Albania built up this page by posting authentic religious information. He managed to get 100,000 likes on the page. Then I paid him 2,000 euros, and he transferred the page over to me.' Another was about abandoned places, another about mobilising communities in a city in the American south. He showed me another that he bought two weeks ago, about dieting and veganism. One was about tiny houses and another was a verified page – it had a blue tick, and a logo – and was something to do with trust. It was quite difficult to actually see what most of Burim's pages had originally been about. But while the groups were bizarre, their audiences were huge: 90,000 likes; 240,000 likes; 26,000 likes. The first step in Burim's trade is to get an audience, and between them, these pages could get his content in front of close to a million pairs of eyeballs. The targets, he told me, were digitally illiterate Americans. 'Thirty and above,' Burim said.

'Stories about killing people – gore, basically – they perform best!' said Burim, cheerfully. He'd dwelt on one page that he was especially proud of. This one he had seriously invested in, spending 20,000 euros building it up using Facebook advertising, and under his thumb, story after story flicked by. 'Dog Groomer Who Kicked Dog all its Ribs Broke Remains Jail-Free' was one story. 'Boy Comes out of Coma after 12 Years, Whispers Dark Secret to Parents [video]' was another. 'Burn Bay Leaves in your Home for these 13 Amazing Health Benefits'. 'The Peanut Butter Test – the Easiest Way to Detect Early Alzheimer's. Everyone must watch this!' Four hundred and sixteen shares; 1,400 shares; 11,100 shares. He paused for a moment, his thumb hovering over a story going crazy, its shares arcing skywards, from the tens into the hundreds of thousands.

How does he decide on the stories? Who writes them? Burim blinked, his face blank, listening hard to the translation. 'I don't care what the content is,' he said, again, a frown frozen on his face as he continued to scroll through the endless content that his operation spews out. This wasn't deliberately fake news. It just wasn't deliberately true either. In the kind of clickbait that Burim published, the truth or lies that he spread to so many people were, simply, an irrelevance. 'This is the first time I've actually read it,' he said. 'I just care about traffic.'

Burim employs seven people to keep the content flowing through his groups. They steal it from an uncountable number of other operations, and know that other people steal their content too. It's a washing machine of people stealing each other's content, until its origin becomes unknowable, irrelevant.

Click on any of these stories, and you're taken to the money-making part of Burim's operation. He maintains around a dozen websites outside of Facebook, constantly changing to avoid detection. Each look like crude versions of an online newspaper, with the full stories hosted under sections called 'Home', 'Health', 'DIY', 'Animals', 'Food Art' and so on. And just like a newspaper, the money is earned from Google Adsense, pay-per-click program-matic advertising.

Burim brought an entrepreneurial mindset to the operation and he spoke about his industry like any other. The business environ-ment was becoming tougher. There were at least two or three hundred people doing this across Kosovo, Macedonia and Albania, he lamented; so much competition for clickbait, it was harder to get the clicks these days when so many people are after them. Like in so many other areas, at the moment there is a profusion of small, agile actors – fake news start-ups if you will. A small number of players are getting bigger and others are dying out. 'I expect it to consolidate,' he said. He also knew that Facebook was working to throttle the endless stream of clickbait, and run him out of business. But that, to him, was just another occupational hazard. It was all about calculated risk, investment and reward.

What Burim was doing was in so many ways the nemesis of journalism: the content was irrelevant, the provenance unimpor-tant, the story recycled, the truth not even worth thinking about. But actually meeting Burim made me see another side to fake news too. He was earning anything from 400 to a few thousand euros per day – good money anywhere, and a fortune in Kosovo. I noticed that underneath the sleeves of his shirt, Burim was wearing a chunky gold watch. 'His accent is from Lipljan,'[31] Bardha said, 'rural, working class.' I couldn't help it; I slightly admired Burim's own enterprise, if not what he had used it to do..

As one of Burim's webpages came up, he started laughing hard, rocking back in his chair, his ribs shaking. 'Look,' he said, turning his phone around so I could see. 'Look who is paying us today.'

31 A municipality of 60,000 people about half an hour's drive south of Pristina.

The banner on the page was advertising Facebook. Still chuckling and wiping tears from his eyes, he got up to leave, and, after a few paces, hesitated, turning back to our table. 'The coffee is on me,' he said.

The Pedant's Revolt

On 17 July 2014, a Boeing 777 disappeared mid-flight somewhere over Eastern Ukraine. Operating as Malaysian Airlines Flight 17, its remains were found shortly after. Fire and thick black smoke billowed out over a bleak, flat field of arid grass and tall weeds. Scattering debris over tens of kilometres, MH-17 had crashed, killing all 283 passengers and 15 crew on board.

From late 2013, a wave of civil unrest had swept across Ukraine. Violence had escalated into running battles on the streets of Kiev, as police clashed with demonstrators calling for the resignation of pro-Russian President Yanukovych and a deepening of ties with the European Union. Not since the Cold War had there been such an obvious clash of East and West, of the influence of Moscow and the beckoning finger of Brussels. The crisis deepened in February 2014 as Yanukovych fled in the middle of the night, finally seeking sanctuary in Russia.

Shortly after Yanukovych's exile, demonstrations began in the Donbass, a region in the Ukraine's south-east and bordering Russia that had been the heart of Yanukovych's power and support. These demonstrations escalated into armed conflict between the Ukrainian army and paramilitaries seeking either the separation of these regions from Ukraine, or their integration into Russia.

By the end of June 2014, the uneasy ceasefire was broken as Ukraine attacked areas held by the rebels. Fighting raged in rebel-held towns, and Ukrainian jets struck rebel areas.

'WHAT HAVE YOU GOT TO HIDE, MR PUTIN?' screamed the front page of the *Daily Mirror*. After the downing of MH-17, news agencies from around the world immediately scrambled journalists to the scene. The focus was intense, as the world's media raced to get to the heart of the story: what had happened to the unlucky aircraft? People living in the area had heard loud noises, and some had seen wreckage fall from the sky. But reports were contradictory, confused, and the truth unforthcoming.

On 21 July, four days after the crash,, the Russian Defence Ministry held a press conference. A giant screen curved behind a panel of uniformed Russian military showed a red line snaking over Ukraine and out of a safe air corridor: the path of MH-17. In a monotone, the Russian official announced a startling finding. Near to the Malaysian Airlines plane, moments before it crashed, another aircraft had appeared, detected only then because it was ascending fast to meet the high-flying jetliner. Kiev needs to explain why their fighter jet was tracking the airplane, said the state-operated TV network Russia Today, covering the press conference. The accusation was there: Ukraine was responsible for mass murder.

The day of the crash, Eliot wrote his first post on hiswebsite. He had already begun to explore a different narrative to the one released by the Russian military. He had found a single video, quickly taken down after the crash, but Eliot had saved it. The video showed, in the far distance, a squat green military-looking vehicle slowly driving up a two-lane road, separated by three trees. Eliot thought the vehicle in the video was a Buk missile launcher, a military anti-aircraft weapon capable of downing a civilian airliner.Eliot shared the video, and the network of like-minded people who had gathered around him sprung into action. They pored over satellite imagery until they found where they thought the road might be: it was a place called Snizhne, a rebel-held town around 15 kilometres away from the crash. It was just a theory, and only one of dozens that had flooded out of defence ministries, the mainstream press, citizen investigators and conspiracy theorists in the wake of the crash. 'I was open-minded at the beginning,' said Eliot. 'But the most interesting thing was the movement of the Buk missile launcher, so we started with that. When Russia gave their 21 July 2014 press conference on MH-17 it was pretty clear they were lying about some of the stuff, so that immediately made them look extremely suspect in my eyes.'

As Eliot's reputation had grown, he had become the centre of a strange new network. One member was a former officer of the Stasi, the East German secret police. There were Masters students from King's College London, someone who used to be an engineer at Microsoft's mobile phone division, someone else who worked on threat intelligence for a bank, people who'd worked in the civil service. They, like Eliot, had developed skills in looking at all the information that was freely available online. They'd been doing their own investigations, and helped Eliot in his. 'People just kinda did it because it was interesting,' Eliot said. In the days after the downing of MH-17, he pulled this network together. They called themselves the Bellingcat Investigation Team.

With some rushed funding from Kickstarter, they quickly grew to a company of five full-time staff members and fifteen volunteers. 'But because of social media,' Eliot said, 'we could discuss what we were finding, look at each others' posts and bring in others to help.' A steady stream of articles began to appear on their website, a kind of volunteer newspaper dedicated to 'open source intelligence' and now focused on finding the murderers of the passengers on MH-17. Over the next few days, the investigation began to find more photos and videos also showing a similar squat, green vehicle, slowly weaving along roads and through towns in eastern Ukraine. It was an oddity, and sometimes people filmed, photographed, and remarked on it as it came past. Sometimes it appeared on camera by accident. A man had a series on YouTube of uploaded dash-cam footage of him driving listening to mournful Russian ballads and occasionally talking to his lucky followers, and on one video the Buk flashed by in the background.

The biggest task that the Bellingcat Investigations Team faced was to work out the exact time and location of each of these Buk sightings. Only by knowing that could they piece together a time-line of the Buk's whereabouts on the day that MH-17 was shot down. One by one, in the days and weeks that followed, they painstakingly analysed each image.

They found a video of the Buk rumbling along a road, on the the back of a red low-loader lorry. The long shadows thrown across the road suggested it was morning, about 9 a.m. An inves-tigator had virtually followed the same route, somehow discov-ering the precise location by finding the same combination of power wires, poles, cables and the silhouette of the treetops. It was in the city of Donetsk, one of the major sites of fighting during the war.

Just before noon, they found the Buk again. The video showed it driving down another road, next to a large, white apartment building surrounded by grassy scrubland and an overgrown chil-dren's play park. They waded through satellite imagery, tallying the location of bins, the layout of pathways, and eventually found the location of the Buk's second sighting. It was 35 kilometres east of Donetsk, in a small town called Zuhres. It was still heading east, still on the truck, but now covered in camouflaged netting.

The rear end of the Buk poking around a corner was captured in a photo by a curious bystander and loaded onto the Russian social media site VKontakte. A member of Eliot's network, a digital forensic researcher called Aric Toler, worked on locating it. Next to the Buk was a shop, obscured by a tree with a yellow facade. Aric knew Russian, so he pieced together the visible letters, searched for chain stores that contained those letters, and discovered that only one fitted: Строй Дом. He found a court document with the name of the shop and, looking on Google maps, he found one near to where the other sightings were. Then he found someone who had been posting videos of himself driving around the area, and found footage of him driving past the store. And so from a single image, just using information that was available online, he was able to establish the exact location of the missile launcher. The Buk was still heading east. They now knew that it had driven along highway 21, and was 25 kilometres away from its last sighting, now in the city of Torez.

The next picture was the first that Eliot had found. After he shared it, several of Eliot's followers on Twitter had pointed to an area south of the centre of Snizhne. 'The road appeared to share the same layout, with the trees in the middle, and the slight turn visible in the video,' Eliot wrote. 'Aside from the road layout, something else stood out in the video, the height of the camera that took the picture.' It seemed the only hills in the area were far in the distance, so Eliot focused on a body of apartment buildings to the north of the road. From that vantage point, comparing the video with a satellite image of the same suspected place, he concluded that the Buk was now south of Snizhne, and heading south. It was only 10 kilometres away from the crash site of MH-17. The next morning, 18 July, the Buk was caught again. The Bellingcat Investigation Team located the photo to the city of Luhansk. It was now speeding north, back on the same red low-loader lorry. However, there was one telling difference: one of its missiles was now missing.

Month after month, they laboriously built up a picture of what had happened. Through this intricate, detailed form of online detective work, they had developed a good idea of the whereabouts of this particular Buk on that day. They knew it had travelled eastwards, through rebel-held Ukraine. They found the field where it had probably fired the missile, and they could show it returning, one missile missing. But now they ran into a new problem. As they waded through all the selfies, shaky videos and blurred photos of military convoys, they realised that Buks were all over the place. They were in Russia, Georgia, Ukraine, Belarus, and across the region of the conflict. Were all their sightings of the same vehicle? Where had it come from? Who was in control of it?

They scoured each Buk for anything that might tell them apart: small white symbols, differently arrangedged cables, perhaps a painted number. Their Buk seemed to have its identifiers painted over, however, and none of the other features seemed quite, enough, by themselves, to help them tell one apart from the others. But then they realised that Buks actually weren't that well designed. A rubber skirting runs above the tracks of the Buk, and they tended to get ripped and damaged. The damage to each one was slightly different. They created a way to trace the dented profile of each Buk's rubber skirting – a unique 'fingerprint' that they could use to tell one from another.

The Buk that they had tracked from Donetsk to Zuhres through to Snihzne had a distinctive fingerprint: a large tear in the rubber skirt. And of all the Buks that they found, only one matched. The Bellingcat investigation team widened their search, and eventually they found its real identity: it was Buk 332 of the 53rd Anti-Aircraft Missile Brigade of the Russian military. The soldiers of the 53rd Brigade, like everyone else, loved taking selfies and putting them up on social media. They found pictures of them, arms linked, standing in front of the Buk. They found them sitting around a fire, grilling sausages, flashing peace signs. They obtained satellite imagery of their camp, and pored over lumps in tarpaulin that they thought the Buk was hidden under.

For over a year, the BIT tracked down over 200 social media profiles from people who were part of the brigade, and who they thought were involved during its trip that ended in the downing of MH-17. Eliot was interviewed as a witness by the Joint Investigation Team, the international task-force set up to investigate the tragedy, and they eventually set out a dossier of names, faces and possible suspects to give to the JIT. Although he hadn't been on the ground, Eliot had been a witness. He and the BIT had played a part. They, like Mukul, had found their own ringside seat to history.

The mystery Ukrainian jet? Some months later, in November, the Russian TV broadcaster Channel One published an explosive revelation that seemed to back up Russia's claims. They had uncovered, they said, a satellite image that seemed to capture the exact moment of a fighter jet in mid-attack on the airliner, a missile actually streaking away from the fighter towards MH-17. But 'the jet was the wrong model', wrote Bellingcat, 'and the two aircrafts were of the wrong scale by an exponential scale. If the satellite was at a normal height when taking this image, it would have meant that the Boeing passenger jet was over a mile long, with its length to scale in the satellite image. It turns out that the satellite image was a crudely made fake posted on an online message board in October 2014, which was then turned into an "exclusive" discovery.'[32]

'I'd say we were definitely ahead,' said Eliot. They weren't the only ones trying to find out the truth behind MH-17, 'which was good in one sense as journalists on the ground in Eastern Ukraine would see our work and follow it up on the ground.' Their investigation both fed off the mainstream press and also helped informed it. They also needed the mainstream press to get their work in front of serious numbers of people. 'Generally we'd have an average of 4,000 readers on a quiet day,' Eliot said, 'which jumps up to 30 to 60k if we have a big story. We might have a 100-page report that is on the site as a PDF that 1,000 people read, 10,000 might read our article on it, but then we might get 1 million people reading about it in coverage on other websites.' But the Bellingcat Investigation Team stayed on this case for three years. 'I think we're one of the few groups who have consistently investigated in such a way. It's really not something that would fit into a traditional media model,' Eliot said, reflecting on their long, dogged pursuit. If not smarts or visibility, perhaps what really marked them out was sheer persistence.

32 www.bellingcat.com/wp-content/uploads/2017/07/mh17-3rd-anniversary-report.pdf

Speaking Truth about Power

It's easy to get nostalgic for the journalism of the past: a rose-tinted time when high-minded editors made professional decisions in the public interest, when investigative journalists had the time and resources they needed to do their jobs properly, and industrious local newspapers comprehensively covered their local patches. Yet pre-digital journalism wasn't a more pleasant or moral world. Press barons wielded enormous influence, and still do. Journalism was not always ethical, high-minded or accurate, and we, the readers, don't need help from an algorithm to apply our own filters and distortions to the world.

Doubtless, amazing journalists are still breaking vital stories, and sometimes precisely because of the opportunities that the internet has thrown open. Outlets like BBC Trending are blazing new trails for what journalism can be. There are so many information sources out there, so many new ways to tell stories and to include the audience. Journalists are often loud, powerful voices on social media too, and use it to get their stories in front of millions.

Yet journalism as a profession has lost much of the power it once held in determining what people see. It is increasingly the tech companies, not the publishers, who decide what we actually this. And this has become harder to pin down, harder to hold to account – harder, even, to understand.

What has happened to journalism commercially is even more worrying, and especially the un-storied rise of programmatic advertising. New, data-driven techniques have seen the market consolidate into just two companies that can best deliver these new technologies. The relationship between the advertiser and the origin of the content has been broken. The amount of money flowing into journalism has precipitously dropped, and online news outlets are struggling, split between living on hand-outs from the tech giants and philanthropists and grasping for new ways to stop losing money.

There's nothing wrong or unusual about one business model replacing another, or of businesses going out of business. That's how things improve. But journalism has never just been just a bald commercial undertaking. The Fourth Estate is the one that can confront the other three, that can stand up to the powerful and the rich. It is what we use to moderate and civilise power, to expose the abuses of it. Investigations are costly and difficult, and journalists simply have less time to chase down stories, less time to be out in the communities they serve. Indeed, there are fewer journalists overall, and fewer newspapers – especially local ones – for them to work for. There is a huge danger that the Fourth Estate now confronts power less well, less avidly, perhaps with a diminished ferocity and vigour, compared to the past.

Take all that to an extreme – and it is still, thank heavens, an extreme – and you have Burim. Clicks are king, the truth is an irrelevance, the originator of the story is forgotten. Within the new online economies that programmatic advertising has created, content doesn't matter. What does Burim care? He is making money. And he is the opposite of a journalist.

But the opposite of Burim is Eliot. He has sprung from redundancy in Leicester to the front page of the *New York Times* in two years. The same technologies that have put such pressure on professional journalists have given wonderful opportunities to citizen journalists – to find information, to form new groups of colleagues, to publicise their research, and indeed to work with the mainstream press too.

'Hobbyists', the embittered hack had said when I'd mentioned Eliot. Hobbyists perhaps, but Eliot to me represents hope among all the difficulties that journalism is going through. The truth is hard graft, a struggle. Confronting power can be grim and tedious. But over years, Eliot and his colleagues have done exactly the kind of gritty, difficult investigative work that is traditionally the preserve of the professional journalist. And the reason they can do so isn't because they are necessarily smarter, or have skills journalists don't possess. There is one thing above all that they need, these 'hobbyists', and it is exactly what so many professional journalists now completely lack: time. This strange, difficult new face of journalism thrives on it. Eliot's is a new kind of stand against churnalism and click-bait. His is a pedant's revolt, a brilliant example of confronting power through the pursuit of the truth.

5

Politics

Sovereignty

On a bitterly cold day in January 1649, a defiant, upright man strode out in front of a hushed and waiting crowd. Charles, by the Grace of God King of England, Scotland, France and Ireland, Defender of the Faith, climbed the wooden steps to the scaffold. He 'is and standeth convicted, attainted and condemned of High Treason' his death warrant read. The king was a condemned man.

He turned to face his subjects. 'I must tell you that their liberty and freedom consist', his voice rang out, 'in having of government, those laws by which their life and their goods may be most their own. It is not for having share in government, sirs; that is nothing pertaining to them; a subject and a sovereign are clear different things.'

For seven years, armies and militias had been raised and clashed across England. They fought and died over the question that Charles addressed in his final words: who should have a share in government? For Charles, the political power that he held was God-given, a divine right that was his alone. But for seven bloody years across Britain, that right had been disputed. As armies struggled for control, Parliamentarian pamphleteers mounted an intellectual and rhetorical offensive against the form of sovereignty on which Charles's crown rested.

Henry Parker was a barrister and pamphleteer, writing for the Parliamentarian side during the war. He produced a short tract, '*Observations Upon Some of his Majesties Late Answers and Expresses*'. Now long forgotten, in that pamphlet he made a ground-breaking, extraordinary, totally radical claim. The subject and the sovereign were, Parker argued, the same. 'When the consent of societies conveys rule into such and such hands, it may ordain what conditions and prefix what bounds it pleases. The king though he be *singulis major* [greater than any individual] yet he is *universis minor* [less than them all].' Now largely forgotten, the claim that Parker made within it was epoch-making: 'Power is originally inherent in the people.'

During that momentous period in the middle of the seventeenth century, the challenge made by Parker and the Parliamentarians cut to the foundations of the political status quo. They challenged, of course, who could make political decisions and how that political power could be legitimately opposed. But the challenge didn't stop there. It went deeper into the heart of politics: by what right could anyone govern? Was political power absolute, in the hands of a monarch? Or was it spread across representatives? What was at stake was not only who should be in charge, but what being in charge actually meant.

This was a struggle for power in its most foundational form: the nature, origin, indeed the essence of political power. A power that could seize fortunes, consign millions to war and death, extinguish liberty, deliver salvation. It is the foundation of power – its core source, from which all other kinds of power exist. Sovereignty: the power to rule.

Conflict would break out again, and again, in the years that followed. But 1649 was a new beginning. With the smell of gunpowder still hanging in the air, Charles stooped down to lay his head on the executioner's block. And with a single stroke, Charles' head was severed from his body. As he was carried back inside, the crowd surged forward, intent on collecting a drop of the royal blood. One vision of political power had been destroyed, another born.

Parker and the Parliamentarians now faced an enormous problem. They needed to put their words into action. They needed to create a form of government that reflected that central claim: political power was inherent in the people. To make democracy – a government of the people – work in a practical sense. But what did it mean in practice for power to be inherent in the people? Which people? Did everyone vote, or only those who held property? And voting for what? Could delegates make their own minds up, or did they have to vote the way they were told to by the people who voted for them? What rights needed to be enshrined?

The victors of the English civil war began to develop a new vision. Before the war, Parliament had been a temporary advisory committee, serving the king at his pleasure. But now Parliament took on a role at the heart of political power. It, and only it, could represent – literally to re-present – a sovereign people. If power was inherent in the people, then it was only through a sovereign parliament, not a sovereign monarch, that it could be expressed. That was the Parliamentarian answer to how you put the people in charge.

The path to democracy was winding and indirect, but Parker's idea – of popular sovereignty through sovereign parliaments – endured and grew, both in the UK and across the world. It had different forms in different places, but bodies of elected representatives became the main way around the world that democracy was practically achieved. It framed, explained and justified political power, deciding who had it and what it could be used for. In democracies the world over, it is the dominant way that political power is expressed.

Yet once again, a fundamental challenge has emerged. More peacefully than in 1649, although not altogether bloodlessly, the core of political power is changing: we are in the grip of another revolution. On the horizon are the silhouettes of new, potential political orders. Around the world, that same basic question that Parker struggled with – how to put the people in charge – is being confronted in new ways, with technology that Parker couldn't have imagined. The status quo is being challenged, from the loudest and most visible surface of politics, all the way to its least visible and most profound depths. The art of winning political power is changing, and so is the ability to oppose it. But the changes run deeper to the system of politics itself: what political power is and what politicians should do, and how entirely new and radically different kinds of political system might emerge.

Labour's Cave

In the decades after Charles's execution, factions within the newly sovereign parliament arose. Alliances were struck, formalised and transformed into voting blocs. New political identities emerged and hardened. As the right to vote slowly spread beyond the exclusively male clique of landowners and gentry, millions began to join new political organisations. For the birth of parliamentary democracy also saw the birth of another political institution: the vote-winning machines of political parties.

In 2015, a long rectangular room sat separated off from the rest of Labour Party HQ. 'We called it the Cave,' he said. I was talking to a senior Labout digital officer that had been there at the centre of the 2015 campaign and had helped build The Cave The team inside the Cave had grown fast. Computers littered a long bank of desks that ran down the middle of the room. 'Creatives', arty types, edited films in small groups, technicians stared at lines of code, jacked into headphones. There were graphic designers, a social video specialist. Digital engagement specialists working on the website. An email team, a social media team. Strategists stood off to one side, writing weekly targets on whiteboard paper hastily flung up on all of the walls. The Cave was Labour's digital campaign bunker.

The team's objectives were written up on the wall: 'Movement, Motivation, Mobilisation, Message, Money'.

'Our first job was acquisition,' he said. Growing the movement. Bringing people into the party's digital orbit as followers and email addresses. 'What we found is that while we could get some traffic by pushing it out through our organic channels, by far the most powerful thing we could do was to use email,' he said. They started with an email list of about 100,000 people. The team in the Cave began to ask people over email to help, themselves, to get the message out. The list grew, to 300,000, 400,000, 500,000. 'We could send our list an email, and build *something* that was interesting on the website. We'd get growth out of that experience. And money. And message push.'

Then, motivation and mobilisation: using digital platforms to recruit and coordinate volunteers, and galvanising and leveraging these online supporters to convert them into volunteers on the ground, phalanxes on the phone banks, and as donors. They launched an online survey that asked their supporters to describe how they felt about Britain, their communities, and the future of the UK under either Labour or the Conservative Party. The final question caused people to dwell for a moment on what a Conservative victory would mean for them. 'We designed the user experience so people would donate at the end,' he said, smiling.

They set up the NHS baby calculator. Type in your date of birth, and it'd tell you what number baby you were born, under the NHS. The shareable graphic that it produced said something about each person who took part; every user had come into contact with a public service that Labour claimed was now fighting for its life. 'We had over a million different people in the UK take part.'

The Cave was fighting a new kind of political campaign, and was filled with a new kind of campaigner. They were younger. They wrote stuff on the walls. They clapped at the end of meetings, whooped when they hit fundraising targets. They high-fived. 'We did things', he said with a wry smile, 'that the other people in Labour took the piss out of. We got a reputation as people who didn't wear any shoes. There was only one personwho didn't wear any shoes.'

Hippy-shoeless-high-fiving-staffers, shut away in their own cave, fighting the election on a front that many veteran campaigns didn't even recognise. The team was like a start-up within their own party, fighting internal battles to show how important their work was. 'We never quite got to the point where we were totally trusted. We were still treated as outsiders.'

They, and campaigners like them across the world, were all reacting to a basic truth. The way in which people engaged in politics, especially young people, had changed. By 2015, half of Brits who used social media were using it in some kind of political way; more than the numbers who were participating in politics offline.[1] A large majority of them – over 70 per cent – reported at least one way they felt more politically engaged as a direct result: variously feeling that it improved the democratic process, that they understood better the issues and debates of the day, understood better what the parties stood for, or generally felt more engaged.[2] And young people – the least likely to vote of all age groups – were the most likely to feel more politically engaged thanks to social media. They were also reflecting a closing of online and offline worlds. Again in 2015, a third of people surveyed said they were more likely to vote because they had engaged in politics on social media – equivalent to an extra 7.1 million people if the results hold true for everyone.

'In the Cave, we had our goals set,' he said. 'We measured everything we did. We tested everything we did.' And compared

1   Contained in work I did, called The Rise of Digital Politics, Demos
2   Carl Miller, 'The Rise of Digital Politics', Demos, 17 October 2016: www.demos.co.uk/project/the-rise-of-digital-politics

to 2010, the dividends were huge: they reached over 15 million people, – a 1,100 per cent increase in money raised (£3.1 million) and a 1,390 per cent increase in online volunteer pledges (over 100,000).

That year, 2015, was a turning point in British elections, the first time that the contest for political power had been systematically fought over the internet, as well as the more traditional arenas of the television, newspapers, billboards and streets. 'It was the first time it had been professionalised. It was the first time that Labour had invested so seriously in it,' the Labour staffer told me. And from 2015, the digital world just became more and more important. In 2015, both the Tories and Labour together spent £1.5m on advertising on social media. In 2017, one estimate put the spending at £3.2 million.[3] Over the Brexit referendum in 2016, the Vote Leave campaign spent almost all their money online. The campaign director, Dominic Cummings, said they spent 98 per cent of their funds (amounting to some £6.9 million), mainly on a final blast of digital advertising.[4] By 2017, Momentum reached one third of UK Facebook users during the six-week election period.[5]

But Labour's wasn't the first Cave.

The vote-winning machines of political parties across the world were all learning that the digital world was a crucial new battleground in the art of winning power. But the first examples of this didn't come from Labour. It had already been proven on the other side of the Atlantic.

3   www.buzzfeed.com/jimwaterson/heres-how-labour-ran-an-under-the-radar-dark-ads-campaign?utm_term=.jo7XkVapKl#.drxreoGq9w
4   https://dominiccummings.com/2017/01/09/on-the-referendum-21-branching-histo-ries-of-the-2016-referendum-and-the-frogs-before-the-storm-2/
5   www.independent.co.uk/news/long_reads/momentum-labour-jeremy-corbyn-elec-tion-result-how-they-did-it-grassroots-movement-a7847421.html

The Obama Train

Step into any major campaign headquarters around the world today, and you'll find a digital war room, something like The Cave. Mainstream political parties around the world are playing to a new rulebook, one that the two presidential victories of Barack Obama in 2008 and 2012 had started to write.

It began in 2002, when the US passed the Help America Vote Act (HAVA). It required all states to maintain a 'single, uniform, official, centralised, interactive computerised statewide voter registration list'. For the first time, American political parties had an accessible list of all voters in the country.

The purpose of the law was to cut down on electoral irregularities, but an intended consequence was that it kick-started the use of data-driven political campaigning. Using the voter registration list as a backbone, both Democrat and Republican parties began to build more and more sophisticated pictures of what American voters were like. And to do this, they started combining more data together – each attached, as far as possible, to the HAVA list. They took data from other public records, joined it with commercially bought data, collected data themselves, and began to build a deep portrait about each of these voters, incorporating just about any angle they could think of. Past voting records. Shopping habits. Gender. Age. Likely income. Likely interests. Browsing history. Whether or not they eat meat. Whether they prefer cats todogs. Propensity to believe in UFOs. The possibilities were almost endless. The Democrat Party created their own database: VoteBuilder. The Republicans, Voter Vault.

By 2012, they began to use huge amounts of data to drive campaign decisions. All political parties had long used data to understand voters by state, possibly even by major cities. But the data scientists that gathered in the original Cave for Obama's re-election campaign began to put each individual *voter* under the microscope. Fed by the thousands of different data points they had collected, they created for every voter two scores for the two actions that mattered to the Obama campaign more than anything else: likelihood to vote, and likelihood to vote for Obama. These were deep and detailed portraits of over 120 million human lives.

It was a perfection of both the very loud and the utterly silent. By 2012, the Obama campaign had a huge digital presence: 45 million Facebook likes, 23 million Twitter followers, and 1 million downloads of its Facebook app. But they had also put the invisible, silent machinery of data at the heart of their work. They created a web of experiments, where every advertisement, every door-knock, every presidential speech was informed by data, and split-tested against alternatives. The campaign team developed the 'Optimizer', which broke the day into ninety-six quarter-hour segments and assessed which time slots across sixty channels offered the greatest number of persuadable targets per dollar.[6] They noticed that West Coast females were easily the most likely demographic group to hand money over to the campaign. They also liked small dinners, contests, celebrities and George Clooney. So the 'Dinner with Barack (and George Clooney)' contest was

---

6   www.technologyreview.com/s/509026/how-obamas-team-used-big-data-to-rally-
     voters/

born. On the East Coast, they did the same with Sarah Jessica Parker.[7] Different campaign mass emails had hugely different levels of success based on the message. The 'I will be outspent' email raised $2.6 million, for instance; ('Do this for Michelle' only about $700,000.)[8] They created and tested thousands of online adverts, chunking people into smaller and smaller groups. In digital politics, gone are the messages that are seen by everybody, and so really speak to no one. If it feels like politicians are speaking directly to you on social media, it's because they almost are.

Data helped to make decisions about where Obama himself needed to go, where advertising money should be spent, where voter turnout drives were needed. Invisible to the voters themselves, campaigns have become cycles of research, modelling, segmentation, digital outreach and feedback. They pivot, change, reshape themselves, re-brand, re-re-brand, re-re-re brand as the data tells them they should.

Politicians around the world watched as Obama converted his digital campaign into the cold hard currencies of political success: money and volunteers, visibility and (probably) votes. Some 358,000 offline events were organised online, and $690 million raised – over half his total. Obama's digital campaign team had proven that digital campaigning could reach and galvanise millions of supporters. But they had also proven that campaigns could be smarter than ever before.

---

7   http://swampland.time.com/2012/11/07/inside-the-secret-world-of-quants-and-data-crunchers-who-helped-obama-win/
8   'Politics by Numbers, *Economist* Special Report, 26 March 2016: www.economist.com/news/special-report/21695190-voters-america-and-increasingly-elsewhere-too-are-being-ever-more-precisely

Digital Campaigns Everywhere

In the wake of Obama's campaigns, political parties scrambled to copy and build on its successes. Each new election brought new tactics and better technology. In 2014, the world's biggest election, India's, saw the Hindu Nationalist Bharatiya Janata Party (BJP) become the first party since 1984 to win an absolute majority in India's parliament. Arvind Gupta, who headed BJP's IT division, led the party's social media campaign. They used a program called 'organise online to assist offline', using social media to recruit 2.2 million volunteers. BJP established IT cells in 350 districts, which recruited citizen volunteers to post supportive messages online about the BJP and their candidate Narendra Modi, as well as to counter anti-Modi coverage. Gupta claims that social media affected outcomes in 30 to 40 per cent of overall seats.

In 2015, Cambridge Analytica was a relatively unknown firm based in Britain, originally working for Ted Cruz and then taken on by Trump after he knocked Cruz out of the race. They collected, they claimed, 5,000 data points about every US voter, searching through all the variables to see which showed people most likely to vote for Trump. They could see in the data that many people who had never voted before now signalled a strong intent to vote, and many non-Republicans said they would too. The key variable they found was that these groups were more likely than any other to drive American-made cars.

Cambridge Analytica joined the Republican campaign a year out from the elections. And their first efforts were to ramp up donations. Then a few months from the election began the 'persuasion element' of the campaign, and lastly the registration and voter turnout initiatives. It was a constant cycle of research, modelling, segmentation, digital outreach, feedback.

'It looked like an uphill battle. Our internal polling showing a slightly better picture, but still, behind.' You cannot make a candidate data-driven, much less a candidate like Donald Trump. Looking at how Trump could win, they ran modelling: an increase in the rural vote, for example, made the Rust Belt much easier to win. They couldn't inspire people with data, but they could work out who might be inspired and how to do it – sometimes making decisions based on their research that seemed counter-intuitive to both sides of the campaign.

Cambridge Analytica has been in the centre of a firestorm since that election. It has been criticised for harvesting Facebook data via a personality quiz and using it for political purposes. The head of Cambridge Analytica was caught on film, boasting of using dirty tricks to swing elections, including creating sex scandals and using fake news. And it has been criticised for its use of 'psychographics' – personality profiling – on social media data in order to work out different messaging strategies for different people.

It may be true that Cambridge Analytica acted illicitly, even illegally, to find Trump every edge they could. But it's also true that they were up against Hillary Clinton's much bigger and better-funded digital campaign team. Much of what they did was unknown to the public, but we can be fairly certain it was also broadly done by many other companies working in this new area. Campaigns, digital or otherwise, might nudge an election a few points this way, or a few points the other. In a close election, it might even be decisive. But the changes to political power are much deeper than that.

Beyond data, the election of Trump showed how political power was changing beyond targeted messaging and data-driven campaigning. The political mainstream just wasn't as powerful as it was before. And he used the digital world to bypass the three Ps of politics: press, pollsters and parties.

For his critics in the mainstream press, of which there are many, Trump's Twitter account has become a ghoulish pick-'n'-mix of quotes, mad, bad, and ugly. But he didn't need the support of the mainstream press. 'I think that maybe I wouldn't be here if it wasn't for Twitter,' he said in one interview. Trump's innovation was to use social media to address his tens of millions of followers directly, rawly, emotionally. And the mainstream media hung on his every word; his Twitter account drove the American news agenda.[9] Likewise, Trump didn't need the backing of established Republican grandees or institutions. His supporters could organise and coordinate on new online spaces they carved out for themselves, on conservative Twitter accounts and forums.[10] He didn't need pollsters, or the wider commentariat, predicting his victory. They too, were part of an establishment that was losing its monopoly.

The reasons for any electoral victoy are staggeringly complex: a mesh of culture and history, macro-economics and psychology, all wrapped together and played out in endless subtleties within the unique lives of the tens of millions of people who make it happen. But if Barack Obama's campaign victories showed how

9 Gaining, by some estimates, almost $2 billion in free airtime through March 2016: https://hbr.org/2017/03/what-trump-understands-about-using-social-media-to-drive-attention

10 www.politico.eu/article/twitter-donald-trump-the-secret-twitter-rooms-of-trump-nation/

political parties could use data-driven techniques to win elections, then Donald Trump's showed something else: that they could also be used to take on the political establishment itself.

Digital electioneering has been revolutionary to campaigning; but it is hardly revolutionary to political power overall. Digital campaigning meant that mainstream political parties – familiar crucibles of political power – had simply found another way to win it. Those who had cash could buy targeted advertising. They could hire data scientists and strategists, bring in a Cave full of the brains that they needed to run the campaigns. Information power and financial power could translate to political power.

Across the world, however, voters have become less deferential and trustful of the people that they elected to wield political power on their behalf. Electoral turnout has generally fallen, and so has membership of conventional political parties.[11] In country after country, anti-politics has become the dominant mood, and there is a pervasive mistrust of power and the powerful. There is a broad sense that our democratic institutions are too distant and remote from our lives and concerns.[12]

Political parties are embracing the digital world. Professional campaigners can see how it can win them influence. But those same tools are in the hands of everyone else as well. The digital

11 In the 1950s, Conservative Party membership peaked at 3 million, and Labour at 1 million. According to a 2015 Ipsos MORI poll, just 21 per cent of Britons trust politicians to tell the truth, less than the proportion of Britons who trust estate agents (25 per cent) or bankers (37 per cent).

12 In the UK, fewer than a third of people were satisfied with the way that parliament works, and just 29 per cent think that parliament is doing a good job of representing their interests. The number of people who feel that they have influence over decision-making nationally is 16 per cent: https://assets.contentful.com/xkbaceojm9pp/1vNB TsOEiYciKEAqWAmEKi/c9cc36b98f60328c0327e313ab37aeoc/Audit_of_political_ Engagement_14__2017_.pdf

world isn't just essential to win political power. It is also essential to oppose it. Underneath the system of parliaments and parties that Henry Parker had originated, an earthquake has been rumbling.

Marianne Grimmenstein

Since 2014, Gregor Hackmack has been the head of the German branch of change.org. Launched in 2007, change.org is a website which allows users to create petitions and mobilise supporters on any issue they feel demands attention. Over 100 million people have signed a petition started on the site, spanning almost every country on earth. They've claimed victories in everything from new anti-bullying laws in the United States, more affordable text-books in Spain, to saving ancient olive groves in Turkey.

Shortly after joining, Gregor sat in his office. 'Where are the good campaigns?' he thought. 'Who needs my help?' He flicked through a pile of newspapers and picked up *Die Tageszeitung*. '*Taz*', as it's known by its readers, is a small German newspaper, and in it was a small article. A woman was trying to sue the German government in the constitutional court over something called CETA. Gregor was a veteran campaigner, but it was the first time he'd heard of CETA.

The Comprehensive Economic and Trade Agreement (CETA) was an enormous trade deal that had been in negotiation for years, aiming to abolish most of the custom duties between Canada and the European Union. It was ready to come into force, and each of the EU's member-states were ratifying the deal.

The woman's name was Marianne Grimmenstein. Seventy years old, she lived in Lüdenscheid, an old, small industrial town nestled among the hills and valleys of western central Germany. Twice a week, she taught the flute to pupils in the music school near her home. She had , taken a great interest in CETA and strongly disagreed with it. She was afraid that it would unleash a free trade zone where the power of big companies would steamroller over the rights of workers and the environment. There was also to be a CETA committee, rather than democratically elected parliaments, that would resolve certain disputes. Mrs Grimmenstein thought it was unconstitutional. So she got a friend with some legal knowledge to help her, and applied to the court to stop CETA coming into force. It failed. The constitutional court – the highest in Germany – wouldn't even hear the case.

'I called her up,' Gregor told me. She hadn't heard of change. org but agreed to give it a try. Gregor helped her set up a petition. 'I thought we might get five or six friends to help and sign,' he said. But word of the campaign spread through change.org's community, and within two weeks it had 60,0000 signatures. Then 100,000. The campaign had begun to tumble into the attention of change.org's boisterous, active German membership.

'Now we needed real legal advice,' said Gregor. Mrs Grimmenstein contacted one of Germany's foremost experts in CETA, a professor in public law called Andreas Fisahn, who agreed to help.

'Oh my God,' Gregor remembered. 'She signed the contract. But we didn't have any money.' Mrs Grimmenstein, semi-retired and by no means wealthy, had contracted Fisahn to prepare the case, committing her to a fee of 14,000 euros.

'I was panicking a bit,' said Gregor. 'I was brand new at change. org.' Bankrupting first-time users of the platform wasn't part of the plan. He knew that they needed to crowdfund the money for the legal case. 'Only one crowdfunding platform actually allowed the campaign. Via PayPal. She didn't have a PayPal account.'

Gregor and Mrs Grimmenstein leveraged the online campaign they'd started to raise money for the legal costs. 'Literally every minute someone was depositing money to the PayPal account – email after email,' said Gregor, letting out a long sigh. They raised 18,000 euros in two days. 'We were actually desperately tying to shut it off,' said Gregor. 'We were getting too much.'

Their next step was to harness the growing popular support in another way: they turned the legal challenge into a 'class action'. This is a kind of lawsuit claiming a harm against an entire 'class' or group of people, and Grimmenstein wanted to bring one on behalf of the entire German people. By October 2015 they invited others to formally join the case. 'We weren't sure how many people could be bothered,' said Gregor. You had to print out a PDF, sign it, and post it to Marianne Grimmenstein's home.

The postman of Lüdenscheid couldn't help noticing that the Grimmensteins were beginning to receive more post than they did before. Single letters turned into bundles, and those turned into sacks, until the post office had to give Mrs Grimmenstein her own postman to handle the flood of mail. Almost 70,000 letters arrived, her whole house full of teetering white columns of paper, neatly bundled together by elastic bands.

Marianne, her eighty-year-old husband Peter, and three volun-teers (also raised by the campaign) sorted through her letters in her living room. 'World politics out of Lüdenscheid,' Gregor laughed. 'Journalists would travel 500 kilometres from Berlin to see Marianne Grimmenstein's living room. For me it was "wow". It's incredible what is possible in the age of digitalisation. There's so many opportunities for the normal person to create massive impact for change. I experienced it first hand and I was blown away.'

In October 2016, Gregor and Mrs Grimmenstein arrived in Karlsruhe, the home of the Federal Constitutional Court. Two years after she was first denied, she had at last got her hearing, and this time she had 68,000 comrades as co-plaintiffs. It was one of the largest constitutional claims in the history of Germany.

Eight of Germany's most senior judges filed into the courtroom, grandly attired in red robes. But then, a hubbub passed through the court. 'We thought the government would send some lawyers,' said Gregor. Instead, a patrician figure swept into the room. Sigmar Gabriel,[13] the German vice-chancellor and economic minister, had, extraordinarily, travelled 700 kilometres from Berlin to be there. At one moment, Gregor remembers, Mrs Grimmenstein and Sigmar Gabriel were standing face to face. You couldn't get a greater imbalance of conventional social and political power. 'You're the woman', Gregor remembers him saying, 'who is causing me all these problems.'

The vice chancellor pushed away the lawyers and ended up defending the government himself – angrily suggesting that the court itself had exceeded its remit. The court ended up approving CETA, but Mrs Grimmenstein was overjoyed. It had also added conditions: it would be parliaments, not the CETA committee, that would have the final say on disputes, and it ordered that the

13 Or, if you remember him from his days as the SPD's 'Representative for Pop Culture and Pop Discourse', Siggi Pop.

Government must always retain the right to withdraw from CETA. 'That's at least a 70 per cent victory' she said. 'I'm really happy.'[14]

An Explosion of Protest

The Egyptian Revolution in 2011 was the moment when many, including me, woke up to how protest was changing. I remember staring at the television, alone in my dark flat half a world away in London, watching the tightly packed crowd in Tahrir Square. I had strolled around there, less than a year earlier, the white-uniformed police of President Hosni Mubarak always standing in small huddles dotted around that enormous central artery. Now it was a sprawling mass of bricks and blood.

Protestors had clung on for days, chanting for a new Egypt. Snipers had climbed the tall buildings that surrounded the square and gunfire sporadically cracked over the chants. They had been charged by camels, and white plumes of teargas hung in the sky over each of the boulevards that opened out in the square. But they had organised themselves: there were food stalls, water points, toilets, a wall of martyrs. And in the heart of the square, a space reserved for the bloggers, transmitting the protestors' message to the rest of the world.

In June 2010, over half a year before the protests began, a Facebook page had appeared, protesting against the torture and murder of a young man, Khaled Said, by Egyptian police. The page was called 'We Are All Khaled Said'. Thousands upon thou-

14 www.sueddeutsche.de/wirtschaft/bundesverfassungsgericht-zu-ceta-ceta-klaegerin-das-ist-mindestens-ein-prozent-sieg-1.3203995

sands of Egyptians joined the page. First, in Alexandria, Facebook users arranged a silent protest, facing out to sea. Then, people started sharing photos and reporting on other violations of human rights. The page's members began to suggest ideas for how to challenge the regime, and voting on them. After polling the page's users, the creator of the page, Wael Ghonim, posted a Facebook event, inviting people to Tahrir Square on 25 January 2011.

Only a quarter of Egypt was online in 2011. But the people that had showed up on the first day, who had made that first sign of dissent, had come from social media. And from those few thousands, the protest avalanched, including people far beyond that early knot of digital activists. Eighteen days later, Mubarak's thirty-year rule had ended.

There were lots of different reason why these movements happened. But with the Arab Spring came the widespread belief that social media and the internet had weakened despotism. Networked publics would overcome coercion. Self-organisation would replace autocracies. Tunisia's uprising had already happened earlier that year. The Libyan civil war came next, and also Syria.

But from the crumbling autocracies of the Middle East, protest continued to spread. 'America needs its own Tahrir,' an email read, sent out in June 2011 to subscribers of *Adbusters*, a magazine 'to advance the new social activist movement of the information age'.[15] A few months later, in September, around a thousand people showed up at a protest against economic inequality and corporate corruption in Zuccotti Park in New York's Wall Street district.

15 www.newyorker.com/magazine/2011/11/28/pre-occupied

And rather than going home, that evening some of the protestors stayed in the park, putting up tents. They called the encampment Occupy Wall Street. Support for the nascent occupation began to build. Hundreds of airline pilots marched in solidarity, as did a rally of postal workers. Mainstream news organisations tended to either ignore or dismiss the protest, especially in America, but it boomed online: protestors streamed live video from Zuccotti Park, and discussion pages on it began to quickly proliferate. Researchers found hundreds of Facebook pages covering Occupy, and hundreds of thousands of people participating in them.[16]

Tented cities began to emerge elsewhere: Tampa, Florida; Columbus, Ohio; Woodruff Park, Atlanta. Occupy Wall Street was joined by Occupy Philadelphia, Occupy Boston, Occupy D.C., Occupy St Louis, Occupy Buffalo, Occupy Baltimore, Occupy Cleveland. Meetings and marches and the signature of the movement – tented encampments – appeared in universities, college campuses, parks, squares. It spread throughout Canada; there were demonstrations in South Africa, Nigeria, Tunisia and Latin America; there were huge demonstrations in Europe. In a handful of months, Occupy became truly global. From Zucotti Park, there were protests in eighty-two countries, 951 cities, involving millions of people.

Occupations began to emerge apparently from no-where, beginning small and becoming booming symbols of collective dissent in only a moment.In 2013, a small knot of protestors were pepper-sprayed and attacked as they tried to stop the demolition of Gezi

16 Zeynep Tufekci, *Twitter and Teargas*, p. 214; Sarah Gaby, Neal Caren, 'Occupy Online: How Cute Old Men and Malcolm X Recruited 400,000 US Users to OWS on Facebook', *Social Movement Studies* 11, not. 2–3 (2012), pp. 367–74.

Park in Istanbul. As the images of the violence went viral, the crowds in the park and nearby Taksim Square began to grow. Calls spread online as people in the park clashed heavily with the police. Molotov cocktails, slingshots, tear gas and dire threats were thrown from one side to another, and a bulldozer was hijacked and chased police vehicles out of the square. Over the days that followed the occupation became entrenched. A library appeared, a medical clinic, both funded by a stream of donations. Like Occupy, it was organised both face to face and online. There was zero preparation, and barely any institutional leadership. The Turkish government themselves estimated that 2.5 million people had been involved at some point in its three-week duration.

There were huge anti-austerity protests in the Plaza del Sol in Madrid, driven by the anti-austerity 15-M Movement, involving over 6 million Spaniards. Southern Europe's 'indignados' staged occupations across Spain, Italy and Greece. In 2014, Hong Kong saw the 'Umbrella Revolution', demanding genuine universal suffrage and the resignation of politicians.

I remember landing in South Korea in 2017 to see crowds glued to the huge television screens at the airport. The pictures showed the presidential motorcade of Park Geun-hye snaking out of her compound. She had been dismissed from her post.

The next day, I walked around the protest encampment in central Seoul, then mainly quiet and deserted. These were the dying embers of the Candlelight Revolution. For months, Koreans in their millions had thronged in the wide boulevards of the city, overlooked by glassy-faced skyscrapers. Activists from the South Korean group WAGL[17] told me what had happened. South Korea,

---

17 The name was phonetic; in South Korea it is supposed to sound like the noise of a crowd.

they said, was a country with little history of political protest. But after thirty years of civil disengagement, they had just kicked out a sitting president.

Partly, this was down to societal change. South Korean society had undergone a 'value shift' towards transparency and integrity, and it was simply less willing to tolerate the corruption of politicians like Park. There wasn't the organisational infrastructure for mass protest or civil disobedience. But WAGL had helped to coordinate the protests using Facebook, Twitter and KakaoTalk (a South Korean version of WhatsApp, a messaging platform). Anti-Park memes appeared on protest banners. Lolcats were printed on flags. Online campaigning led to unprecedented grassroots mobilisation, which in turn led out onto the streets of Seoul.

Protests became known for their hashtags. #blacklivesmatter began online in 2014, after the acquittal of George Zimmerman over the shooting and killing of African-American teen Trayvon Martin. In what became a broader protest against police brutality and targeting of black communities, public marches in the name of Black Lives Matter have happened all over the States. Over 2,000 demonstrations have been recorded, more than one per day.[18] Likewise, the #MeToo campaign arose in 2017 in response to more than a dozen allegations of sexual assault against Hollywood mogul Harvey Weinstein. Millions of social media users, mainly women, began to use the hashtag, in order to share their own experiences of sexual harassment and assault, to empathise with others, and to challenge how sexual assault is handled, spoken about and policed.

18 https://elephrame.com/textbook/BLM

Mobilisations and counter-mobilisations happened across the far reaches of the political spectrum. In response to #blacklivesmatter, for example, #bluelivesmatter (supporting police officers) came into being. The internet has allowed feminists to mobilise in news ways, but in turn an online 'manosphere' has emerged, populated by men's rights activists, pick-up artists, paleomasculinists (who believe male domination is natural) and many others.[19] As early as 2011, far-right movements across Europe were active on Facebook. The English Defence League in the UK mobilised to 'defend English culture against Sharia law'. Other nationalist movements grew elsewhere: the Swedish Democrats, the Dutch Freedom Party, the Front National Party in France, Italy's Lega Nord, the Danish People's Party, Flemish Interest in Belgium, CasaPound in Italy. All were different from each other, of course – some had ambitions to enter formal politics, others were focused on street protests. But they were broadly united in their antipathy to multiculturalism, globalisation, immigration and what they saw to be the erosion of western culture. And in most cases, their online Facebook following dwarfed their formal membership.[20]

Technology doesn't make protests; people make protests. Many of the largest public demonstrations took place in the aftermath of the recession in 2009, as people raged against austerity and demanded more equality, jobs and opportunities. Likewise, protests also occurred after decades of autocratic governments, in the face of police brutality, and in the wake of globalisation and other sweeping social trends.

19 Alice Marwick and Rebecca Lewis, 'Media Manipulation and Disinformation Online', *Data & Society*, p.14
20 Jamie Bartlett, Jonathan Birdwell, Mark Litter, *The New Face of Digital Populism*, Demos

Technology, however, is making different human actions possible. Political mobilisation used to be expensive and difficult. Reaching people – painstakingly building lists of members and supporters – took time and effort. Organisations such as political parties, trade unions and charities needed money, contacts and experience to get their message out. Today, protests have taken on a different character.

New protests come seemingly from nowhere, spontaneously. The trigger now tends to be an event – a scandal or tipping point – rather than an organisational decision. They spread unbelievably quickly. A movement that hadn't existed a few days ago could be millions strong tomorrow.

The mainstream is being challenged by everything that isn't itself. Feminists, meninists, animal rights campaigners, anti-corruption activists in Romania, ultra-nationalists in Russia – there seems to be no particular political direction that has benefited more from the internet. Both anti-authoritarian and authoritarian, mobilisations and counter-mobilisations have erupted all over the world. It is not just one side – either left or right – that is being strengthened by these changes. Instead every political opinion outside of the mainstream political consensus has gained prominence. Movement after movement has emerged to unsettle the incumbent political powers around the world.

Protestors now have the power to organise without organisations.[21] People can protest, mobilise, coordinate and act without needing to have institutions in place beforehand, andthat has ripped politics wide open. This drastically alters the relationship

---

21 This was the argument (and subtitle) of Clay Shirky's influential book on collective action, *Here Comes Everybody*.

between the powerful and the powerless, those with their hands on the reins of power, and those that disagree with what that power is used to do. Monopolies are toppling everywhere, all over the world. The money, experience and machinery of the political mainstream matter a lot less than they used to. As mass movements and mobilisations challenge the consensuses, institutions, the very underlying assumptions and practices of mainstream politics, they are starting to change what the mainstream itself is. But the ability to oppose political power is one thing . . . what about the ability to use it?

For Colin Megill, an activist and technologist, both Occupy and Tahrir Square were huge wake-up calls. They showed how powerful digital life was going to be for politics. But also that mobilisation without consensus was dangerous. Moments of awakening, and moments of warning. 'At Occupy, we saw mobilisation,' Colin told me. 'likewise Tahrir Square and Green revolution. We saw the huge potential. The frustration was that you had all that passion, but there was no way of a decentralised community getting to a consensus and discovering who is and is not speaking on behalf of everyone.'

Protests without formal organisations can find it difficult to turn an opposition to something into an agenda for something else. Without such organisations, it is difficult to resolve disagreements and collectively make decisions. It is easier to protest, but harder for that protest to define itself, harder to react to offers and overtures made by authorities. And that has meant that protest has also become fragile. Fast, cheap and fragile.[22]

22 A view that I share and owe to Zeynep Tufekci in her book on digital protest, *Twitter and Teargas*.

The Occupy Movement knew what it didn't want. But the protesters struggled to come together to say what it was that they did want. All the individual voices created a cacophony. The lack of consensus caused people to naturally move into tighter balls of people similar to them. It created division, and eventually polarisation. As more and more people came into Zuccotti Park, they concentrated into smaller, homogenous groups. Separate 'uptown' and 'downtown' areas developed. Uptown had a library, an Apple pop-up store, bicycle-powered espresso machines. Downtown, a drum circle. 'Up is where the college hipsters go,' said a protestor interviewed at the occupied site, 'where they try to rule the park from. Down here it's more a poor people's encampment. It's kind of contentious.'[23]

Colin was one of a new kind of person entering politics from the world of technology – loosely termed 'civic hackers'. They knew that there needed to be ways not only to challenge and oppose decisions, but also to make new ones. And they needed to do it in ways that didn't reflect (in the eyes of many of the protestors themselves) the flawed, rigid hierarchies of the very institutions they were seeking to oppose. It wasn't only a question of protesting the old politics, but also the making of a new politics too. Protest could challenge political power, but consensus was needed to remake it. In addition to opposing political power in its current forms, new groups of people were also turning to digital technology in order to provide the answers to the perceived problems. It was a challenge to the political status quo that was more subterranean; quieter than Trump's tweets or the popular hashtag campaigns. But it was also reaching deeper, into the very fundamental levels of what political power really was.

23 https://vimeo.com/148680935

The Civic Hackers

Audrey Tang had always been fascinated with programming and computers. She came from a family of activists, and her parents said she was reading classical literature in a variety of languages and solving simultaneous equations in first grade. With all the hallmarks of a child prodigy, she left school at fourteen, and by sixteen had founded her first company, a start-up that built a search engine for Mandarin-language song lyrics. She moved to Silicon Valley and worked as a consultant for Apple, reportedly earning one bitcoin an hour.[24]

In 2012, Audrey was back in Taiwan. Then in her early thirties, she announced her 'retirement' and moved back see how the internet could be used for the public good.[25] The world economy was reeling from the recession, and the Taiwanese government announced a massive stimulus package that they hoped would reinvigorate the economy. They called it the Economic Power-up Plan.

To promote the Economic Power-up Plan, the government produced an advert. It showed four people: a young man, a ship owner, a female office worker and an elderly woman, all staring cluelessly at a sign reading: 'The Economic Power-up Plan'. 'What exactly is the Economic Power-up Plan? We would very much like to explain it to you in simple words,' a voice cuts in. 'But it is impossible due to the complexity . . . The most important thing is that a lot of things are being done. We might as well run until our legs break instead of just simply talking,' the voice concludes.

24 At the time of writing, that would mean she had earned roughly £12,000 an hour.
25 www.taipeitimes.com/News/taiwan/archives/2016/08/28/2003654031/2

'It was insulting,' said Audrey. What had really been advertised was a government who saw no value, no way, in explaining complicated policies to their citizens. It wasn't just the tone of the message that was insulting; it was the message itself. This wasn't the way that politics should work.

Taiwanese YouTubers began to flag the video as fraudulent. So many, indeed, that YouTube removed the video, and suspended the government's account. 'A government account being suspended by YouTube . . . Our government has became a global joke,' a legislator said later.[26]

In the wake of the video, a group, including Audrey, came together with a call to 'fork the government'. It was the language of software developers, in which a 'fork' means to take a piece of software down a different path, forking off from the main version. They called themselves Gov Zero – or just Gov – and they wanted to build new ways for citizens to understand what government was doing – and to challenge government to become more open to citizens too. It was a fork, in their eyes, towards a government that was more transparent.

Gov was intended to be one button press away from government: a ghost, a shadow to the official websites. Throughout 2013, dozens of new 'civic remixes' got off the ground. Often they simply scraped government websites and found ways of making the data they found more accessible to normal users. They set up fact.gov. tw, a website for presenting complicated information in the form of simple timelines. They set up the Deaf Welfare Portal, which helped hearing-impaired users to find the relevant laws, welfare

26 DPP Legislator Tsai Chi-chang (蔡其昌).

channels and aid packages relevant to their specific hearing condition. On each gov page – on subjects as diverse as congress,
tenders, geography, weather, healthcare and electricity – was a
mix of the data, tech or new thinking they wanted to use to open
up government.

For most of her life, Audrey and her Gov colleagues had been
involved in a culture that had formed on the internet, primarily
between those making technology, especially software. Called the
open source movement, it was nothing less than a parallel political
system. As Audrey said, reflecting on it: 'I am a conservative
anarchist. It may seem contradictory: anarchy is often associated
with utopia, a dream world set in the future. But I've experienced
this "utopia" for over twenty years: it is the anarchy of the net I
want to keep.'[27] And it was a system that was especially hostile to
the top-down fiat of the Economic Power-up Plan.

The open source movement had, for decades, largely stayed
away from the mainstream politics of offline life. But movements
like gov were a sign that this was changing. The values of the
open movement were beginning to become demands for mainstream political reform. The group could see that new forms of
political deliberation, representation and decision-making were
possible for the politics of states, not just the internet. They began
to call, with increasing volume and urgency, for open politics as
well as open source.

Audrey began to foment her own ideas. If you don't like it, she
thought, then build a better way. Audrey believed the public could
change how politics worked not just by complaining about the

27 http://blog.openculture.org/2015/10/12/audrey-tang-brilliant-programmer-hacks-
   politics-in-taiwan/

status quo, but by building new alternatives to it. Audrey wanted to open the process of government as much as possible, so people could see who made decisions, on what basis, reflecting what evidence, and so on. She wanted to challenge how decisions should be made. Consensus, not majorities, was at the heart of the belief system of the open movement, and consensus produced by having as many people as possible involved in the process. Top-down decisions should not just be announced by the government; ideas should be cultivated and encouraged.

So it wasn't just that political parties could use the internet to campaign for political power. And it wasn't just that groups had found new ways to oppose political power. Something else was happening too. New ideas, new demands were emerging on the internet that began to look like a new political philosophy, a new way to do politics. It was an emerging ideological challenge to the very fundamentals of the status quo. As two Taiwanese members of the movement, Mei-Chun Lee and Po-yu Tseng, put it: 'Open government is not just a slogan of reform but a political movement. It redefines the relationship between government and civil society'.[28]

The Sunflower Revolution

In 2014, two years after the fiasco of the Economic Power-up Plan, the Cross-Strait Service Trade Agreement (CSSTA) was tabled in the Taiwanese Parliament. It aimed to open up more trade

28 Authors of the *Taiwan Open Government Report*.

between China and Taiwan, to allow investment and business-people to move more easily between the two countries. There had been simmering concerns about the bill among the public. There were fears that it was laying the groundwork for the eventual unification of the two countries and in response the government had promised that it would open the bill up to over a dozen public hearings for careful scrutiny.

But then, the ruling Kuomintang Party acted. Before the review had begun, they forced the agreement onto the floor of the parliament for a final vote, ignoring previous promises they'd made to subject the law to a line-by-line review, or citizen assemblies. It was a unilateral, politically aggressive move.

The next evening, protestors surrounded the Taiwanese parliament. There were academics, students, civil society organisations, protest groups. A few hundred protestors climbed over the fence, broke a window, and burst onto the floor of the parliament. They had physically entered into the place from which they felt recent events had excluded them.

Stuffing rucksacks full of electronics and wires, members of Gov dashed around the parliament offices. Among the crowd, weather-proofed racks of servers appeared, and satellite dishes. Out of the open windows of the building snaked thick electrical cables. Gov had scrambled together a ramshackle infrastructure to broadcast the occupation on YouTube and on giant screens outside. Media had reported the occupiers as 'mobsters', having fights, drinking beer. Yet Gov now provided 'zero-hand' reporting. 'Reality itself speaking to you', Audrey said.

Over the next few nights there were violent clashes outside the executive chamber, where the government was housed, and the protestors were eventually beaten back by riot police. But in the legislative chamber itself, with the protestors refusing the leave, there was stalemate. The world was watching, on the internet and on huge screens, and the police simply couldn't allow a bloody brawl to break out on the floor of the parliament.

Day after day, the occupation continued on.[29] Sitting in circles, taking turns to speak, the occupiers began to debate policy. In fact, political debate was taking place everywhere: online, outside on the streets, as well as on the floor of the parliament itself. It was becoming a demonstration of another way that the CSSTA decision could have been made: by scalable listening, empathy-building, and consensus-making. The values, indeed, of the open source movement.

After the Revolution

The occupiers eventually left the parliament only after the government promised to postpone the trade pact. But that didn't end the government's crisis of legitimacy. Confidence in Taiwan's president was barely above single digits. Beyond the trade pact itself, the actual practice of democracy had become a political issue. The occupiers had demonstrated in front of millions how to conduct transparent democratic process at scale, and in the municipal elections that followed, the Kuomintang Party suffered heavy defeats. By the end of 2014, city-level elections brought many occupiers into local government. And the premier, Jiang Yi-huah, the old foe of the occupiers, resigned by the end of that year.

29 https://civichall.org/civicist/vtaiwan-democracy-frontier/

The government began to pivot towards a platform of opening itself up to regain trust. Then something extraordinary happened. Jaclyn Tsai, a minister in the new government, came to a Gov hackathon. 'We need a platform to allow the entire society to engage in rational discussion,' she told them. The government never wanted to see another Sunflower Revolution again. They didn't want citizens to feel so shut out of parliament that they felt they needed to break in. They knew they had to find new ways of making decisions. The government was asking the civic hackers for help.

In return for Gov's help, the government offered their most precious commodity of all: power. If this new process, whatever it was, could create consensus, then the government would be bound to enact it in law. The civic hackers had tried to hack into the corridors of power. Now they were being brought inside.

And Audrey. She had dropped out of school at fourteen, and had her own technology start-up at fifteen. She had been a Silicon Valley entrepreneur and by thirty a civic hacker. But then, in 2016, to bring this new politics into being, she was appointed by the new incoming government first as a minister without portfolio, and then, in October 2016, as the Digital Minister of Taiwan. She was the youngest minister in the cabinet, and the first transgender politician ever to hold office in Taiwan. But the thing that set Audrey most apart was that she was a completely new kind of politician. One that wanted to change not only what government did, but government actually was.

Audrey and the civic hackers saw the challenge of democracy as a problem of information. Voting was a single opportunity for a citizen to give off a political signal. But it was an incredibly weak signal. It wasn't enough to let the government know what citizens felt about any issue, and it wasn't enough for citizens to feel that they were being involved in the outcome. During an election, the choice facing the voter was already framed. The agenda already set. And the vote itself, in any given electoral system, might matter little to the outcome and therefore little to the candidates.

Audrey brought Gov into government. They called their new organisation the Public Digital Innovation Service (PDIS). Their values were the same as the open source community: participation, accountability and transparency.

The changes were tangible and wide-ranging. They worked on increasing the information flowing out of government. They made government data 'open by default'. They created a dashboard to share government information to allow everyone to track fluc- tuations in vegetable prices during the typhoon season. They constructed a portal to share real-time information about disasters and emergencies. They built a working forum system to bridge the gap between officials and civil society, where ministries are required to respond to questions within seven days. They created participation officers – volunteers across the government who regularly meet to learn the ways of open government.

As important as it was to increase the flow of information going from the government to citizens, they also needed to deal with the thorniest question of all. 'Democracy', said PDIS, 'is defined as government by the people, but it is also the active participation of the people, as citizens in politics and civic life.'

They needed to find a way for Taiwanese citizens to give off more political signals back to the government. They need to collect the beliefs of the Taiwanese public on the issues that mattered to them. But beyond simply sharing their beliefs, the process needed to allow them to deliberate with each other constructively. And beyond even that, they needed to find a way for citizens to find what they had in common: to build consensus.

VTaiwan

Throughout the frustrations of Tahrir, Occupy and mobilisations elsewhere Colin Megill thought a lot about the democracy: 'why do humans have difficulty coordinating their behaviour?' Why is it so complicated?

Colin, like Audrey, saw democracy as basically a problem of information: 'Democracy is coarse-grained. Voting is compression – it's removing information. We want to make it a little more fine-grained, moving beyond voting to the agenda-setting stuff.'

After Occupy, Colin set out to find a way of solving this information problem. He began to collaborate with technologists to build new ways that opinions could be seen and consensus reached. They drew on insights from machine learning and computational biology, and beganto build a platform that could move beyond polarisation, polemics and dogma. 'I call it a router,' said Colin. It was a way to help groups understand themselves, to help government understand how these groups relate to each other, and to see where there is consensus between the groups. It was called pol.is.

Gov began working with the team around polis on a new way to make political decisions. As they would with any piece of software, they edged it forwards, constantly tweaking the process, constantly evaluating it and acting on feedback. They glued together the workings of government, the media and civic technology, especially pol.is. It was called vTaiwan. Before long, it faced a difficult test. The twelfth topic it was directed towards was, a political controversy that Audrey called 'an epidemic of the mind'. The issue was Uber.[30]

As PDIS got going, Uber had recently opened in Taiwan. Within the usual chorus of conflict and division, it was the job of vTaiwan to resolve how it should be regulated. Gov knew that direct democracy didn't work if people didn't agree on the basic facts. All sides needed to start deliberating based on a shared grounding of evidence. Under the vTaiwan process, the first stage was the 'objective', with the aim of simply laying out the basic facts of what was known. Important articles and facts were put onto a Wikipedia timeline, and validated independently.[31]

The next stage was the most difficult: 'reflection'. People from all sides came to share their feelings. Taipei taxi drivers, representatives of Uber, members of the government, business leaders, trade unions, taxi users, Uber services, all came to share their views.

It was here that vTaiwan used pol.is. People with opinions across the Uber divide were asked to log on to the site. As they did so, a white screen appeared, and a single statement: 'I think passenger liability insurance should be mandatory for riders on UberX private vehicles.' No one could give an individualised response to this – you had to simply agree, disagree or pass. 'Basically, replies at scale don't work,' said Colin. 'We did away with replies. That's part of the core idea.' Replies means trolling and division. And polis was built to avoid that.

30 https://medium.com/@richdecibels/how-taiwan-solved-the-uber-problem-29fd2358a284
31 http://fact.gov.tw/wikipedia/優步時間軸#18

As people responded to the statement, pol.is showed them a map. On it were small circular avatars for each of the people that had answered the question. The people that agreed with you appeared in one group and people that disagreed in another. Then people were asked to draft their own statements, beginning with 'My feeling is . . .' 'The aim', said Colin, 'was to give the agenda-setting power to the people. In voting, the cake is baked. The goal is to engage citizens far earlier, when everyone is arguing over the ingredients.'

Participants were asked to keep drafting statements and answering them.[32] As they did so, each person's little circular avatar started bouncing around the map, staying close to the people that they kept agreeing with, and moving away from people where disagreements had emerged. The software created and analysed a matrix comprising what each person thought about every comment. This is an algorithm,[33] making sense of what Colin called a 'combinatory space'. 'We wanted a comment system to be able to handle large populations and stay coherent, while preserving minority opinions and producing insights automatically. AI made that possible. We wanted people to feel safe, listened to and be able to jump in and out as they please. Overall, we wanted to make it easier to success-fully decentralise power in organisations of all kinds.'

Over the first few days, pol.is kept visualising how opinions emerged, clustered, responded, divided and recombined. At first people shared strong feelings that appealed to other groups close by. Four broad groups of people soon emerged: taxi drivers, Uber drivers, Uber passengers, and other passengers.

32 Or you may prefer Colin's phraseology: 'Getting high-dimensional, organic feedback from the population during a problem identification phase.'
33 A dimensionality reduction algorithm, more specifically.

Eventually, those four groups turned into two. Group One clustered around a statement that wanted to flatly ban Uber. Seventy-five per cent agreed with: 'Since the Ministry has already rejected Uber's administrative appeal, I think Taipei city government should cancel the company registration of Taiwan Uber Inc.' Group Two had clustered around another, completely different view: 'When I am not in a hurry, I prefer to call Uber even if there are plenty of taxis in the street' (77 per cent of Group Two thought this).

But while majorities of these two groups held these opinions, there were more people disagreeing with these two statements overall than agreeing with them. This is the opposite of a consensus. This is polarisation. And if this was Twitter or Facebook, we'd see echo chambers, spats, competing online petitions and massively contradictory information flowing into politicians. We'd be getting nowhere.

But pol.is produced something more useful than just feedback. 'When people started using pol.is, we found that it became a consensus-generating mechanism,' said Colin.

People were asked to continue to draft statements, but the ones that were given visibility, that other people could see, where those that found support not only from the drafter's group, but the other groups as well. The process encouraged people to start posting more consensual, more nuanced statements. 'Change the information structure,' said Colin, 'and you can tweak power.' Group One toned down their original statement: 'I think it is the responsibility of the Ministry to actively outlaw unlicensed passenger vehicles' (87 per cent agreed). The main concern was the lack of registration.

So did Group Two. For them, the main concern was that getting registered was difficult, as it was practically a closed shop:

'Currently, the only way for traditional taxis to survive is to join a taxi fleet . . . UberX has subverted this unwritten rule. I think it is quite awesome!' (93 per cent).

By the fourth week the groups had come together and a consensus statement had emerged: 'The government should leverage this opportunity to challenge the taxi industry to improve their management and quality control systems so that drivers and riders would enjoy the same quality service as Uber' (95 per cent across all groups).

The aim was to find a consensus statement that had a 'super-majority' – your group agreed with it, and at least 50 per cent of other groups too. This made it very difficult for any of the interest groups to flood the process.

Those consensus items fed into the next stage of vTaiwan: 'interpretation'. The authors of the consensus statements joined other representatives and stakeholders who met face to face – livestreamed, published in open structured data, fully transparent. They went through the facts and the consensus items shared on the pol.is platform, and tried to agree recommendations to be passed over to the government.

Finally, the outcomes were coded into legalese. On 23 May 2016, the Taiwanese government pledged to ratify *all* the pol.is consensus items: taxis no longer needed to be painted yellow; app-based taxis were free to operate as long as they didn't undercut existing meters and so on. This was the 'decisions' part of the vTaiwan process.

The process didn't only give everyone a chance to speak. It also created empathy between the groups. When the Taipei High Administrative Court rejected Uber's appeal on one of the finer points of the ruling, the Ministry's press release stated:

'We are grieved for and pity them; we do not feel joy at our own ability.'[34]

On 26 July 2016, Taiwan's new premier declared that 'all substantial national issues should go through a vTaiwan-like process'. VTaiwan's success over Uber was followed by another shortly after. It broke a six-year deadlock over the sale of alcohol online. It has been used to conclude about twenty disputes now, involving around 50,000 stakeholders, experts and members of the public. Five new cases, PDIS tell me, are on the way; two are under discussion. Eight times it has changed the law, and seven times it has changed regulation. So far, the issues have been primarily digital, affecting least the people least likely to use it. Baby steps? Perhaps.

Technology has opened up new possibilities for how to answer that same basic question that Henry Parker struggled with over five centuries ago: how do you put the people in charge? How can democracy practically work?. Sometimes triggered by crisis, sometimes by generalised democratic discontent, groups of people around the world have begun to experiment with new systems. The philosophy of open source, joined with the technology that can make it happen, has begun to slowly shift the practices of governments around the world.

In Seoul, I met with Kim Sung Kook, a member of the city's government. 'In the past,' he told me, 'we made policies with other public sectors and provided service to the citizens. It was mainly

34 The quote is notable, Audrey points out, for its preceding text in the original *Confucian Analects* from which it is drawn: 'The rulers have failed in their duties, and the people consequently have been disorganised, for a long time': https://blog.pol.is/uber-responds-to-vtaiwans-coherent-blended-volition-3e9b75102b9b

a government-led approach. Now, we want to make service *with* citizens, private sectors and academics.' They called the plan Global Digital Strategy 2020, and introduced the Smart Complaint App, which allows the city's inhabitants to complain about anything. Every day, 25,000 complaints or requests flow into City Hall's servers, handled by 400 staff members.

The 'Pots and Pans Revolution' occurred in Iceland in 2009 as a reaction against the government's handling of the financial crisis. The Best Party was founded by the comedian Jón Gnarr, originally as a joke, stating that while all other parties were secretly corrupt, they were openly corrupt, and wouldn't honour any of their election promises. They won the 2010 city elections, and Gnarr became mayor of Reykjavik. The party jokingly committed itself to crowd-sourcing ideas, which led to a platform called 'Better Reykavik'. Every month, the city agrees to formally respond to the top fifteen ideas on the platform, and it's led to some tangible outcomes, including a public stairwell down to the beach and more homeless shelters.

Much like protest, new ways of wielding political power also spread. Parlement et Citoyens in France is a website which brings together representatives and citizens to discuss policy issues and collaboratively draft legislation.[35] In Finland, a new Citizens' Initiative Act enshrined the right of Finnish citizens to submit proposals for new legislation. In Brazil, the e-Democracia portal was set up in 2009 by the Chamber of Deputies to open up lawmaking to citizens.[36] In all these developments, public contribu-

---

35 Ten thousand participant contributions (proposals, amendments and comments), 85,000 registered votes and 23,000 registered users.

36 By September 2016, the portal had attracted about 37,000 registered users, more than 23,000 forum posts and more than 52 million visits.

tions can inform and shape the legislation that is put before their national parliament.

Most people do not want to participate in politics –. Shaping and debating laws takes time, can be costly and (I say this with some experience) boring. And the people who can and do participate are often not drawn equally across society. Lots of activists are students, because they have the time and energy to be. People who speak up in meetings are often more confident and experienced in doing so.

However, what vTaiwan did has sent shockwaves through activists and technologists across the world. It included many more people in the process than normal, and the process itself was open and transparent. It defused situations and promoted empathy, not enmity. And it showed that people do want to be heard in the decisions that really matter to them. VTaiwan was a first: it was changing power because it was also tied to power.

Audrey, too, was a completely new kind of politician. Although she holds executive office, Audrey doesn't see her job as making decisions at all. Instead, she sees herself as a 'channel for collective intelligence' – a convenor, moderator or chairperson within a much wider discussion. 'I bring what we do in the open source communities . . . I don't take commands. I don't give commands,' she said.[37] Every meeting that she has is recorded, transcribed and published for anyone to see. I communicated with Audrey – let's remember, a minister – on an open website, accessible to anyone with internet access.[38]

37 https://sayit.pdis.nat.gov.tw/20170208-rufus-pollock-visit
38 https://talk.pdis.nat.gov.tw/t/questions-to-audrey-tang-from-carl-miller-demos/1311/2

Gov in government has also begun to change the habits of compromise. Beyond campaigning, they have shown that there are new ways of talking to the people who you disagree with.

It's hardly the storming of the Winter Palace. No king has lost their head. No armies have been scattered on the field of battle. But this is a revolutionary moment. Henry Parker gave a new vision of parliamentary democracy to the world, but now it is being challenged again.

The pressure on governments will grow. Audrey's example is a powerful one, and the message of radically opening up politics and doing democracy differently to a parliament – at a time when so many feel so distant from it – is something that will only become louder and more difficult for conventional politicians to resist. For the first time in centuries, the basic order of parliamentary democracy is being challenged. And if it works, if the vision of people like Audrey spreads – as I think it will – political power will leak out of parliaments and out of governments. Politics will become more open, and citizens more powerful.

Start-Up Politics

I pushed into the air-conditioned cocoon of a Starbucks off Stevens Creek Boulevard in San Jose. Bigger than its more famous northern neighbour San Francisco, San Jose is a city that sprawls around both sides of the head of the Bay Area in California. It is the home of old-school Silicon Valley – the Dells and Intels rather than the Googles and Ubers.

Immediately, I see who I'm looking for. He is sitting rigidly, his legs curled into a lotus position on the high stool. His name is Patri Friedman. Patri has been a serious poker player and had graduated from Stanford in computer science. He was also the grandson of Milton Friedman, the Nobel Laureate.

'I was always a libertarian, always dissatisfied with the country. And being, like, young and ambitious, rather than giving up, I was like, all right, is there any way to fix it? Is there any way to change it?'

Patri spoke about politics in a way that I had never heard before. In his eyes, it can be directly equated to technology. A social technology. '[American political academic] Larry Lessig says code is law. And I say law is code. Law is an algorithm. Institutions are social technology.'

In Patri's eyes, the problem with government is that it can't do what other kinds of technology can: be updated. 'We're using best-of-breed governance technology from the eighteenth century right now. If I were driving a car from 1776, it would be a horse. From a programmer's perspective, we're using technology that hasn't had a rewrite for hundreds of years.'

What government needs is a start-up sector; its own Silicon Valley. The Valley had disrupted transport, advertising, healtcare. Why couldn't the same thinking be brought to disrupt the largest industry on earth: Government?

The problem was that it was hard to apply an entrepreneurial, Silicon Valley mindset to Government because there weren't any opportunities to start again and try out radically different alternatives. Governance, Patri argued, is one of the slowest technologies to advance because there aren't blank slates where people can try out new political systems. At some point, Patri said, we need to stop and do a rewrite from scratch. 'Re-architect your system,' was how he put it, 'because the problems you face in the twenty-first century are different.'

There needs to be opportunities to start again.

Patri wants to bring a Silicon Valley start-up culture to politics by ... creating new countries. In 2008, Parti founded the Seasteading Institute. Seasteading is the creation of new landmass on the ocean. Mainly floating concrete boxes, Patri told me, or concrete filled with foam. The ones that Patri drew for me were large, circular and flat layers of land, hundreds of metres across and surrounded by a floating breakwater, and tethered to something to stop them floating away. Imagine just a flat plane a few metres above the lapping waves.

The point of building seasteads is to create entirely new political blank canvasses that people can use to create entirely new forms of political organisation. Get a small passionate group of people, start with no users, design a new political system from scratch and scale it over time. 'What could be more Silicon Valley than that? It's taking the Silicon Valley mindset and applying it to another industry – one that's much bigger, much more broken and much harder to fix.'

'We need diversity and experiments. We need a bunch of people trying out a bunch of different political systems to see how it actually works in practice. Not arguing about them on the internet, and trying to get people to hack them into our existing country or start revolutions or whatever.' If it works, seasteads will create a start-up sector for governance. Building governments out on the waves – to see which ones work and which do not – is like a proof of concept. And if they succeed, they could possibly export successful models back to the mainland.

'The point of seasteading is not to make any one vision of society,' Patri argued. It isn't just libertarians that have become interested in nation founding. 'There are all kinds of utopian-communal traditions too.'

In January 2017, the Seasteading Institute signed a Memorandum of Understanding with French Polynesia, to create a 'SeaZone', carving out, as I understood it, some kind of partial sovereignty. Nothing seemed bound, everything still uncertain. It will be a decade, predicted Patri, before a hundred people are living on a seastead. Between twenty and fifty years before 100,000 are. We shall see. Their biggest challenge isn't, I think, building the island itself. It is convincing a country to part with what the whole project is about: sovereignty.

Seasteading is, again, the application of tech thinking to political problems. But here it isn't the values of Audrey's open source community that shine most clearly through. It's the creative, innovative muscle of Silicon Valley. While Audrey is working to change politics from the inside, Patri wants to open up a whole new frontier. And he isn't the only one.

The State Itself

Toomas Hendrik Ilves is, reports say, something of an unlikely sex symbol in his native Estonia.[39] His signature sartorial flourish

39 www.theguardian.com/world/2011/nov/03/president-ilves-made-estonia

is the bow tie; something he is never caught in public without. But he appeared on my computer screen only as a black box, with an explosive clearing of his throat. We were using Skype but he'd stuck tape over the webcam mounted on his laptop.

Ilves spoke in long, wandering paragraphs, with a flawless American accent, stopping only, from time to time, to cough. His family had fled Estonia in 1944 as the Soviet Red Army rolled in to end four years of Nazi occupation. Born in Sweden, he grew up in New York. After two psychology degrees, directorship of a Vancouver arts centre and teaching at an 'alternative arts school' in New Jersey, Ilves ended up on the Baltic desk of Radio Free Europe during the Cold War In 1993 he became Estonian ambassador to the United States, then foreign minister, then an MEP.

The digital world had changed how political power was won. It had changed how political power was opposed. It was changing how political power was used. But I wanted to know whether it was changing what political power flowed through – the instrument of politics: the state. And from 2006 to 2016, Toomas Hendrick Ilves had been the president of Estonia – its head of state.

'My contribution to this began with despairing of the state of affairs with Estonia,' he began. Before the Second World War, Estonia and its closest cultural neighbour, Finland, were equally rich. But as Estonia emerged from Soviet occupation in 1991, Finland was thirteen times richer. Estonia was independent, but poor.

'I was reading a book called *The End of Work*,' Ilves told me. 'There is discussion of a steel mill in Kentucky that had 12,000 employees and produced X million tonnes of steel. And then the Japanese bought it and automatised it and employed 120 people and produced the same number of tonnes of steel each year.' For the author, this was proof of how bad everything was. People were going to be driven out of work. But for Ilves, it was a great insight. 'Yes, we can be small and do things more efficiently,' Toomas kept going, his voice rising, 'but in order to do this we need to take this leap and digitise.' It was a backwards reading and, for Estonia, an incredibly important one.

Shortly after Estonia became independent, Ilves picked his first fight. Finland's capital, Helsinki, was updating its telephone exchange, and they offered the old, 1979 (analog) system to replace Estonia's even older system for free. 'I fought against that. I was "no way",' said Ilves. 'A lot of other countries in the post-communist world tended to hold onto both technological and other social legacy systems.' But he knew that Estonia needed radical change that could only come with new technology. He won, and they ended up going directly to a modern digital system.

The fight over the telephone system was really a fight over the kind of state that Estonia was going to be. Ilves and his allies saw digitisation as Estonia's escape route from poverty and backwardness, and they pushed hard for Estonia to embrace it.

The first step was education. By 1997, the 'Tiger Leap' programme equipped every Estonian school with a computer lab and internet access. In 2000, the government declared internet access to be a human right. In 2009, they launched a large project for computer education for the elderly, rural populations and lower-income people, and by 2012, five-year-olds were being taught coding.

Then the economy. 'Hugely important to the development of Estonia was the astounding success of Skype,' said Ilves (over Skype). Skype was one of the first telecommunications applications that let people video chat over the internet. Invented by four Estonians, it was sold to Ebay in 2005, pouring billions into Estonia's economy. 'Suddenly the mindset that we had just been a poor, backward, cold and grey backwater of Europe changed. Suddenly you saw a worldwide brand being invented locally.' Skype's success created a whole generation of Estonian entrepreneurs. 'They saw you could actually do something if you studied the dreary STEM subjects which young people everywhere had eschewed. That certainly led to a sea change in attitudes as people saw you could accomplish a lot if you did something digital.' Thousands upon thousands of new digital companies emerged in Estonia, intent on becoming the next Skype. It is here, not Silicon Valley, that holds the record for the most start-ups per person.

Education and business were important, but it was the third part of Ilves vision that I found the most significant. Estonia began to digitise the workings of the state. The first step was to tell citizens apart. The government gave everyone a constant, unique ID across all different services. The 2000–2001 Digital Signature Law issued chip-based digital identity cards to all residents aged sixteen or over, and made digitally signed documents legally equivalent to paper signatures.

Estonia then pushed service after service, function after function of government onto a digital platform, to an astonishing degree. There are no paper copies or records. The court system was digitised, and the police, lab technicians, judges, lawyers, prison wardens and defendants each had their own portal. Medical prescriptions were computerised, and an e-ambulance service introduced so paramedics could access relevant medical histories as they were rushing to save lives. Pets were digitally registered on the pet registry, houses on the land registry. An e- or an i- was put in front of everything: i-Voting, e-Tax, e-Business, e-Ticket, e-School, e-Governance. The entire bureaucracy moved online. In 2005, Estonia became the first country in the world to allow online voting nationwide. Now, around a third of all votes are cast this way.

This all, from 2001, became bundled into something called the X-Road. As the Estonian state became digital, X-Road became its backbone. Rather than a giant central server, the X-Road is a way for hundreds of different databases to link up. Data is stored where it is created, whether at the bank, the police station or a school. Other parts of the state request the information as they need it, and as they're authorised do so. When a child is born, information is sent directly from the hospital to the population register, and from there automatically to the health care system.

Almost 700 public sector institutions use the X-Road and, since it was created, 3 billion requests for data have been made using it. The vast majority of them are automated; Estonia estimates that only 5 per cent of requests for data on the X-Road actually involve communication between people.[40]

This sounds strange and technical. But as Estonia followed the digital path that Ilves had set it upon after independence, it arrived at a startling destination. It was drastically different from the United States and Silicon Valley, from Patri's vision or Audrey's. While in America the tech giants are becoming more like states, here, the apparatus of the state was dissolving into the digital aether. The main services that government is involved with – legislation, voting, education, justice, health care, banking, taxes,

40 www.ria.ee/x-tee/fact/#eng

policing, and so on – were becoming digital. And as they became digital they began to change what the state was.

Now, it seemed, the state of Estonia itself was becoming virtual. In 2014, Estonia created something called e-residency. 'A new digital nation for global citizens, powered by the Republic of Estonia,' says the website.[41] Citizens of other countries can become e-residents of Estonia for 100 euros. They can set up a company, access business banking, declare taxes. You do not have to live in Estonia – you don't even have to have visited Estonia – to work and pay taxes under it. It is location-independent.

They were starting again with the very notion of statehood.

'We need', Ilves told me, 'to redefine what a state's role is. The standard view is that states were formed in the crucible of war. Well, maybe it's time to move beyond that.'

Estonia was disrupting a settlement that was as old as Parker's parliamentary democracy. In 1648, in the middle of the English civil war, a series of peace treaties were signed in continental Europe, collectively called the Peace of Westphalia, that marked the beginning of the modern system of international relations. At its heart, the treaties recognised states as being sovereign but also territorial units. The primary building blocks of politics were pockets of physical land.[42] Since then, the basic unit of political power has been the state. And the basic essence of the state has been control of a geographical slice of the world.

Estonia is a place where geography matters a lot. Over its history, the territory has been passed from empire to empire like a chip at a poker game. Sweden gave it to Russia in 1700.

41 https://e-resident.gov.ee
42 Graham Evans and Richard Newnham, *The Penguin Dictionary of International Relations*, p. 572.

They fought a war of independence in 1918. They were invaded by the Soviet Union in 1940, Nazi Germany in 1941 and the Soviet Union again in 1944. Now a member of NATO, western troops are constantly present in the country to deter a Russian invasion.

It may be that it is exactly because Estonia is geopolitically cursed that they have done more than any other country on earth to detach geography from the state. In 2017, they set up the world's first 'data embassy'. It is a server closet in Luxembourg, and technically, like any of its other embassies, Estonian soil. For the first time in its history, if Estonia is invaded, the state will continue. Its political leaders could continue running Estonia from the cloud. The X-Road would survive. 'One aspect of power that has changed due to digitisation is that geography no longer matters,' Ilves continued. 'The North Atlantic Treaty Organisation is the North Atlantic Treaty Organisation because of bomber range, jet fighter range, tank logistics . . . If we do want to develop some kind of defence in the digital era, we need to develop something beyond geography.'

'So what is the state now?' I asked Ilves.

'A service provider. Of course, among the services defending territory, protecting citizens, maintaining rule of law, police – that will have to stay. But on the other hand, maybe there will be other things that will become less important. I don't know what they are. I don't know how this is going to play out.' The Estonian state has heralded, in the way that Patri Friedman has longed for, the beginning of a new market: where countries compete for citizens.

This seems like the most fundamental question of all for modern politics: what does political power give you power over? For centuries, political power has meant control of a territory. But maybe that settlement is beginning to wither away.

This deepest level of political power is also the most unknowable. Ilves quoted Jesus: 'He who is first will later be last.' Estonia had risen from being one of the poorest, most primitive countries in Europe to becoming the most digitally advanced. It had thrown off the legacies of the old world. But where it was all going was very, very hard to say. And for Ilves himself, whose vision has done so much to lead Estonia to where it is, that vision is now less clear.

'We're in about 1520 trying to work out the ramifications of moveable type. Thirty years after Gutenberg, you can't really . . . what does all of this mean? Well, one thing that happened was the Reformation. We're there. That's where we are. Thirty years afterwards. And thirty years after Gutenberg, that's when the Reformation started to take place, and that started the Thirty Years War. So who knows?'

A Crumbling Status Quo

Patri was right about one thing, at least – politics is one of the least disrupted things in the digital age. Ranged against a system that hasn't changed much since the eighteenth century are a series of formidable challenges. Political power has become more easily opposed, as protest has embraced all the possibilities that digital technology has given it. The future is uncertain, as states mobilise their own financial and technical might to control the internet.

But the mainstream, at least for now, has lost its monopoly on political mobilisation.

Part of the story is the changing expectations that people have for a different kind of government. The open movement was born on the internet, but is now stepping into mainstream political life, with new demands for transparency and a deep hostility to hierarchies and commands. Across the world – whether with Patri and his libertarian seasteaders, in formal political parties, activist cells or simply in the minds of a growing number of voters – those ideas are spreading.

Political power isn't simply being opposed, however. Technology has opened up new ways for decisions to be made. So far, the example of vTaiwan shines as a lonely beacon, one of the few places where the digital democrats have found political power, and where it has worked. But the experiments will continue.

Power over *what*, is the final question. On the far horizon is the possibility that states become less about territories, and more about the people who choose to be citizens of them. As the Estonian state became more digital, it also became more borderless, reflecting the mobility of the modern world. New social contracts and new citizenships might emerge that, rather than challenging states, simply make them passé. But Ilves is right; it is too early to tell. A world of post-nation states remains, as yet, a possibility and nothing more.

Henry Parker's idea of sovereign parliaments – an idea that has stood for centuries – is, I think, just beginning to come to an end. A parliament is sovereign because its people are. But politics is trapped in the twin clutches of apathy and polarisation. It struggles to respond to citizens, to convince them that it is expressing their will.

If politics has been one of the least disrupted things of the digital age so far, I think it will be one of the most disrupted things in the years to come. Political power is shuddering through a transformation, layer by layer, from how it is won, how it is opposed, what it really is, and what it controls. Of all the uncertainties, however, one thing is clear: the days of Henry Parker's grand, centuries-old political settlement are coming to an end.

6

Warfare

'Not to have [television] broadcasting for abroad is like not having an MOD [Ministry of Defence]. When there is no war, you do not need it. But when the war starts, it matters.'

Margarita Siomonyea, head of RT [formerly Russia Today, an international Russian television network funded by the Russian government]

'[Our enemy] has said that 50 per cent of the current struggle is taking place in the arena of public information. That may be an understatement.'

Donald Rumsfeld, former US Secretary of Defense

War does not belong in the realm of arts or sciences; rather it is part of man's social existence

–Clausewitz

The 77th Brigade

Nestled among the gentle rolling hills of Berkshire in England is a military base called Denison Barracks. From the outside it looks just like any of over a hundred others dotted across the UK: a barbed-wire fence sternly traces the perimeter, enclosing row after row of brick, low-rise buildings within it. A guard's hut blocks the road, and the Union flag whips and twists in midsummer gusts of wind. But the soldiers that casually stride in and out of the base wear on their arms a particular insignia – a small round patch of blue encircling a snarling golden creature that looks like a lion. It is the emblem of a unit of the British Army called the 77th Brigade.

The snarling lion is a Chinthe, a mythical Burmese beast that protects the entrances to sacred sites. 'The 77th', as they're called, were named in tribute to the Chindits, a British and Indian guerrilla force formed during the Second World War to protect Burma against the advancing Japanese army.

The Chindits' purpose was to take on an enemy much larger than themselves. They acted quickly, unpredictably and unconventionally, infiltrating deep behind enemy lines into Japanese-held Burma, destroying supply depots, enemy communications, and spreading ripples of uncertainty and confusion throughout Japanese high command. They shed many of the conventions and structures of the regular military along the way, an army of irregulars fighting the war in a different way.

Inside the base, everything was in motion. Flooring was being laid down, work units installed; desks – empty of possessions – formed neat lines in offices still covered in plastic, tape and sawdust. The brigade is only months old, thrown together from various older parts of the British Army to form something new – a 'media operations group', a 'military stabilisation support group', a 'psychological operations group'.

'If everybody is thinking alike then somebody isn't thinking' was written in foot-high letters across a whiteboard. There was a darkened editing suite with large, electronic sketchpads and multi-screened desktops loaded with digital editing software. The men and women of the 77th Brigade were people who knew how to deploy cameras, record sound, edit videos. They had been plucked from across the British military because they knew about graphic design, social media advertising and data analytics, and they used phrases I had heard countless times from digital marketers: 'key influencers', 'reach' and 'traction'. I'd found similar things inside viral advertising studios, in digital research labs, indeed in grander form within the huge technology giants of Silicon Valley. But the skinny jeans and long beards of East London had been replaced here by crisply ironed shirts, neat hairstyles and the light patterned camouflage of the British Army. Next to a digital design studio, soldiers were having a tea break, a packet of digestives lying open on top of a green metallic ammo box.

The soliders of the 77th were spread across different depart-ments. One focused on understanding the audiences they wanted to reach. Another developed 'attitude and sentiment awareness', and another produced video and audio content to be shared. Teams of Intelligence specialists were closely watching how messages were seeing how messages were being received, and discussed how to make them more resonant. I looked over to another sign. 'Behavioural change is our USP.' What on earth was happening? Much has been written about the 77th Brigade. These are Britain's 'Facebook Warriors'. It is a 'trolling task force', a 'division of disinformation agents'.[1] I saw, at least, none of this. In fact the legal and ethics of their work was clearly something they thought about a lot. Yet, walking through the headquarters of the 77th, the strange new reality of what warfare is today became a little clearer.

'The character of the conflicts in which we could be involved is changing,' I was told. I'd heard a lot about 'cyberwarfare' – about how states could attack their enemies through computer networks, damaging their infrastructure or stealing their secrets. But that wasn't what was going on here. This wasn't about making things go bang in new ways. What I was seeing was the army desperately reacting to the realisation that an engagement now doesn't just happen kinetically, on the battlefield, but it also plays out publicly in the media. A victory is won as much in the eyes of the watching public as between opposing armies on the battlefield.

Information Warfare

The idea of warfare constantly changes as society changes around it.[2] From the sixth through to the sixteenth centuries, warfare was the primary tool used by members of the wider Christian assembly to resolve internal disputes. The *Respublica Christiana* was held together by divine law, and warfare within it could only be waged to uphold that divine law. 'The one thing it could not be', wrote

1   https://www.look-up.org.uk/77th-brigade/
2   Martin van Creveld, *Technology and War: From 2000 BC to the Present*, p. 1.

the distinguished theorist of warfare, Martin van Creveld, 'was a manifestation of naked interest.'[3]

By the seventeenth century, warfare became something only carried out by the state machine. Modern armies began to take a shape still recognisable today: formed by systematic conscription, paid by the state, and under one commander, answerable to the monarch.[4] Under Napoleon in the nineteenth century, war became 'total war'. It was no longer waged just to protect the dynastic property of a monarch; it was seen as defending values as much as interests – liberty, equality and fraternity. During the French Revolutionary Wars, crops were requisitioned, ration cards distributed, a national bread – *pain d'egalite* – created, all to support a form of *levée en masse* in which, under Napoleon, 600,000 men invaded Russia.[5] From the French Revolution to the two world wars and Cold War of the twentieth century, warfare was understood to be a form of defence of fundamental political values: populism against monarchism, or liberal democracy against totalitarian fascism.

Now in the Information Age, militaries are beginning to reconceive warfare as increasingly a problem of information, to be solved using information. Country after country has updated its own military doctrine – the guideline for how their militaries fight wars – to put information at the heart.

In 2014, an important memo was sent across the British military by the commander of Joint Forces Command, called 'Warfare in the Information Age'. 'We are now in the foothills of the Information Age,' the memo explains, 'in which the combined

---

3   See van Creveld, p. 129.
4   Under Frederick William I of Prussia and Gustavus Adolphus of Sweden.
5   Howard, Michael, *War in European History*, 2nd edn. (Oxford: Oxford University Press),ch. 5.

power of exponential growth in processing power, data and connectivity will fundamentally shape the way the world lives and works. We should be clear that we do not hold the initiative over this: it is driven by commercial and societal forces that will determine how the technology unfolds and is used.

'The execution of Full Spectrum Effects will have information at its core ... Influence activity will often be dominated by the imperative to act in open source and social media, it will be necessary (it is necessary now) to engage 24/7 in social media in the reciprocal, real-time business of being first with the truth, countering the narratives of others, and if necessary manipulating the opinion of thousands concurrently in support of combat operations.'

The British Army had a new doctrine, an overarching guide for how conflicts should be fought. It was called Integrated Action, and weaved throughout was a central idea: 'part of the whole purpose of Integrated Action is to change attitudes and behaviour *in our favour*'. It was 'integrated' because it folded how the British Army would fight on the battlefield together with how it would fight its perception. And here in the 77th was a warfare of storyboards and narratives, videos and social media. Several hundred strong, and growing fast, the 77th Brigade was fighting in the battlefield of ideas, information, beliefs and opinions.

In December 2014, the Security Council of the Russian Federation published a new Russian military doctrine. Answering to the threats ranged against it from the West, Russia, the document said, needed to use new non-traditional methods and information operations. Paragraph 15A stated: 'the characteristic features and specifics of current military conflicts are ... military force, information, political and economic measures, the use of the protest potential of the local population; and the use of special forces.'

AJP 3.10 is NATO's Allied Joint Doctrine for Information Operations from November 2009. 'Increased attention on Info Ops is also due to the realisation that we now live in an information-dominated environment . . . There is an increased reliance on, and desire for, information,' the doctrine started. 'The ever-increasing use of technologies such as the internet have resulted in a world where information plays an increasingly important role.' The document explains that information operations should be used to target an enemy's 'will': 'For example, by questioning the legitimacy of leadership and cause, information activities may undermine their moral power base, separating leadership from supporters, political, military and public, thus weakening their desire to continue and affecting their actions.'

In other parts of society, again and again, I had seen institutions that were conventionally powerful undercut and undermined. Whether it was professions like journalism, traditional political parties or even states themselves, the people that used to hold power now held much less. But in warfare, states are fighting back – they are changing how they operate to reflect the realities of the digital age. Deception and rumour, intelligence and communications are all longstanding elements of warfare, but what is now happening in the 77th isn't just a case of using new tools and technologies to update these traditional forms of propaganda. It is a change of what war actually is. Information warfare.

What I didn't know, leaving Dennison Barracks on that pleasant summer's day, was how central we all were to this new kind of information warfare. I didn't know then that as militaries around the world have begun to focus on and fight through information, it is we who are in the crosshairs. Our opinions and beliefs, what we hold to be true and what we think is right and wrong have all become strategic objectives. I didn't know that warfare, redefined, isn't something that happens far away. Each of us has been brought – face to face – to a new frontline.

Cats

Long before the creation of the 77th there was another and very different group of people who had begun to see the power in the new methods of influencing. But they didn't come from militaries, or even companies. It may sound strange, but information warfare began with cats.

In 2003, a fifteen-year-old called Chris Poole created an image board site named after a Japanese trend: 4chan. It was simple set-up. Just a forum where you could upload a message, an image or some video. 4chan grew quickly. In its early years, the servers groaned under a tidal wave of extreme porn, Japanese anime and long-running arguments,, all of it impenetrable to anyone not steeped in the thickly woven layers of lore, slang, inter-board trolling, in-jokes and running feuds that each of the different boards on 4chan quickly developed.

4Chan passed a million posts, then a billion. And somewhere out of theendless content churning through the site, new cultures were forming. New feelings of identity and collectivity began to set the inhabitants of that anonymous pocket of the internet apart from the mainstream. Online life was a chance to break free, as they saw it, from the strangling influence of political correctness in wider, offline life. And they knew the internet better than almost anyone else.

An early member of 4chan was a British man called Mike. Now in his late twenties, he runs his own cybersecurity company. But throughout his teens, Mike was a bored kid, with what bored kids have in excess: time. He spent almost every waking moment on the internet, in hacker forums, in IRCs and on 4chan.

'What most people don't understand', Mike said, 'about the whole cat picture thing. It was a joke, but it was also deadly serious. They're also all over the internet because people wanted them to be.'

Cats were about ownership. 'For us back then, a lot of us felt this was our internet. When normal people and companies came in and tried to be really serious on the internet, it just created a massive game,' Mike told me. The game was to use the internet to spread cats as far as possible. As the mainstream invaded what they saw as their territory, these members of 4chan were working out how to use their knowledge of the internet to invade the mainstream.

'Getting anything onto TV, into the newspaper – that was the Holy Grail,' Mike said. A military would call that 'media operations'. They just thought it was a win, and one of their first was over Oprah Winfrey. Many felt that *The Oprah Winfrey Show* sensationalised anxieties about paedophilia. A 4chan user trolled the show, writing on their message board:

WE DO NOT FORGIVE

WE DO NOT FORGET

WE HAVE OVER 9,000 PENISES[6] AND THEY ARE ALL RAPING CHILDREN

Ridiculous, over the top – and *The Oprah Winfrey Show* completely fell for it. Oprah herself, on the show, warned her

---

6 One of 4chan's enormous number of in-jokes. This one referred to the television show *Dragon Ball Z*. 'It's over NINE THOUSAAAAAAAND!' became a meme from the show – referring to Goku's power level, if anyone's interested.

viewers that a known paedophile network 'has over 9,000 penises and they're all . . . raping . . . children.'

It was a deliberate undertaking. They wouldn't have called this information warfare. They might have called it attention hacking. They looked at social engineering, psychological manipulation, much of it taken from mainstream academic literature, and they worked together, tested things, and began to find ways to could reach through the computer and change what people saw or even thought. *Time* magazine ran an online poll for its readers to vote on the world's 100 most influence people. 4chan used scripts to rig the vote so that Chris Poole – a.k.a. 'moot' – came first. They arranged =ged the poll's webpage so that, read downwards, the first letters of the next twenty spelled 'Marblecake, also the game' (a 4chan in-joke). They worked out ways of manipulating search engines so that their pages came up top. 'We hated Sony,' said Mike. 'If you googled Sony, all you got was a bunch of websites that we'd made.'

Then there were the 'actions' where 4chan members would coordinate to swarm a target. In 2006, rumours spread on 4chan's busiest and most notorious board, /b/, that the moderators of the online game Habbo Hotel were banning avatars based on their skin colour. They began a series of organised raids on the game, putting together instructions for how to cause maximum disruption by blocking the entrances to some of the most popular hangouts. They also built 'bots' and 'sockpuppets' – fake social media accounts – to make topics trend and otherwise appear more popular than they were.[7]

7　In a notorious case, in 2014, the #notyourshield hashtag began to trend on Twitter. It was related to the GamerGate controversy, demanding that 'social justice warriors' stop using allegations of misogyny to deflect 'genuine criticism'. But journalists uncovered chat logs that showed that only a small number of 4chan members were at the centre of it. 'It took a few days of four to five of us doing it, but it's taking off,' one of the organisers said in the log: https://arstechnica.com/gaming/2014/09/new-chat-logs-show-how-4chan-users-pushed-gamergate-into-the-national-spotlight/

4chan celebrated each victory with an endless deluge of memes. This was another part of attention hacking, a key way to make information more likely to spread. Memes, Limor Shifman, an Associate Professor at the Department of Communication and Journalism at The Hebrew University of Jerusalem, told me 'create subcultures'. On the internet they are usually just a single illustration, often using consistent images, taglines, fonts – something that makes it clear the image is a riff on a bigger theme. 'They are community binders and builders' she said. what they do is they help you feel like you're part of a community that you feel part of it, but you can also express your individuality.'

Memes are also the ideal way to spread ideas across the internet, and 4chan became a meme factory. They knew that content that isn't sticky quickly dies. Cat memes were the perfect method to capture attention. 'The Oprah Winfrey Network is Now Owned by Business Cat Enterprises,' said one meme. 'YOU GET NOTHING.'

Long Kat is Long
Ceiling Cat
Hacker Cats Hacking
Grumpy Cats

Each one a cat in a meme that spread virally around the internet.

As it got bigger, the soup of different online subcultures began to define themselves more firmly from one another. There were the anti-corporate hacktivists, techno-libertarians, conspiracy theorists, paleoconservatives, incells,[8] white nationalists, and an endless array of others. Each had their own language, in-jokes,

---

8 Involuntary celibates.

moral codes, and eventually politics and they spread across a wider ecology of wikis, IRC channels and internet forums. But each brought with them the different techniques to use the Internet to exert influence as they saw fit.

The lulz became more and more political. On 8chan (the 'free speech' 4chan alternative), savvier members mentored newer ones on how to craft effective anti-Semitic memes: 'You need to make the message short and simple, so that the reader has already intaken [sic] all of it before their brain shuts it down. And you need to make it funny so that it sticks in their brain and circumvents their shut-it-down circuits.'[9]

Daily Stormer, a white nationalist site, has 'Memetic Monday', where they post dozens of racist memes to see which die and which spread rapidly. One far-right meme showed Hillary Clinton, a Star of David, and in the background piles of money – 'Most Corrupt Candidate Ever!' it screamed. Donald Trump retweeted it. So the meme travelled from the backwaters of the white nationalist internet to Trump's millions of followers, and then even further due to the mainstream media backlash to that tweet.

Some of these splintering online subcultures also continued to hijack and swarm their opponents. During the French presidential elections of 2017, an international coalition of alt-right groups descended on pro-Macron hashtags with a pre-prepared armoury of 159 pro-Le Pen, anti-Semitic and Islamophobic memes.[10] From spreading funny pictures of cats, memes had become political weapons, the tools of a subcultural insurgency that was raging

9 Alice Marwick and Rebecca Lewis, 'Media Manipulation and Disinformation Online', *Data & Society*, p. 34.
10 https://motherboard.vice.com/en_us/article/4xe9nn/trump-shitposters-twitter-bots

against the mainstream. Almost any hashtag of any significance is hijacked, now.

They continued to find ways of breaking into the mainstream too, with agenda-setting hoaxes. In November 2015, Andrew Anglin, the founder of the Daily Stormer, directed his followers to set up fake 'White Student Union' pages on Facebook, then contact local media. His plan was to use the moral outrage of journalists to lure them into the covering the story. He targeted local journalists – perhaps hoping they were too strained to sufficiently check the facts – and as they covered it, hoped to trade it up to larger, national outlets. It worked: the controversy built and the story ended up on *USA Today* and in the *Washington Post*.[11]

Attention hacking wasn't only about fake news, but when those techniques were applied to spreading lies, they had a surreal, fantastical effect – and most bewildering of them all was Pizzagate. Across the 4chan forums, conspiracy theory websites, Twitter and Facebook, rumours spread during the US presidential campaign in 2016 that Hillary Clinton was involved in a child sex ring and Satanic rituals. After key Democrat emails were hacked and leaked earlier that year, sites masquerading as newspapers published story after story claiming that the emails had revealed details of high-ranking Democrats connected to a human trafficking ring; 4chan zeroed in on a pizzeria in Washington called Comet Ping Pong as the apparent headquarters of the gang. On 4 December, a man actually entered the restaurant with an assault rifle to investigate the claims himself. This controversy brought all the different techniques of influence together: hacks, fake news, swarm tactics,

11 Alice Marwick and Rebecca Lewis, 'Media Manipulation and Disinformation Online', *Data & Society*, p. 50.

a deluge of memes, and the creation, online, of a story that then burst out into the mainstream press and physical world.

These different cultures, then, had developed new ways to use the internet to obtain power. Whether it was for the lulz, or whether they had sharper political motives, attention hacking could grip the mainstream – which was only dimly aware that it was happening – in enormously influential ways. It was a new route to power, and these online subcultures were probably the earliest innovators, but other groups would never stay out of questions of influence for long.

Disinformation on Demand

In 2002, browsing the internet as usual one day, Mike's inbox pinged. He'd received an email inviting him to buy into the Money Tree. It suggested that you buy reports that contained the secret of making a fortune. You physically sent the money to five people on the list, and each one sent one of five reports to you. You then sent the reports onwards and urged everyone to send theirs on too. It was a simple pyramid scheme: buy into it, sell it on to others, get rich – but to a naive teenager, it looked like a great business opportunity. He bought it, sent it out to his friends – but no luck.

Fifteen-year-old Mike might have been socially naive, but he spent his entire waking life on forums sharpening his technical skills. To make the Money Tree work, he thought, he needed turn it into an Electronic Money Tree. Mike rewrote some of the reports, with topics like 'how to market yourself online', 'how to build a website'. He set up an online payment process using PayPal, so people didn't have to send envelopes of cash around to each other. But the biggest change was how he sent the report out to people.

He'd noticed that there was a vulnerability in the basic protocol that makes the internet work. Before computers start talking to each other, they ping each other little messages; basically telling each other that they're ready to start speaking. It's the digital equivalent of a handshake, or picking up the phone receiver.

Mike worked out how to use this to check whether millions of emails really existed. He used a 'crunch list' – a systematically unfolding list of letters in every possible combination, some of which would generate genuine email addresses – and sent each a ping. If it pinged back, he sent an email, inviting others to buy into the Money Tree. He woke up the next morning with £30,000 in his bank account.

'I sent hundreds of millions of emails,' Mike said, laughing. He booked every PC in a local cybercafé, all sending emails from the crunch list. He started a company too, helping others to send millions of emails of their own. 'I was fifteen and had this fortune in PayPal. They had locked the money in, so I had to go to America with my dad to try to get the money out. I thought it was a legitimate business. I thought I was made for life.' Eventually the police turned up at the cybercafé. They thought they were there to arrest a huge criminal gang.

Mike had started a spam marketing company. 'This was before people had sussed out how to advertise on the internet,' he said. He had realised what many others had realised too – some decades earlier than Mike himself.[12] Using the internet to illicitly grab

12 The earliest case of email spam was in 1978, although back then it was only sent to a few hundred others.

people's attention could be done for culture and kudos – but it could also make an enormous amount of money too.

Advertising on the internet is the multi-billion dollar industry that fuels Facebook and Google. And of course it's entirely legal. But the techniques that 4chan and others had developed – techniques we now understand as influence operations – were monetised as the murkier, more illicit side of advertising. A whole new global industry has emerged selling over-the-counter digital propaganda; a whole subterranean ecosystem of services and tools. And this means that the techniques that 4chan developed have become available to everyone, if they can pay for it.

If you want to create fake crowds on social media, you now have plenty of commercial options. There is software for sale to create your own fake social media accounts. On Alpha Bay or Hansa Market you can buy a 'HUGE MEGA BOT PACK' for $3. For that, you get software to make Alibaba message bots, a Badoo account creator, Googlebot fetcher script, Yahoo account creator bot, YouTube views bot, YouTube video uploader, and over a hundred others.

Or you can buy accounts that others have created for you. A website called buyaccs.com has an entire marketplace of precreated social media accounts across all major social media platforms. In Russian, the site lists the social media accounts they have 'in stock', and the sale price. They sell fake accounts on every social media platform that you've ever heard of. Special offers include:

'On sale, new Instagram.com FB accounts are tied to Facebook profiles, with and without photos. Excellent price – from only $100 for 1,000 accounts !'

'Reduced price of Reddit.com Aged accounts – now only $6 per piece!'

'Added Reddit.com accounts – regular and seasoned.'

There are ninety-eight other types of 'bundle' on offer.

You can also buy software to manage this new digital-zombie army. Go on www.Tweetattackspro.com and you can buy software designed to run thousands of Twitter accounts at the same time. The software is the command console for a huge online army of Twitter accounts. You can scroll down your list of fake accounts, checking how many tweets they've sent, whether they're suspended, how many followers they have. And from it, you can issue commands, following, unfollowing, tweeting and sending messages to any people duped into following one of your zombie accounts. 'The software can simulate human operation perfectly!' it promises. There is similar software for running Facebook, Instagram, LinkedIn, Reddit, Tumblr and Pinterest accounts.

There are also copywriter services who will throw together huge numbers of blog posts pushing a single line or message, purportedly written by different people. BlackHat World, 'the home of internet marketing', is a huge forum packed with intricate discussions about keyword stuffing – loading a webpage with keywords – and link farms (a set of webpages that link to a target page to move it up the search engine results). On closed forums in the darker corners of the internet, top consultants promise to give your campaign the sharpest edge.

The most expensive end of the market was exposed by researchers from the University of Oxford in 2017. An anonymous source who worked for a political communications firm told Oxford's researchers that over ten years, his firm had been responsible for creating 40,000 unique identities, each one with multiple accounts on social media, a unique IP address, its own internet address, even its own personality, interests and writing style. Each employee manages fifteen identities at a time, building their own comment history. It would be almost impossible to link accounts built in this way to each other, or to know if any of them were fake. 'The amount of work which goes into these efforts is staggering,' the researchers wrote.[13]

Overwhelmingly, the language when selling these services isn't the 'mind hacking' of 4chan, nor is it the 'information warfare' or 'influence operations' of the military. It is social media marketing. Marketing, too, has dipped into the murky world of spam, search engine optimisation (SEO) and fake accounts. Small PR firms, political communications consultancies, specialist services and dark markets have all begun to offer the same tactics and techniques that 4chan pioneered.

To Prague

I climbed into a car that was waiting for me outside the glass hangar of Vaclav Havel airport, Prague. During his life, Havel was a dissident, playwright and eventually the president of the Czech Republic. Once passed secretly as *samizdat*, hand to hand under the nose of Soviet authorities, one of the pamphlets he had written was called *Power of the Powerless*, a furious denunciation of the Communist regime.

'The centre of power is identical with the centre of truth,' Havel wrote. 'Government by bureaucracy is called popular government;

---

13 http://comprop.oii.ox.ac.uk/wp-content/uploads/sites/89/2017/06/Comprop-Poland.pdf

the working class is enslaved in the name of the working class; the complete degradation of the individual is presented as his ultimate liberation; depriving people of information is called making it available; the use of power to manipulate is called the public control of power, and the arbitrary abuse of power is called observing the legal code.'

Havel's point was that when power could control the truth, it could last forever, however abusive it was. The Soviet regime could only exist within a reality of its own making. 'Individuals need not believe all these mystifications, but they must behave as though they did . . . they must live within a lie. They need not accept the lie. It is enough for them to have accepted their life with it and in it. For by this very fact, individuals confirm the system, fulfil the system, make the system, are the system.'

Militaries cannot stay out of questions of influence, and eventually the power that had been opened by 4chan's attention hackers, and monetised by the spam marketers, finally made its way to armed forces around the world. Now the same body of techniques has become known by militarised terminologies – influence operations, media operations, psychological warfare, covert online action and, indeed, information warfare. And here in Prague, a diverse group of hounded Finnish journalists, angry US spies, Balkan dissidents, idiosyncratic British diplomats and NATO officials had arrived from all over the world to examine the very same abuses of power that interested Havel.

The techniques of 4chan and the marketers were being used by militaries to control the truth. The kind of information warfare that the 77th were being built to fight had already broken out. The summit was about a new offensive that Russia had launched in the struggle for control over information, opinion, people's beliefs.

An American, sitting next to me in the car, was on the way to the conference too. As we pulled up outside our hotel, he turned to me. 'I'd be *appalled*,' he said, '*appalled*, if the Russians *weren't* listening to every word that we'll say tomorrow.' A vast, spike-peaked central tower loomed over us, each wing sprawling out in a blank-faced frontage of light brown-pinkish stone. We'd arrived at Hotel International, formerly Hotel Družba, 'friendship' in Russian. It was like something out of a spy novel.

The summit was held in the Czech Ministry of the Interior, and among the crowd of neat suits, there was a man in a crumpled tweed jacket, smoking and looking both tired and incredibly worried. His name was Yevhen Fedchenko and he had suddenly found himself on the strange new frontline in this war of information.

'Maidan', he said, referring to the Ukrainian public demonstrations against Russia in 2013 and 2014, 'was a starting point.' Amidst the turmoil of the protests in Kiev, Yevhen noticed that there was an influx of propaganda. There were faked photos, forged documents, fake witnesses, hoax experts appearing on television and online. He let out a hoarse laugh. 'I mean, on the television, some self-proclaimed "geo-political expert" was paraded around for a while. He turned out to be a used car dealer from New Jersey.' The biggest source of disinformation, Yevhen told me, was Zvezda TV (which belongs to the Russian Ministry of Defence) and ukraine. ru, which belongs to the Russian state-owned Novosti Information Agency. 'All Russian media started to describe Maidan using the same words, and the same kind of perspective. It was massive.'

In the months that followed the influx of information continued, even increased. New messages, new narratives appeared on TV bulletins, online stories and across social media. In story after story, interview after interview, tweet after tweet, a case was being put together: that the Ukrainian authorities were a western-backed junta. That Ukraine was a failed state, a fascist state. Not only a puppet of the West, but also forgotten by them. There had been 'Ukrainian fatigue' – the withdrawal of western support. But the war in Eastern Ukraine was also actually clandestinely conducted by the United States through private military contractors. And they were connected with ISIS anyway.

The arrival of these stories was sudden, unexpected. But, Yevhen said, raising a finger, 'A decision was made.' All the different accounts, interviews and reactions on social media seemed too . . . coordinated. It was almost like a preordained narrative had just been turned on.

By the early 2000s, Russia found itself surrounded; in its own eyes, besieged. The Arab Spring, the 'colour revolutions', NATO enlargement – each had chipped away at the crumbling edifice of Russian power. In 2004, the Orange Revolution had (temporarily) defeated the political ambitions of the pro-Russian Viktor Yanukovych as protestors thronged amidst the snow and optimism of Independence Square in Kiev. Riots in Estonia had broken out in 2007 over the relocation of the 'Bronze Soldier', a Soviet-era war memorial. Then came the 2008 war in Georgia and, in 2011, unrest came to Russia itself. The parliamentary elections of that year saw, by Russian standards, large demonstrations against Putin and the following year Putin's re-election saw further protests. NATO and the EU were pushing up to their border, and soft western influence was spreading into Russia itself.

The problem, Russian decision-makers realised, could not simply be fixed with new military equipment and training. The problem also lay in how Russia was seen. The crowds thronging Independence Square in Kiev in 2004 had been drawn there by Europe's beckoning finger, the promise of prosperity and new opportunities that would come with integration with the West. There had been an outpouring of support, internationally, for plucky Georgia's resistance against the clumsy might of the Red Bear. And during the Maidan protests of 2013, people hadn't braved the snap of sniper fire because they had been ordered to. They were fighting for the future they wanted. The protests against Putin had been organised online, as the liberal opposition in Russia found powerful new alternatives to the mainstream media outlets that had been throttled by state control.

Russia had a large conventional army – lots of soldiers and tanks – but that seemed to matter less than in the past. And anyway, they had an economy smaller than Spain or California and they couldn't hope to beat the West in a conventional military arms race. How could they achieve their overall aims in a world with far fewer cases of armies storming across a border?

A year before the Maidan protests, the Chief of the Russian General Staff, Valery Gerasimov, gave an answer.[14] There were easier ways of confronting the United States than through its military, Gerasimov argued. Warfare, he argued, was now

---

14 His comments appeared in an article in *Voyenno-Promyshlennyy Kurier*, the 'Military-Industrial Courier'. There are lots of arguments about what Gerasimov really meant. It's important to note that he was outlining what he perceived as the changing way that *America* fought conflicts. He had in mind the US-led interventions in Kosovo, Iraq and Libya, the Arab Spring and of course the colour revolutions, which are all widely believed by the Kremlin to be US-manufactured conspiracies. So reforms to the Russian military were all couched as a defensive response – an act of describing what the enemy is doing to 'us' to justify what 'we' should do to them.

'hybrid' – it blurred the lines between war and peace, civilian and military, state and non-state. Biker gangs, NGOs and cyber-weapons as well as columns of tanks should all now be used to advance Russia's interests. Alongside military tools, Gerasimov argued, Russia needed to pull all the other levers at its disposal to get the outcomes it wanted.

Among all these different levers, Gerasimov saw 'moral-psycho-logical-cognitive-informational struggle'[15] as taking a leading role. Warfare through information. That, he argued, was how you could neutralise an enemy's superior military strength. And the key to informational struggle was *maskirovka* – subterfuge – the manip-ulation of the enemy's picture of reality.[16] In the same way as the British Army, he was conceiving war as something much wider than military conflict. It was as much about thoughts as actions. Russia could achieve its geo-political aims with a strategy based, as Soviet foreign affairs minister Eduard Shevardnadze put it in 1991 on the 'force of politics' rather than the 'politics of force'. It was an idea that became known as the Gerasimov Doctrine.

Yevhen found himself on the receiving end of that doctrine. In mid-July 2014, a gruesome story appeared on Russia's most popular station, Channel One: Ukrainian officials had nailed a three-year-old boy to a wooden board in the city of Slovyansk. His terrified mother, a 'witness' said, was then tied to a tank and dragged around the city's central Lenin Square.

Yevhen and his colleagues knew that Ukraine was under threat. They got together to decide what they could do in this moment of peril. The dean of a journalism school, Yevhen decided to do

15 For the record, I think this is a horrible phrase.
16 www.ifri.org/sites/default/files/atoms/files/pp54adamsky.pdf

what he had always done: report what he saw. And what he saw was a propaganda campaign being waged against Ukraine. So they started stopfake.org to try to monitor, watch and debunk sources of propaganda and deception wherever they saw it.

A few years later, stopfake.org has two television channels, is broadcast in eleven languages, has published two textbooks and produces a radio show. Debunking fake news became, in Yevhen's hands, an entirely new genre of news. His site – entirely dedicated to rooting out fake stories – has become one of the top ten news websites in the Ukraine.

Vasili Mitrokhin spent thirty years working in Russia's foreign intelligence service. He was an archivist there, keeping records on the KGB's activities and operations. And, after the collapse of the Soviet Union, he walked into the British embassy in Riga to bring both himself, and his files, over to the West.

You only need to dip into this Mitrokhin Archive to know that 'active measures' are nothing new for intelligence agencies. Forged speeches, letters, front organisations, planted stories, salacious rumours, manipulative slogans, even carefully selected true information deployed maliciously were all tactics that were *par du jour* during the Cold War. The promotion of an anti-nuclear agenda, the secret bankrolling of youth movements, these were the everyday. Both East and West did whatever they could to influence the attitudes and behaviour of both their own people and the watching publics on the other side of the Iron Curtain. Sometimes that was digging wells, setting up radio stations and distributing leaflets. All were different kinds of 'influence operations', and sometimes they included falsehood and fakery. Stagecraft has long been a feature of statecraft.

Yet something was new. As the summit in Prague swirled around us, I spoke to Mark Laity, the chief of strategic communications at NATO. 'Stratcomm', as they call it, was set up by NATO in 2007, an attempt to pull together the different ways that information matters to a conflict, *was* in fact the conflict. Mark seemed possessed of a cold anger. 'Russia Today', he said, his finger marking each syllable with a thud on the table in front of us, 'is psy-ops' – short for psychological operations.

'Absolutely.' (Thud.) 'Absolutely.' (Thud.) 'It is run directly from the Kremlin. It's following Kremlin's narratives. It's a psy-ops operation. And it's black psy-ops.' (Thud.)

'There is nothing in principle illegal or even immoral in governments trying to influence each other. It's how you do it,' Mark continued. In other words, it's not the Russian aims that are the problem. It's the Russian methods.

Mark and the other experts had gathered not just because a new wave of disinformation is happening, but because it is happening in a new way. Officials, researchers, journalists – each came forward, like Yevhen, to talk about how informational struggle has broken out across the media landscape of their country. And in each case, they spoke about how the old tools of information warfare – radio channels, television shows, leaflets, letters – have now been joined by digital tools that make it more powerful. 'The way that we can be got at and influenced has radically changed,' Mark concluded, 'and it is radically more effective.' Mark got up to go, and turned back towards me. 'That's all on the record, all right? No issues with that at all.'

Country after country has been hit by a wave of Russian digital and mainstream propaganda. In Swedish-language Sputnik (a Russian state-owned media outlet), Swedish researchers tracked an editorial line that meandered from story to story not on the basis of newsworthiness, but on the priorities of Russian foreign policy. The 'dominant meta-narratives', as they called them, were 'crisis in the West', followed by 'positive image of Russia' and 'western aggressiveness'.[17], [18] In Latvia, NATO had themselves issued a report on internet trolling as a new tool of 'hybrid warfare'. 'The same messages', the report says, 'are reported again and again.' Primarily directed at the third of Latvians who speak Russian as their first language, the messages were that Latvia was a failed state dominated by social problems, that it treated non-Latvians badly, and that Russia wasn't responsible for the conflict in the Ukraine. In Lithuania, hundreds of online 'elves' skirmished with pro-Russian trolls on Facebook, and the Russian-language social media platform VKontakte, and in the comment sections of Lithuanian news articles. It was happening from the Baltic in the north, across central and eastern Europe, and stretching into the Balkans in the South.[19]

The highest-profile case of all was Russian involvement in influencing the outcome of the 2016 presidential election in the United States. Probably using techniques honed and perfected elsewhere, it was 'the boldest yet in the US', said the US intelli-

---

17 Martin Kragh and Sebastian Åsberg, 'Russia's Strategy for Influence Through Public Diplomacy and Active Measures: The Swedish Case', *Journal of Strategic Studies*: DOI 10.1080/01402390.2016.1273830

18 My personal favourites, however, were the inept forgeries. A letter appeared on social media, apparently from the Swedish Minister of Defence to the CEO of Sweden's largest weapons manufacturer and supposedly revealing that Sweden was selling arms to the Ukraine. But for reasons beyond anyone's comprehension, the letter, from one Swede to another, was written in English.

19 A 'Kremlin Influence Index' scored countries by their vulnerability to it. In front of the Czech Republic (a score of 48), Ukraine (49), even Georgia (54), it was Hungary (61) that the report spotlighted as most influenced: http://osvita.mediasapiens.ua/content/files/dm_iik_engl_pravka-compressed.pdf

gence community in their declassified report. They didn't mince their words. 'We assess Russian President Vladimir Putin ordered an influence campaign in 2016 aimed at the US presidential election. Russia's goals were to undermine public faith in the US democratic process, denigrate Secretary Clinton, and harm her electability and potential presidency.' US prosecutors alleged that members of the GRU (the Russian military intelligence agency) gained access to the Democratic National Committee's networks, and then threw compromising emails out into the public via Wikileaks.. Russian media then leapt on the story, accusing Clinton of corruption, poor physical and mental health, and ties to Islamic extremism.

When it looked like Clinton would win, Russian diplomats and pro-Kremlin bloggers began impugning the fairness of the election. They prepared, a social media campaign screaming that the vote was rigged, reaching a crescendo on election night itself. Our own research found that it abruptly went silent, the moment that Trump won.[20] They circulated an exclusive interview with Julian Assange claiming that 'Clinton and ISIS are funded by the same money' and another headlined: 'How 100 per cent of Clintons' charity went to . . . themselves'. They had littledoubt that Russia was behind these stories. 'We have high confidence in these judgements,' the US intelligence community concluded.[21]

But Russia didn't just have to pretend to be journalists. The internet gave them a new opportunity: they could pretend to be everybody else as well. In 2015, journalists exposed a 'troll factory'.

20 How Twitter fueled the wild rise of vote rigging allegations, Mashable, https://mash-able.com/2016/11/07/rigged-elections-donald-trump/#FQNVU4SpHmqY
21 Intelligence Community Assessment, 'Assessing Russian Activities and Intentions in Recent US Elections', 6 January 2017.

In downtown St Petersburg, they found an office where salaried employees worked twelve-hour shifts to post on the internet pretending to be members of the public. Called the Internet Research Agency, hundreds of its employees worked to quotas, bonuses and report cards. There were different departments for VKontakte, Facebook, Twitter, Instagram and the comment sections of news websites. Over an average working day, they were expected to post on news articles fifty times, keep six Facebook accounts going, run ten Twitter accounts and tweet at least fifty times, all evangelising opinions that were handed out to them every day. The point, wrote Adrian Chen, the *New York Times* journalist who exposed it, 'was to weave propaganda seamlessly into what appeared to be the nonpolitical musings of an everyday person'.[22]

One of the Facebook communities secretly run by the Internet Research Agency was called SecuredBorders. It was churning out memes that were packaged to travel across the digital world. These memes were virulently anti-immigrant. 'New modern warfare by birth rate,' said one, 'taking over countries without single bullet.' 'Oh you want to practice Sharia law in America?' said another meme, the text framing the smiling face of Gene Wilder, in character as Willy Wonka from *Charlie and the Chocolate Factory*. 'Let me fix you a warm cup of get the fuck out of here.'[23]

A friend investigating Russian influence operations mailed me some examples of articles on the blogging site Medium, which were almost certainly written by paid Russian propagandists.[24]

---

22 www.nytimes.com/2015/06/07/magazine/the-agency.html
23 www.thedailybeast.com/30-batsht-crazy-mostly-racist-facebook-memes-the-russians-used-to-corrupt-your-mind
24 They were flagged by Twitter themselves, in evidence to the US Congress: @TheFoundingSon, @WadeHarriot, and @jenn_abrams.

Their accounts have been suspended now, but one was by a man supposedly called John Davis. He described himself as a 'Business Owner, Proud Father, Conservative, Christian Patriot', adding the hashtag #WakeUpAmerica. He had 39,000 followers on Twitter. The piece was called 'Totally Non-Political March for Science', written on 23 April, and it was about the March for Science that had happened the day before. John's main point was that although the march was non-partisan, in fact it wasn't at all, because people were holding placards that were critical of Trump. One man was pictured holding a sign that equated Trump with cavemen. A woman was pictured with a placard suggesting Trump needed a brain transplant. 'So that's what science looks like when liberals get their hands on it. Pretty much like everything else they have already screwed up,' said John.

Wade Harriot was another. 'Christian, Husband, Father, etc etc'. The article called for Clinton to be disqualified from the race to be president. Wade wanted to support a petition to prevent the 'dynastic succession of the Clinton family in American politics [which] breaches the core democratic principles laid out by our Founding Fathers . . . turning American democracy into a monarchy.' There was nothing to indicate this was Russian propaganda.

And so, under great pressure from US lawmakers, the technology companies disclosed what they knew about Russian influence activity. It transpired that Russian agents had created inflammatory posts that reached 126 million users on Facebook, they had published more than 131,000 messages on Twitter, 120,000 Instagram posts, and uploaded over 1,000 videos to YouTube.[25]

25 www.nytimes.com/2017/10/30/technology/facebook-google-russia.html

Twitter notified almost 700,000 Americans that they had likely interacted with content from the Internet Research Agency.[26]

Journalists who challenged these disinformation campaigns often faced terrifying harassment. Jessikka Aro is a journalist who works for the Finnish state broadcaster Yle. In September 2014 she started to investigate paid, anonymous social media commentators. 'Trolls', she wrote, 'are part of the Kremlin's propaganda system and technique of information warfare: these recruited commentators distribute the messages of Russia's political leaders online.' She wanted to see how they impacted Finnish public debate.[27]

When Jessikka Aro started to investigate these Russian trolls, she drew a furious retaliation from them. Speaking in a dull monotone at the Prague summit, she described the campaign that was put together to discredit her. Online articles began to claim that she was compiling an illegal database of Putin supporters. One day her phone rang, and when she answered she heard a gun being fired. She received texts claiming to be from her dead father, saying he was 'observing' her. A music video appeared on YouTube in which an actress played Aro, wearing a blonde wig, waving NATO and US flags in President's Putin face. She became the target not only of intimidation, but a full-blown counter-investigation. Her opponents had found court records of a twelve-year-old, 300-euro fine for drug use. Protestors appeared outside Yle's headquarters, demonstrating against the 'NATO information expert drug dealer' who was 'mentally ill'.[28, 29]

*

26 http://adage.com/article/digital/twitter-notifies-700-000-users-russian-tweets/312023/
27 Jessikka Aro, 'The Cyberspace War: Propaganda and Trolling as Warfare Tools', *European View*, 15:121–132.
28 Ibid.
29 Our friend Eliot Higgins of Bellingcat (from Chapter 3) has been constantly attacked too. The anti-Bellingcat group emerged in Russia, composed of 'really independent' experts, and picked up by Sputnik in multiple languages.

Russia's techniques are a mixture of the very visible and very secret, a sophisticated blend of cyber-operations and covert influence involving paid spies, hacker groups, state-funded media, third-party intermediaries, paid social media commentators and an unknown number of people around the world who simply agree with what they were all saying. Some of it isn't organised at all, but some of it is part of a new kind of apparatus, built to stretch Russian influence by extending its narratives – sometimes truth, sometimes fiction – all over the world.

The apparatus stretches all the way from the mainstream media to the backwaters of the blogosphere, from the President of the Russian Federation to the humble bot. A network of state-owned and semi-official Russian news outlets feed off each other, often reusing the same stories or text directly. They refer their audiences to each other. And time after time, the line they are pressing is the one most useful to the Kremlin.

The internet is a crucial part of this apparatus. There are hackers – perhaps Russian intelligence masquerading as activists, criminals masquerading as Russian intelligence, or a strange combination of all of them. There are troll factories that are either financed by legitimate businessmen or Russian organised crime. There is a changing tapestry of newly influential voices online, including 'independent' experts, front groups, real groups, activists, united fronts, real documents, forged documents, academics, journalists, and people posing as either or both – and they all come together online around certain stories and narratives.

Online, however, disinformation can take a new direction. It is no longer just a means of disrupting traditional journalism.

Now it is possible to also fake being the public itself. There are troll factories and 'bots'; there is the use of automation to make stories appear more popular than they are. But alongside salaried antagonists and bot armies are simply real people with pro-Russian opinions. It has become incredibly difficult to tell apart the people who genuinely believe what they write and the people who are paid to believe it. Online, salaried propagandists mix easily with heartfelt, genuine opinions. And some of it is even true. Disinformation mixed up with information; truth with lies.

This apparatus apparently tries to do different things in different places. It seems to have different narratives and tactics for different nations and regions. Some of it is directed internally, some of it to Russophone and ethnic Russians abroad, some to the West. Messages are targeted at environmental activists and racists, Wall Street financiers and radical egalitarians.

The themes it touches on cover everything from police brutality, racial tensions, online privacy concerns, alleged government misconduct, gun rights, transgender issues, conspiracy theories, isolationism and anti-interventionism. Some themes dwell on the glorious never-was of Soviet Communism, others offer caricatures of contemporary western politicians. Brexit and the EU, anti-vax, anti-Zika spraying, anti-GMO, the 9/11 'Truth Movement' are all touched on too. In the Baltic, the message aims to exploit fears of US abandonment and Soviet nostalgia. In Romania, that EU accession was a failure. In the Czech Republic, anti-war and anti-corruption themes. In the US, long-time fatigue with democracy, and raging polarisation between red and blue. In the UK another dividing line: Brexit.

Killing the Truth

Whether in Ukraine, Latvia or the UK, it isn't clear whether any of his has actually made Russia any more attractive to most of its viewers – but perhaps that isn't the point.[30] Contradictory stories – even from within the same media outlet – flow out from these sources and into the internet. There is no single version of the truth. There are hundreds. That, I think, is the point.

The primary aim of all of this isn't to replace one truth in people's minds with another, but to undermine the idea of truth at all – to kill the truth, the very idea of trust, facts and credibility. What can we believe in any more? Who do we trust? On the whole the propaganda doesn't seem to be about intellectual judgement, but more about mood, how people feel. It is a softer, more invasive, more attritional aim: building a sedimentary bedrock of feeling that everyone is corrupt, everything is rotten. If there is a general aim, it seems to be to destroy the public's belief in truth itself. A war on information as much as information warfare.

The summit in Prague spent days dissecting the realities of information warfare that people from across the West are convinced is now happening. It uncovered more questions and puzzles and mysteries than it did answers, but as I left, one thing was crystal

---

30 In April 2014, Gallup polls found that only 2 per cent of Ukrainian respondents named Russian federal broadcasters among their three most important sources of information. In fact, the Russian news channels that enjoyed a weekly reach of almost 19 per cent in Ukraine in 2012 are now reduced to around 9 per cent. Russia's role in the crisis was perceived as 'mostly positive' by only 35 per cent of respondents in the east and 28 per cent in the south of Ukraine. In the centre, west and north, less than 3 per cent of respondents considered Russia's role to have been 'mostly positive'. See Joanna Szotek, 'The Limitations of Russian Propaganda in Ukraine,' *Russia List*, 11 June 2014: http:// russialist. org/the-limitations-of-russian-propaganda-in-ukraine-russian-tv-is-waging-a-propaganda-war-against-ukraine-but-is-it-working

clear. The internet and social media have changed how states influence populations. The speed, openness and anonymity of online life, its love of the headline and controversy, all make it ideal for influence operations. Small, little-known news outlets can reach huge audiences. Online, the 'public' of one country can constantly talk with and influence the public of another. Entire fake publics can be conjured from thin air. I could understand why the 77th Brigade was in such a hurry. Information warfare has already broken out.

A Trip to GCHQ

In Cheltenham, UK, there is a building affectionately known as the doughnut, a giant, multi-floor circle, with a grassy hole in the middle. I squeezed through a turnstile and a checkpoint, another checkpoint and then another. Inside, a sweeping white marble concourse with a glass roof gently follows the curve of the building. Some of the people striding along this artery look incredibly young: dyed hair, skinny jeans and T-shirts. Others are in full military uniform. Lots are anonymous, in suits. I was inside Government Communications Headquarters, invariably called GCHQ. It is the UK's technical spy agency, only admitted to exist by the government in 1994.

On the top floor there's a large banner on the wall: 'GCHQ Never Sleeps'. At the top of the building is the Event Management Centre, a long oval room, probably about 25 metres long. Huge television screens are mounted on the walls, and hundreds of smaller monitors show graphs that tick to the beat of some unknown metric. The atmosphere is relaxed when I walk in. Analysts are sipping tea, and the cricket is quietly playing on one of the big monitors. It looks like a cross between an open space office, and NASA launch control.

Deep underneath the Event Management Centre is a long concrete tunnel, 15 feet tall. Fluorescent lights throw a lurid orange glow onto the blank, smooth walls. The corridor opens onto an enormous room, half the size of a football pitch, with rack after rack of computers stretching through the gloomy interior. Cocooned within concrete, this is the blastproofed brain of GCHQ. It is its underground data centre – the heart of Britain's cyberwarfare capability.

A vast amount of power is fed into the computers in this room. Each is a large, loudly humming silhouette and each is billions of times faster than a normal computer. Under the floor, pressurised cold air is forced up through gratings to flow over the racks of the machines. There's enough cabling to go to the moon and back. To most of us, the digital revolution might be slick, smooth, silent and non-physical. But here among the flashing orange lights, pipes and ventilators, it is like a factory. The hot air that is thrown out of this room, I was told, is sometimes so great that it creates a rain cloud above GCHQ.

It is of course not just Russia that has realised how warfare is changing. Governments around the world have all built something like GCHQ to project power and influence out into the digital world. GCHQ has many jobs: to crack the transmissions of foreign states while keeping the UK's transmissions secure; to protect the UK from cyberwarfare, to track down terrorists. But ever since Edward Snowden's explosive disclosures about the realities of western intelligence, we have known that GCHQ, too, has been building capability to influence opinions and beliefs through the internet.

A group that Snowden exposed in 2013 was called the 'Joint Threat Research Intelligence Group', or JTRIG. As is common in the world of intelligence, the name itself is unrevealing. But in the documents that Snowden leaked, JTRIG is described as 'lying at the leading edge of cyber influence practice and expertise'. Its core function is to use the internet to achieve 4Ds against any enemy: deny disrupt, degrade, deceive. It is a group dedicated to online covert action for information and influence operations. 'Using online techniques to make something happen in the real or cyber world,' they explained.

JTRIG achieves the 4Ds through a number of now-familiar techniques. Propaganda. Deception. Mass messaging. Pushing stories. Fake accounts. Psychology. To discredit companies, they could 'leak confidential information to the press through blogs etc', as well as posting negative information on other appropriate forums. They could change social media photos ('can take "paranoia" to a whole new level', a leaked slide said). They could use masquerade-type techniques – placing 'secret' information on a compromised computer.[31] They could bombard someone's phone with text messages or calls.

Also leaked by Edward Snowden (and this was dated way back to 2009) was the operational toolkit developed by JTRIG. It detailed around 200 tools that JTRIG were building, from in-development to fully operational. 'Badger' allowed the mass delivery of email. 'Burlesque' spoofed SMS messages. 'Clean

---

31 https://snowdenarchive.cjfe.org/greenstone/collect/snowden1/index/assoc/ HASH7b20.dir/doc.pdf

Sweep' would 'masquerade' Facebook wall posts for individuals or entire countries. 'Gateway' gave the ability to 'artificially increase traffic to a website'. 'Underpass' was a way to change the outcome of online polls.[32]

As with Russia, this was the use of human psychology and the internet to shape the 'human terrain' in furtherance of the policy goals of the country.[33] JTRIG had operational targets across the globe: Iran, Africa, North Korea, Russia and also the UK. Sometimes the operations focused on specific individuals and groups, sometimes the wider regimes or even general populations.[34] Operation Quito was a plan to prevent Argentina from taking over the Falkland Islands. A slide said 'this will hopefully lead to a long-running, large-scale, pioneering effects operation'.[35] Another operation aimed for regime change in Zimbabwe by discrediting the current regime.

To learn more about JTRIG, I travelled from the blastproof corridors and incessant humming of GCHQ's data centre to the hushed, marbled interior of the Reform Club, Pall Mall, London. A domed glass ceiling rose above me, surrounded by discreet marble collonades, red leather and stained wood. And in front of me was Sir David Omand GCB, the former director of GCHQ. He chuckled when I told him that I wanted to talk about disinformation and influence operations. 'It's a fashionable subject.'

32 https://snowdenarchive.cjfe.org/greenstone/collect/snowden1/index/assoc/
    HASHd34e.dir/doc.pdf
33 https://snowdenarchive.cjfe.org/greenstone/collect/snowden1/index/assoc/
    HASH9098.dir/doc.pdf
34 https://snowdenarchive.cjfe.org/greenstone/collect/snowden1/index/assoc/
    HASH01d8/d1780c95.dir/doc.pdf
35 https://snowdenarchive.cjfe.org/greenstone/collect/snowden1/index/assoc/
    HASH01ab/d97e2af9.dir/doc.pdf

A quietly spoken man, with rimless spectacles, David spent most of his career inside the Ministry of Defence and then GCHQ during the height of the Cold War. 'Influence operations' – what JTRIG, Russia, or anyone else are doing – have long been used by the state as a way of avoiding the earth-shattering consequences that a direct confrontation would inevitably have. 'You always had two different levels of battlefield,' he told me. 'You have the intelligence battlefield where the adversary's intelligence agencies would be slugging it with us. And you have the campaign for influence through propaganda. Both happening under the threshold of armed force.'

During the Cold War, GCHQ had been primarily a signals intelligence agency – listening to other people speaking on wireless, telegrams or the telephone, and trying to stop others doing the same to their own side. In the post-Cold War era, GCHQ had, like everyone else, pivoted towards the Internet, and JTRIG was part of that. 'As far as I know,' Sir David Omand said, 'JTRIG was the first time GCHQ specially organised for action in cyberspace. The important step here is "specialisation". The principle of weaponising information is much older. But it was probably the first time they organised a group especically for this purpose.'

Global War

As researchers delved deeper into these new methods of state control, they began to uncover the same kinds of techniques that Russia used happening across the world, but especially in authoritarian states. Unlike Russia, these efforts were often directed

primarily at domestic audiences. In each case it seemed coordinated, and working to protect the interests and reputations of
the incumbent government. It became a way not only of one
state struggling with another, but of the powerful defending their
avantage.

In China, a Harvard paper estimated that the Chinese government is suspected of employing 2 million (this is not a typo) people
to write 448 million social media posts, primarily aimed at their
own populace to distract the public, change the subject, and keep
online discussion away from sensitive political topics.[36] Researchers
exposed thousands of fake Twitter accounts operating in Saudi
Arabia, generating 'anti-Shia and anti-Iranian propaganda' and
'generally lionising the Saudi government or Saudi foreign
policy'.[37] In Bahrain there is evidence of spam-like operations,
aiming to stop dissidents finding each other or debating politically
dangerous topics online.

In Mexico, an estimated 75,000 automated accounts are known
locally as Peñabots, after President Enrique Peña Nieto. Similar
to the case in Bahrain, they overwhelm the political opposition on
Twitter in vast, inhuman hoards. When a new hashtag emerges
to raise awareness about a protest or corruption scandal, Peñabots
jump into action: either causing other hashtags to trend, or something called 'hashtag poisoning' – flooding the protest hashtags
with irrelevant, annoying noise burying any useful information.[38]

In the Philippines, the journalist Maria Ressa found all the tactics
that are now becoming familiar from elsewhere. She uncovered
salaried social media commentators, similar to the Internet

36 http://gking.harvard.edu/files/gking/files/50c.pdf
37 https://exposingtheinvisible.org/resources/automated-sectarianism
38 https://freedomhouse.org/report/freedom-net/freedom-net-2017

Research Agency in Russia, but mainly focused on a domestic audience. 'They share the same key message,' Ressa wrote in her expose of them, 'a fanatic defense of Duterte, who's portrayed as the father of the nation deserving the support of all Filipinos.' She found huge bursts of automatically generated tweets. She found technical manipulation of online polls. But she also found entirely genuine and real-person threats made by supporters of Duterte to campaigners, journalists and political opponents.[39] After she wrote the story, she came under attack herself – receiving ninety hate messages an hour, many with the hashtag #arrestmariaressa.

In Thailand, politicians encouraged and incentivised followers to report 'unpatriotic' content. Police officials reportedly offered a $15 bounty to those who report users who have opposed the military government. Over 100,000 students have been trained as 'cyber scouts' to monitor and report online behaviour deemed to threaten national security.[40]

In Turkey, there are reports of 'white trolls' that rumble out in support of the ruling Justice and Development Party. Some 6,000 people have allegedly been enlisted by the party to manipulate discussions, drive particular agendas, and counter government opponents on social media. Journalists and scholars who are critical of the government have faced orchestrated harassment on Twitter by dozens or hundreds of users.[41]

The independent watchdog Freedom House assessed sixty-five countries for online 'manipulation tactics'. They found that thirty had evidence of paid pro-government commentators. Twenty showed evidence of political bots. Sixteen had seen deliberately

39 www.rappler.com/nation/148007-propaganda-war-weaponizing-internet
40 https://freedomhouse.org/report/freedom-net/freedom-net-2017
41 https://freedomhouse.org/report/freedom-net/2017/turkey

misleading news pumped out during elections and in ten accounts had been 'hijacked' – forcibly taken over to spread information against the owner's wishes. And these were, of course, just campaigns that could be seen.

Information Defence

Warfare is an arms race between offence and defence. So what about the defence? Journalists around the world, like Yevhen Fedchenko in Ukraine, have started their own efforts to report on disinformation when they see it, and to fact-check the claims that other journalists or prominent commentators make. The *Washington Post* has the 'Fact Checker' column by Glenn Kessler. There is PolitiFact.com, FullFact.org, Chequeado in Argentina, the BBC Reality Check. The European Union has set up the 'Disinformation Review' that collects examples of pro-Kremlin disinformation every week and flags overall trends.

Fact-checking, however, is never going to solve the problem alone. You only visit the EU's database to combat disinformation if you do, indeed, believe that it is disinformation in the first place. You only believe the fact-checking column from the BBC if you believe the BBC. It is that trust that influence campaigns around the world have both sought to reduce and to exploit. They promise to bring their audience the 'real truth' that the 'MSM' (mainstream media) are too corrupt and compromised to report on themselves. But on a deeper level, disinformation campaigns don't seem to really focus on rational judgement. They want to change how people feel, to promote a general, underlying feeling that everything is rotten. Fact-checkers work at the level of evidence, but not feelings and mood.

Education is the obvious answer to raise the resilience of a whole population. Digital literacy is a vital response, perhaps the only true solution to the problem. But it also takes a huge amount of time, and as a formal curriculum could only really reach people in school Time during which influence operations will get smarter, more constant, and probably more ambitious. What about now? What about everyone else?

As militaries around the world scramble to weaponise information, the burden of protecting the online spaces that militaries increasing contest has largely fallen to the technology companies that own and run them. The tech giants are, of course, formidable adversaries for even states to take on. They have huge amounts of money and some of the greatest concentrations of technical talent in the world. So what are they doing about the problem?

Andrew Smart is an American data scientist, and used to work for Twitter, in a team called 'Information Quality' – or IQ. It was their job to safeguard Twitter as a platform against all the different attempts around the world to subvert and manipulate and information that passed through it. 'Twitter is under-resourced for this,' Andrew told me.' My team was a seed project – never more than a dozen strong. And information warfare wasn't even a large part of what the IQ team actually did. 'We would discuss the warfare aspect,' Andrew said, 'but very peripherally. It was more misinformation, rumours. When people brought up the weaponisation aspect, it was ignored or dismissed – not in a malicious way, but it was just seen as something Twitter couldn't control.'

*

There is something called a re-CAPTCHA, a little button to tick, that is widely used across the internet to prove you're not a bot. Twitter does not include this when you sign up for an account. Why? There is possibly a case of mixed incentives. Twitter cares about metrics. It cares about user-base. More tweets and more users are good for Twitter as a business; that's understandable. Digital marketers use metrics like numbers of followers, 'reach' and 'impressions' as ways of measuring the success of their campaigns, and companies like Twitter get rewarded by delivering big numbers. Thus it gets penalised for adding any kind of 'friction' like a re-CAPTCHA button. Quantity of information is easy to measure; quality, of course, much more difficult. Bots, spam, manipulation and misinformation, if they remain unidentified as such, are 'activity' on the platform. Of course, companies like Twitter do genuinely remove spam, because they know that it harms the user experience and might in turn reduce the number of people that use their product. But over-expansive solutions to information warfare, removing millions of accounts or tweets, will rub up against these basic market incentives. Twitter won't reveal how many of its 313 million active users are automated bots, semi-automated spam accounts or state-based trolls. It probably doesn't know. But Andrew said, 'I found one IP address – one source – from Russia that had made some Twitter accounts follow other accounts on 26 million occasions.

There are – I know them – good people in the tech giants working unbelievably hard on this problem. And it is hard to tell whether they privately share Andrew's frustrations. They are our best line of defence – the only people capable. But it doesn't sound like there are enough of them, or that their work has enough priority across the whole of their organisations. While militaries have started to see platforms like Twitter as a key tool, most people in Twitter aren't worried about the military. It just isn't part of their conceptual framework.

'It's a naivety about the ruthlessness of military people,' said Andrew. 'Most people in tech just don't come from intelligence and defence backgrounds – it's incomprehensible to them that people would go to these lengths to manipulate mass psychology.' The world of information warfare sits completely at odds with the thinking that makes Silicon Valley tick: the liberating power of networks, the freedom that comes with more tools, the individual emancipations that their platforms provide. Information warfare has been a blind spot to the tech giants. And until that changes, the level of challenge that Twitter currently poses to intelligence agencies will be low. It isn't because the offensive side of information warfare is simply better resourced. It's that the defensive side barely recognises that war has been declared.

Target: You

It started as pranks on 4Chan, but they were only amongst the first to realise the potential of online tools to influence what we see and think. Spammy marketers used it, and fringe and splinter political groups. And last, militaries too. What began as ways of spreading cats aeound the internet became militarised, systemised and weaponised, turned into acronym-laden military-speak.

We live in a more peaceable world than most of our ancestors would recognise. But what we haven't realised is how warfare has transferred outside the kinetic arena, and into battlefield of ideas, information, beliefs and opinions. Militaries and intelligence agencies have redefined warfare for the information age. The battlespace now extends from a muddy field all the way to online blogs – it's all been conceptually folded into the same, militarised space.

The year 2011 was the high point for those believing the internet would spread freedom around the world. Popular uprisings in Egypt and Tunisia, the 'Twitter and Facebook revolutions'. Protests in Moscow too, and newly empowered civil societies around the world organising and protesting in ways that they had never been able to before. We were moving, we thought, towards a world where everyone would have a voice.

After the Snowden revelations, the idea was cemented that the internet was a giant western surveillance machine. Authoritarian states around the world began to assert domestic control and localise and nationalise data. Now, we are confronted with another hard realisation. The internet is not just a surveillance machine; it can also be a manipulation engine. Being online doesn't necessarily set you free, and being connected with others doesn't necessarily deliver you the truth.

Things changed when militaries got involved.

We are waking up to the capacity for state power to control networks. Special technology and honed techniques in the hands of the well-equipped few can have great influence, online, over the many. A decentralised network is actually very vulnerable to centralised control from outside forces, and that's before you even count the internal influence of the tech giants who own them.

The concerted, systematic exploitation of these techniques by militaries puts the scale and impact of influence operations into a different league. Compared to building a tank or a missile, creating fake accounts on a social media platform is trivially cheap and technically very easy to do.

It is inescapably true that, for influence operations, offence is beating defence. It's far easier to create information than to ascertain if it's true. It is easier to create a fake identity than it is to expose one. And the internet, at the same time as making all these new forms of influence possible, has also undermined the commercial basis of journalism, whose reporters might otherwise have checked and exposed these attempts.

In a sense, there should be nothing surprising about this. The internet has become just like any other sphere. It is where we live out our lives – like the air we fly through, the ground we walk on. However, the moment that information was defined as a theatre of war, the game changed. It is a sphere where we are all very, very vulnerable, and where the power is the hands of the well-equipped, well-financed few.

This is a form of power that is tremendously unrecognised. The full scale of attempts by militaries to conduct influence campaigns on the internet is not well known. The techniques they are using are, we can be sure, constantly changing and improving. Most people do not know it is happening, and it is hard for anyone to know exactly what *is* happening. It is a form of power that works best when it operates from the shadows.

Furthermore, it seems to be benefiting more from technological progress than the attempts to stop it. Automation will become better. Bots will become smarter. Computers will keep learning how to mimic human beings and it will become harder and harder

– and at some point impossible – to tell whether or not you're speaking to a real person or not.

Finally, it is a form of control that inherently benefits authoritarian states more than liberal, democratic or rights-respecting ones. It is not technical difficulty that constrains how states deploy influence operations; it is the law. I asked Sir David Omand what the difference between Russian disinformation and JTRIG was. He said: 'The actual methods of the SVR are bound to be almost identical to the GCHQ. The distinguishing feature doesn't rest essentially in the methods. I would draw a distinction between methods and intentions.'

'In the UK, you need the right authoirty' he continued. The Security Services Act, the Intelligence Services Act – almost certainly, the Foreign Secretary is accountable – you have to ask and get authority. Otherwise you're opening yourself up to conspiracy to commit a criminal offence.'

'But what's the right role of misinformation?' I asked.

'There has to be a very good reason for it. Proportionality and necessity. It's the legal framework, the safeguards, the independents courts, judges, and the rest of it. That, in Russian eyes, seems to be totally inconsequential.'

The internet was designed with democratic principles in mind, especially freedom of speech and assembly. Non-democratic states have staged a counter-attack in the second decade of this century using the very infrastructure on which freedom has flourished. Rather than suppress openness, the aim is now to exploit openness.

This is fundamentally disempowering. The message isn't an uplifting or optimistic one, but it is only by hearing it that its effect could be diminished. The democratic potential of the internet – the integrity of the internet itself – is threatened as it becomes a platform to shape influence. Through it, an assault is being made on your beliefs and opinions. You have become a strategic objective.

7

Hidden Power

'*Whoever becomes the leader in the sphere [of artificial intelligence] will become the ruler of the world.*'
Vladimir Putin

'Never view a tuna.
Suns sail like misty girls.
Moons fall like cold masts.'
From 'A Tuna', a poem by a bot[1]

'*If there's a recipe for virality, it looks like it needs a dough of spectacle and farce held together by a crust of narrative, a sprinkling of schadenfreude and a dusting of bourgeois taboo.*'
The Peng! Collective

---

1   http://botpoet.com/vote

We hear more and more every day about how addicted people have become to technology and how predictable we are when we use it. We hear about algorithms dictating how we behave online: what we buy, what we read, where we go. We read about how smart bots influence elections. About fortunes locked in crypto-currencies. About computers replacing humans in the workplace. Out there in the world, these are all examples, I think, of the same basic trend: at exactly the same moment that technology is becoming more sophisticated and unknowable to us, we are becoming more open and understandable to it.

There is a collection of phenomena that aren't just examples of power, but are also examples of how difficult it is to see power when it is working through technology. And not just to us, but sometimes to the very creators of these forces themselves.

This isn't about artificial intelligence taking over the world, or robots rising up against us. But it raises a question crucial to the reality of power both today, and in the future. Have we lost control?

The Algorithm

'I'll lose my job if anyone knows about this.'

There was a long silence which I didn't dare to break. I had begged to make this meeting happen. And now the person I had long been trying to meet leaned towards me. 'Someone is going to go through your book line by line,' he said, 'to try to work out who I am.'

He'd been a talented researcher, an academic, until his friend started a small technology company. He had joined the company and helped it to grow. It eventually became so big that the company had been acquired by one of the tech giants. And so, then, was he.

He was now paid a fortune to help design the algorithms that were central to what the tech giant did. And he had signed solemn legal documents prohibiting him from speaking to me, or to anyone about his work.But as the years passed, his concern – indeed his guilt – grew. 'It's power without responsibility.' He paused. 'There's *so much* power, and so little responsibility. This is not notional abstract power. This is real power about day-to-day lives. It's both material and cultural and financial. The world has to know that this is how it works.'[2] 'There's something rotten in the state of Denmark,' he said, quoting *Hamlet* a little melodramatically.

So he had decided to take a risk. 'If they find out I'm doing this,' he said, 'I'll be marched out of my office and I'll never work in technology again. That's the best-case scenario.' He wasn't just going to talk to me about his work. He was going to show me it.

From his satchel, the researcher pulled out his laptop. He tapped for a few minutes and, with a sense of occasion, turned the screen to face me. 'It's all there.' And there it was: a white

2 Each tech giant has built teams and infrastructures to wage war on an internal enemy: the leaker. Apple, as one example, has the Global Security Team that employs an undisclosed number of investigators to prevent information from reaching the press (and competitors). Members of this team have previously worked for the NSA, the US military, the FBI and the US Secret Service. The Global Security Team in China has been 'busting their ass' to solve the problem of leaks stemming from Apple's factories. 'Trench warfare non-stop,' said the head of it.

screen with instructions arranged in neatly arranged in a series of boxes.

'In [3]' the first step says
'In [8], in [9]' says the next.

There were words in different colours, some green, some purple, some in red, in bold, in italics.I looked at the researcher, a proud grin spread across his face. There it was. An algorithm that really influenced people's lives. And it was . . . totally underwhelming.

Twenty-three centuries ago, the Greek mathematician Eratosthenes sat in the great library of Alexandria and tried to find a way to identify prime numbers. He wrote every number from one to 100 in ten rows, and crossed out the one. He circled the two, crossed out all the multiples of two, circled the three and continued. He had created an algorithm, in essence something very simple. His 'sieve', as it was called, did what all algorithms so. It took an input, followed a series of well-described steps and produced an output. Input, process, output: that's all an algorithm is, and has ever been.

Throughout their history, algorithms have been built to solve problems. They have been used to make astronomical calculations, build clocks and turn secret information into code. 'Up till the nineties,' the researcher said, 'algorithms still tended to be RSAs – Really Simple Algorithms. Previously it was pretty clear how stuff happened. You take the original Google algorithm. It was basically a popularity study. You'd just surface (or rank more highly) things that people clicked on more. In general, the people who made it understood how the thing worked.' Some algorithms were more complicated than others, but the input > process > output was generally transparent and understandable, at least to the people who built and used them.

The algorithm he had brought up on his screen was built to solve a problem, too. It ordered and organized reality in an important way, trying to separate what was important from what was irrelevant. But it was different from the RSAs.. 'It's way more complicated than it looks,' he said, hovering a pencil over some of the short words in square brackets. 'But I need to show you why.' And with that, we started to journey through his creation.

First, it imported 'libraries', a specific language of definitions, instructions and actions. Next, he showed me how it brought in data. 'There's a bit of a macho thing about feeding your algorithms as much data as possible,' he said. 'The more data you feed it, the better. We work with a lot more data than most teams, actually,' he said, drawing his cursor longingly over the script that brought the huge, churning quantities of data that fed the algorithm. Gigabytes, terabytes, petabytes of data were ordered, there on the page.

By instruction fifteen, 'functions' were added. 'A function is a little factory,' the researcher said, highlighting each one. 'These are the building blocks of the algorithm: a sub-algorithm, basically.' He showed how he built each of these building blocks, stringing together phrases like 'get component', 'filter by station', 'sort_nodes_in_degree'. Then, the main stage. 'This is the business end of the algorithm,' he said. 'This is where I stack up the building blocks.' He was supposed to be showing me how the functions were connected together. But

I was lost. 'I don't get it,' I said. 'How can you keep track of what's doing what?'

Each of these sub-algorithmic functions, his building blocks, was really another complete house. Each was a complex tangle of instructions and processes, and some were themselves made from sub-algorithmic building blocks. The screen looked simple, but I was looking at a blueprint of building blocks within building blocks within building blocks: millions of instructions in just a few pages of code. Its builder was sitting next to me, but even he struggled to explain the stages, retracing steps and correcting himself as he tried to hold the layer upon layer of abstraction in his head. He seemed to finish, but then paused. 'I don't really remember where that last bit comes from,' he said.

The researcher knew, of course, what data he'd fed into the process. He knew why he'd designed it, the problem it was trying to solve and the outputs that it produced. However, after he'd been trying to explain it for over an hour, he sat back in his chair, exhausted. 'Yes, as you can see, the gap between input and output is difficult to understand,' he said. He'd flooded the algorithm with a huge amount of information, 'a trend', he said, because in the tech giant he could, and everyone did. But the amount of data meant it was hard to tell what the salient inputs within it were. 'From a human perspective you're not sure which of the inputs is significant; it's hard to know what is actually driving the outputs. It's hard to trace back, as a human, to know why a decision was made.'

Within his tech giant, algorithms rarely stand alone. Instead, they exist within webs. 'I rely', he said, 'on signals that are produced by other algorithms.' His algorithm was fed by outputs that were shaped by other algorithms. It was like a car assembly line. He, like his colleagues, worked on a small, specific part of a much larger process.

The algorithm was also constantly changing. The data inputs were flowing into the algorithm in real time, but the actual weights, measures and trade-offs that the algorithm made weren't static either. Some of the functions that the researcher had woven in used machine learning – techniques where the machine constantly learned and adapted to what the most important patterns, correlations and relationships were. It meant that the algorithm was constantly changing and moving as the world moved around it, and its diet of data changed to reflect that.

We sat there, looking at the computer, his creation laid out in multi-coloured type. 'This is all to do with complexity,' he said contemplatively. 'Complexity of input. Complexity of analysis. Complexity of how outputs are combined, structured and used.' One of the reasons that he'd been employed to build a process like this was exactly because it could handle complexity by being complex itself. It grasped the blinding number of factors, signals and influences that bounced off each other at every moment in ways that we simply cannot.

Algorithms have changed, from Really Simple to Ridiculously Complicated. A web of new technologies is changing the possibilities of algorithms. They are capable of accomplishing tasks and tackling problems that they've never been able to do before. They are able, really, to handle an unfathomably complex world better than a human can. But exactly because they can, the way they work has become unfathomable too. Inputs loop from one algorithm to the next; data presses through more instructions, more code. The complexity, dynamism, the sheer not-understandability of the algorithm means that there is a middle part – between input and output – where it is possible that no one knows exactly what they're doing. The algorithm learns whatever it learns. 'The reality is, professionally, I only look under the hood when it goes wrong. And it can be physically impossible to understand what has actually happened.'

From Truth to Output

With a triumphant flick of his wrist, the researcher tapped a key and the algorithm began. Twenty seconds later, the algorithm was finished. There in black and white, was an output. One, of course, that I cannot specifically describe, but an output that many of us use every dayThe algorithm had produced a kind of reality, really – one that we make decisions from, that can even change our lives.

The researcher scrolled through the bundle of instructions, and changed a single one to a two. A single value. The algorithm reran, and reality popped out again, but this time, a quarter of the results had ceased to exist.

'OK,' I said, 'what happened there? Why did you change it? You know the two is wrong. But how do you know the one is right?'

'That', he said, gesticulating at the sabotaged result, 'is the point. It's a heuristic. I tried it, and it seemed to work. Then I tested it, and the result looked right. I can't say the one is true. I can only say that it passed minimum evaluation criteria. The whole algorithm is full of parameters that could have been something else. Truth is dead,' he sighed. 'There is only output.'[3]

'Who checks these?' I asked.

'Me.'

'What about your boss?'

'You've seen how difficult it is to really understand. Sometimes I struggle with it, and I created it. The reality is that if the algorithm looks like it's doing the job that it's supposed to do, and people aren't complaining, then there isn't much incentive to really comb through all those instructions and those layers of abstracted code to work out what is happening.' The preferences you see online – the news you read, the products you see, the adverts that appear – are all dependent on values that don't necessarily could be something else. They are not necessarily true, they've just passed minimum evaluation criteria.

---

3   Changing the values of the algorithm had felt trivial, and so easy for him to do. But even the smallest changes have enormous capacity to change the realities that they produce. Back in 2009, some books started dropping off Amazon. One of the authors affected by it was Mark Probst and, when he investigated, he found that the books affected were ones, like his, with gay and lesbian themes. He made his concerns public and, when journalists looked into it, they eventually found that 57,000 books had been affected, including not only LGBTQ titles but also ones appearing under the headings Health, Mind and Body, Reproductive and Sexual Medicine, and Erotica. Remembering that Amazon is the world's largest retailer of books, this was a huge cultural shift in the books that people see and buy. But the cause was remarkably small. It turned out that a single Amazon technician working in France reportedly altered the value of a single database-cataloguing attribute – 'adult' – from false to true in these categories. And 'adult' material is excluded from some Amazon searches. Human thought and expression had been influenced by a database value because it had been algorithmically expressed. See Ted Striphas, 'Algorithmic Culture', *European Journal of Cultural Studies*, vol. 18.

High Stakes

Jure Leskovec spoke with a strong Slovenian accent, softened slightly by the rolling Rs I had become used to in California. Jure had spent time at Facebook and as chief scientist at Pinterest before moving back to academia. We were sitting in his office in Stanford which, like the other centres of tech in California, seemed to be expanding rapidly. As we spoke, clouds of hot, white dust drifted up past his window from drilling below.

He grabbed a pen, and sprung toward an enormous white board that took up a full wall of his office. His latest work was building an algorithm to help criminal court judges make better decisions over whether to grant a plaintiff bail. 'You have a judge,' he said, drawing a large, black rectangle on the board with a J in it, 'and a defendant. The judge is trying to make a single determination: if bailed, will the defendant commit crime or no crime? So I can train a machine learning algorithm to answer the question, "If I release you, will you commit another crime or not?"'

The scribbling on the board became more profuse, as Jure excitedly sketched out the study. He'd gathered criminal records data on people who, when bailed, committed another crime, and other data on people who hadn't. He also found a way, by comparing lenient and stricter judges, of constructing data on people who were released but who normally would have been locked up, and whether they committed another crime too.

'The point', he said, 'is that our algorithm outperforms human judges by 30 per cent. So far, these machine learning algorithms have mostly been used in, y'know, recommendations, the online world. And I would say that these types of domains are low stakes.

You might get a bad ad. You have a bad Friday night because you've watched the wrong movie. That's the worst that can happen to you. But if you think about applying these algorithms to high-stakes domains . . .'

'Which is increasingly happening?' I cut in.

'Which I think is increasingly happening. Then you have to make sure that the methods that we develop, and the standards about the way we use these methods and the way we verify them, are incredibly rigorous.'

Already, according to the *Wall Street Journal*, at least fifteen states in the US use automated risk-assessment tools to aid judges in making parole decisions. Predpol is, amongst others, a company that uses algorithms to predict areas where crime in the future is likely to happen on the basis of crimes committed in the past. Pegged is a company that offers this kind of technology (powered by artificial intelligence and fuelled by huge amounts of data) to help find the best candidates for any particular job. Algorithms are being used as contract negotiators, making split-second decisions over which terms to offer and accept. Algorithms are not only becoming more complex, they are also taking on more and more important jobs.

'I think there is a huge revolution to come,' Jure said. 'In how decisions are made in society.' He wasn't saying that algorithms should take over, only that they should be used to support human decisions. 'This bail example – I can say algorithms do better. I'm advocating, let's use these algorithms to help the human judges. They have a really hard time; they have like a minute to make a decision. They often have no feedback on whether they made the right decision, and there is no knowledge-sharing between the judges. I think it's clear that when human and machine have access to the same data, machine will beat the human. We see this over and over. Just give it enough data.'

'The algorithm', like 'artificial intelligence', has become a phrase that means more than what we say. It's become a kind of shorthand to describe the general use of advanced computation to learn and find things in ways that we don't fully understand.

Power here is buried somewhere within a process too complex for humans to grasp. Built by humans, driven by humans, only given expression and agency through humans, algorithms ultimately become powerful exactly because their analytical powers – in certain data-rich contexts – surpass humans. Like any technology, advanced computation is not an independent agency unto itself. It is how humans use it that is important. But humans have given agency, genuine decisional power, to processes that are so complex they are hidden.

'Weapons of math destruction' is how the writer Cathy O'Neil describes the nasty and pernicious kinds of algorithms that are not subject to the same challenges that human decision-makers are. Parole algorithms (not Jure's) can bias decisions on the basis of income or (indirectly) ethnicity. Recruitment algorithms can reject candidates on the basis of mistaken identity. In some circumstances, such as policing, they might create feedback loops, sending police into areas with more crime, which causes more crime to be detected.

The problem is that in many cases, we simply don't know. The researcher had taken a personal risk to show me what he had created, because his algorithm, like most that really affect us, is proprietary and hidden; they are expensive pieces of intellectual property that we cannot understand, and we cannot challenge. A 'black box society', as the academic Frank Pasquale describes it:

a society harmed by a whole new kind of secrecy that obscures the automated judgements that affect our lives.

If, as Jure suspects, machine judgement will become measurably better than human judgement for important decisions, the argument for using it will only grow stronger. And somewhere in that gap between inputs and outputs – the actual decision-making part of the process itself – is something that can shape our lives in meaningful ways yet has become less and less understandable.

'We need', Jure said emphatically, 'to step up and come up with the means to evaluate – vet – algorithms in unbiased ways. We need to be able to interpret and explain their decisions. We don't want an optimal algorithm. We want one simple enough that an expert can look at it and say nothing crazy is happening here. I think we need to get serious about how do we get these things ready for societal deployment, for high-stakes decision environments? How do we debug these things to ensure some level of quality?'

There is something happening here that is deeper than any single algorithm. They are at the forefront of what, at times, appears to be almost a new philosophy. 'God is the machine,' the researcher told me. 'The black box is the truth. If it works, it works. We shouldn't even try to work out what the machine is spitting out – they'll pick up patterns we won't even know about.'

Bots

Consumer Key: generated
Access Key: generated
App: created

I had shaped its personality. I had given it purpose. I had defined its world, its life. 'We bleed the red of patriotism,' Trump stormed from the television. It was the day of Donald Trump's inauguration, and I was ready to let my creation free.

It was a day of anger, raw recrimination and high emotion. Social media was a battle-zone. Hatred flowed across political fault lines both in America and the rest of the world. And amongst all the anger, I had an idea. Today, of all days, we needed to something to cool temperatures. We needed a peacemaker.

The American lawyer and technology advocate Mike Godwin had described a law in 1990 that seemed more relevant today than ever before: 'As an online discussion grows longer,' said Godwin, 'the probability of a comparison involving Hitler approaches one.' *Reductio ad Hitlerum* – the reduction of any dispute on whatever topic to an association with the Nazis. And as Trump spoke on the stage, as online protests and celebrations clashed with each other, everyone was calling everyone else Nazis.

Just on Twitter alone, there were too many arguments, too many *reductio ad Hitlerums* for me to handle alone. But I was with Tom Feltwell, an academic from the University of Northumbria. Tom makes 'bots',[4] robotic personages on social media that interact with users and say things according to a pre-programmed, automated script. 'Just a few lines of code,' he said to me as we watched the speech, 'and we can do something politically powerful.'

---

4 An enduring confusion is that 'bots' are used to describe another thing too: if a computer has been seized by a hacker to remotely execute their commands, these hijacked computers are also called bots, and large networks of such computers are botnets. Many of the same basic principles of automation apply to both, but here I focus on bots that are built, not computers that are stolen.

I intended to make a robotic personality that would step in when anyone was calling anyone else a 'fucking Nazi' and politely interject. It would remind them about Godwin's Law, that the person they were insulting had human feelings, and was probably not a Nazi. I was going to create my very own robo-pacifist. I called it ReductioAdHitlerBot.

First, we'd created a Twitter account. I'd found a funny image and given it a name. ReductioAdHitlerBot was now a blank slate. But rather than pilot the account manually, as a normal person would do, I needed to program its personality.

One line of code told my bot to only go after Twitter users in conversation with other Twitter users. One line defined its target: tweets that contained the phrases 'fucking hitler' or 'fucking nazi'. One line told it to reply, and another line provided a message, in the form of a clipped rebuke: 'As an online discussion grows longer, the probability of a comparison involving Hitler approaches one.' This would be followed with a link to Godwin's Law. Finally, a bit of limiting: I needed to make it a bit un-botty. So last, there was some code to tell it to limit and randomise its tweeting.[5] I threw out some chaff to camouflage its identity; I made it follow Holly Willoughby.

A click of the button, and the script started rolling. It was alive! RiductioAdHitlerBot threw itself into the wilds of Twitter, and began to execute my instructions. It was far louder, far faster than I could ever be, jumping into hundreds of conversations, sending tweets faster than I could read them. But in a split-second, my

5   For any aspiring bot developers: we used a little (free) box of tricks called Twython. It gave us – like the algorithm I'd already seen – a library of pre-made instructions that we could use.

pride melted into horror. Pounding CTRL-C, I called for help. My bot had gone rogue.

Twitterbots probably began more as art than politics. There is just something funny, surreal, poignant or cheeky about a lot of bots online, especially when they're not even trying to appear human. Botpoet writes poems, and challenges users to tell the difference between ones written by humans and bots. Another creates (rather beautiful) emoji-haikus,[6] and neuralgae, another bot, creates stunning artworks of swirling colours.

Far beyond Twitter, however, different kinds of bots have long conducted all kinds of janitorial work across the net. Google couldn't work without bots, and most of the traffic now swirling around the internet is not human. It is automated, programmatic, algorithmic.[7] Wikipedia is the largest collection of human knowledge available to anyone with the internet, for free.[8] But its sheer size means that it crucially relies on a cloud of defensive bots. There are anti-vandalism bots (ClueBot), bots that detect copyright violations (EranBot), bots that categorise articles (Cydebot) and those that report suspicious edits (COIBot). About 10 to 15 per cent of all Wikipedia edits are performed by bots: this amounts to more than a million a month. Wikipedia has a Bot Approvals Group, who sanction approved bots on Wikipedia and who also block malfunctioning ones. Members of the BAG offer 'sound bot-related advice to bot operators, admins, bureaucrats, and editors alike'.[9]

6   http://botpoet.com/vote/back-yard-heroes/
7   www.incapsula.com/blog/bot-traffic-report-2013.html
8   And for what it's worth is, in my view, it is the first digital wonder of the world, up there with the Great Pyramids or the Ancient Library of Alexandria.
9   https://en.wikipedia.org/wiki/Wikipedia:Bot_Approvals_Group

However, automation is increasingly being thrown into a new arena: politics and influence. Far more successful than mine was the Twitterbot ilDuce2006. It was born in November 2015 with only one purpose: to talk to Donald Trump. Every few hours, it sent him a quote on Twitter, always signing off with a cheery #MakeAmericaGreatAgain. Months passed and nothing happened. ilDuce2016, just like RiductioAdHitlerBot, was only a few lines of code; it was crude and elementary, but it was also patient and tireless. Finally, in February 2016, it got what it wanted – a retweet from Trump himself. But ilDuce2006 was a digital ambush; all its quotes came from strutting fascist strongman Benito Mussolini. The trap had been sprung, and Trump was promptly hauled onto the TV networks to explain his views.

Automated activists like RiductioAdHitlerBot and ilDuce2006 have some strong advantages over their fleshy counterparts. Bots can shout constantly, tirelessly and indefinitely. They can be inhumanly loud. Another, DroptheIBot, could go after every Twitter user who used the words 'illegal immigrant' with the snapped reply: 'People aren't illegal.'[10] They also make the perfect data activist, and are much better and faster than humans at scooping up data from one place and pointedly making it visible in another. @EveryTrumpDonor hooks into the Federal Election database, and tweets the name, location and occupation of – yes – every Trump donor. @stopandfrisk tweets each stop and search conducted by the NYPD in 2011. The potholes in Panama City weren't getting fixed, until they became 'botholes' and started tweeting complaints to the Department of Public Works every single time a car ran over them (via small pressure pads).[11]

10 http://migrantreport.org/twitter-shuts-down-the-illegal-immigrant-police/
11 www.adweek.com/creativity/ogilvy-gets-potholes-tweet-asking-be-fixed-every-time-theyre-run-over-165097/

Bots are also being weaponised within information warfare. Automation is a power in the hands of states and militaries as well as activists and artists. A cyber-security specialist (who didn't want to be named) has been looking at the rise of bots for influence. 'The malign use of bots is in an early stage of development,' he told me. 'It is boosted by the considerable global pull of digital media-savvy merchants who are weaponising their knowledge of commercial social media manipulation services in a political context, supported by huge surface and dark web supply chain.' He described how entire bot-maker teams have formed in the shadows. There will be a programmer to keep up with the latest developments in automation. An editor to keep track of the political environment and direct the content the bots produce. A team of content producers form the content itself, supported by graphic designers who knock together memes and other shareable images. A procurement team might buy bots from the dark net, and a liaison figure is the go-between between the bot group and the client.

'It's like an assembly line,' he said. These teams often enjoy significant human resources; they are well managed and well funded. They prepare the campaign, penetrate the target audience, maintain the operation, and then they strategically disengage. In each of the stages, the balance between automation and human intervention can vary, depending on what the bot is being used for. 'The bot market has solid fundamentals' he said. 'There's a ready supply of them and also a consistent demand. The market is only going to get bigger'.

Much like algorithms, the use of bots – automation – is only going to grow, and bots themselves are only going to get smarter. Some will become more personalised, targeting *you* on the basis of what you say. Others are learning how to sound more and more like humans, and it is inevitable that sooner or later the smartest will become indistinguishable from humans unless you meet them face to face. People will use bots to push boundaries, change the way we look at things, create public outcry, fake public outcry, skewer candidates, even try to become candidates.

I suspect that the bots' primary use as pranksters and artists is behind them now. It is commercial and military actors that are probably making the greatest investments in bots now. But whatever their purpose, they are one small window into a far more general effect that automation has on society. Actions, like decisions, are moved a step away from human beings. They too become less accountable and confined by rules and laws.

Take the case of Jeffrey van der Groot. His bot was programmed to tweet random chunks of its own tweets, until one day, at random, it came up with: 'I seriously want to kill people.'[12] He got a knock at the door from the police (the kicker here: the death threat was directed to another bot). Bots have also been alleged to drive up airfares by buying low-priced seats.[13] But as power turns into a stranger form, it also becomes less accountable, and the morality less clear. It is another case of technology causing power to exceed the cages that have been built for it; it is moving faster than the moral codes and public understanding that keep it tame.

And as for my bot – from promising beginnings, it went skipping through Twitter, self-importantly reminding complete innocents of Godwin's Law. They weren't saying 'fucking Hitler'; they weren't even talking about Nazis at all. Even worse, often the

12 https://splinternews.com/who-do-we-blame-when-a-robot-threatens-to-kill-people-1793845324
13 www.nbcbayarea.com/news/local/Bots-Driving-Up-Airfare-SF-Company-Fighting-Them-473678153.html

people being called Nazis really did look like Nazis. 'You know,' said one Twitter user, using a logo that said 'Anti-fascist All Stars', 'with all the actual Nazis running around, I think it's time to shut down the @GodwinsLawBot [its actual name]. It has outlived its usefulness.' Moments later, Twitter suspended the account.

Protocols

Every year, representatives of all the far-flung tribes of the internet journey to a single place. The tech giants arrive, and so do police agencies, diplomats and spies. There are activists whose friends have been murdered by brutal regimes for what they've said online, network engineers, and representatives of an alphabet soup of international groups – IAB, IETF, IRTF, W3C, ISOC, ISO. They stand in the same lines at passport control and check into the same hotels. Invited by the United Nations, they are here for something called the Internet Governance Forum (or, another acronym: the IGF). In 2016, I too joined the annual pilgrimage – to the winter heat of Guadalajara, Mexico.

Thousands upon thousands of people gather for the IGF. To the sound of trilling mariachi, I'd turn in my chair to see a diplomat from the US State Department chatting to an Icelandic pirate, joined by a European MEP and a central African activist. From the deep philosophy of what the internet stands for, to how website naming should work, almost everything to do with the internet is discussed over a four-day dance of meetings and workshops, consensus-building and favour-currying, alliance-building, back-room deals and parlays.

I thought the IGF would be where the decisions were made. I had hoped that at the IGF I would find the internet's beating heart. But it was only there that I realised that what I was looking for didn't exist. Everything is discussed at the IGF, but hardly anything is actually decided.

The only way that change happens is through something that the IGF calls 'multi-stakeholderism'. The single most important principle of the IGF, it is the idea that no single group or interest should dominate the internet. If there is enough input from all different groups, it is hoped, a consensus will eventually emerge. Everyone is considered a stakeholder as long as they buy into this basic principle, and provided you could get to Mexico, you could go to the IGF and say your piece too.

The IGF is a radical departure from the manicured world of traditional international statecraft. It is a brave experiment in international diplomacy that only the internet could have created. The IGF has no central authority because the internet has no central authority. This idea of multi-stakeholderism is so important because it recognises the basic reality of the internet: no single group is in charge. And the reason for that is because of another hidden source of power: protocols.

The two fathers of the internet were Bob Kahn and his colleague Vint Cerf. Both were defence scientists during the Cold War, and it was to them that the US government turned to work out a way of getting the small number of computers that then existed to talk to each other. Kahn and Cerf had a particular vision for how this should happen. They imagined a network that was free to use, which any computer could join, where all data would be treated equally and where there would be no reigning authority or centre.

The vision was executed. But it was not guaranteed by any kind of international treaty or foundational document. It was instead woven into the very basic way that the internet worked, perhaps the most important protocol ever invented: TCP/IP.[14]

When more and more computers joined up to the internet, they were making an agreement, of sorts. They were implicitly signing up to the rules that TCP/IP set. It defined the actions that were possible and not possible to do online.

Over the years, however, TCP/IP has come under greater and greater pressure. Without a central authority, TCP/IP also made the internet difficult to fully secure. Actually finding out who someone really is on the current internet is difficult, time-consuming and easy to spoof. With the 'Internet of Things' just around the corner, fears continue to grow that we're about to go from hacked passwords to hacked pacemakers. A question has begun to be asked: 'Is TCP/IP fit for purpose?'

Bob Kahn also invented another protocol. It was called Digital Object Architecture (DOA), and it was another way to find and retrieve information. Created in the early 1990s, DOA works as a 'super-identifier'. Under DOA, every 'object' has a unique identifier that never changes. Under that protocol, you, me, our devices, even our documents all have an immutable digital fingerprint. Kahn's invention found an important if lower-profile role underpinning library catalogues and online journals.[15] But as the problem of cyber-security continued to intensify, Digital Object Architecture

---

14 Internet engineering experts will at this point notice that Transmission Control Protocol/Internet Protocol is, in fact, a suite of different protocols. There is a wealth of information on how it works, but this is all getting complicated enough already.

15 This is based on an investigation that I originally did with the *New Scientist* on Digital Object Architecture. See: www.newscientist.com/article/mg23531383-300-we-can-stop-hacking-and-trolls-but-it-would-ruin-the-internet/

was dusted off as a protocol that might be able to make the Internet of Things more secure.

DOA has many supporters. But it is a centralised system, and one that others are worried could prohibit transparency and increase state control. A system that could be 'subject to geopolitical concerns rather than technical efficiency'.[16] While it has received UN approval, DOA isn't backed by tech giants, the market or consumers, and has been met by a cold, blank stare by most of the technical community.[17] Its biggest fans are governments.

The internet itself, and the way it is governed, has long been a thorn in the side of a number of states. The way it is built has always been hostile to concentrations of power, and very difficult to control, to find out who people really are and to block content. For its backers, I suspect that Digital Object Architecture might fix a bigger problem than cyber-security. The crucial implication of DOA is that it creates a master global database, where every digital object is uniquely tagged, and where information is added, tracked and queried. Whoever controls the DO registry becomes the centralised gatekeeper to all the information, resources and devices on the internet. DOA turns the internet into a giant library, where everything, including its users, are the books. And in this library, governments are the e-librarians who can ban you from the library, or stop you taking out a book as they wish. It would create an unprecedented concentration of power to control and manage online life.

Under DOA, it's possible to imagine a world where the state gives you a digital identifier at birth. Where any time you get a new device, it is registered to this unshakable number that will

16 www.internetsociety.org/doc/overview-digital-object-architecture-doa
17 www.w3.org/blog/TAG/2016/11/01/the-tags-concerns-about-the-digital-object-architecture-and-the-web/

track your movement through online space the same way you track a book in a library. Information, devices, people without this unique identifier would become invisible. And the gatekeeper would decide who gets an identifier and what that identifier would let you do. Done 'right', it would function as a layer on the internet that would enable the gatekeeper to do granular censoring of individuals and individual devices, and to control the flow of information both inbound and outbound. This may be the opportunity that some governments have been looking for to to firmly bring the internet to heel, to get it under control and re-owned by statutory power.

China may have been first to adopt DOA when it became one of the top-level managers of the system in 2014.[18] In May 2016, the Russian Minister of Communications, Nikolay Nikiforov, said: 'Russia is interested in designing alternative ways of addressing on the internet, such as the DONA (Digital Object Numbering Authority).'[19] On 16 October 2016, South Africa signed an agreement to use DOA.[20] The South Africa signatory was Minister Siyabonga Cwele, who said: 'Our cabinet approved that South Africa participates in the development of the Digital Object Architecture (DOA) or an alternative way of managing information on the internet.'[21] Also in October, the Rwandan Minister for Youth and ICT signed an agreement to use DOA.

It could be the world's most boring coup. Buried in technical documentation, an alphabet soup of obscure international organisa-

18 www.miit.gov.cn/n1146312/n1146909/n1146991/n1648536/c3489529/part/3489530.
    pdf
19 www.telecompaper.com/news/russia-mulls-back-up-in-case-sanctions-cut-off-world-
    wide-web-1143262
20 https://afigf.org/sites/default/files/2016/Draft%252520Agenda%252520for%252520t
    h%252520AfIGF%252520016%252016%252520Oct%252520016%252509am.pdf
21 www.gov.za/speeches/african-internet-governance-forum-16-oct-2016-0000

tions and impenetrable legalese, a serious power-play might be underway to finally bring the internet under state rule. It would see the replacement of an internet with many approaches to identity, many different owners and decision-makers, to, possibly, a system owned by governments and directed by the decisions that they make.

The point is that it's being fought not by politics or international law – this is geopolitics by protocol, and the emergence of blocs defined by the protocols that they use. Protocols like TCP/IP can decentralise power, and others – like DOA – might centralise it. But the power over protocols is hugely important too; for this is the power to set the rules of digital life. With algorithms and automation, fields of human activity are now being carried out by machines. As they've done so, they are slipping out of the rules that have governed them. But the rules themselves, at least the ones that really matter, are another example of new power. Even the rules are now arcane, difficult to understand and obscure – far away from public understanding.

The Viral Factory

A shaky camera nervously pokes out of a window, to see an enormous wooden mannikin storming down the streets of Reykjavik. Dangling on giant strings carried by Chinook helicopters, the 30-foot-high puppet rises from its knees, towering above the buildings. You can hear the beat of the propeller blades above agitated, excited Icelandic voices. Hang on . . . it seems to be wearing a pair of snugly fitting jeans. Then comes the catchphrase, 'Freedom to Move'.

At the same moment, ten different films all containing the giant wooden doll were uploaded to social media by planted users. Each uploaded video claimed to be a different eyewitness snapshot of the same surreal event – a huge puppet lumbering through the streets of Reykjavik directed by a cloud of helicopter puppet-masters. 'Over the following weeks,' a promotional write-up explained later, 'fierce debate raged at the authenticity of the films, driving the viewers to discover the hidden branding concealed within the films and embracing the advertising message at the heart of the campaign.'

I stared at the puppet, shrunk to about a foot now but otherwise the same and still wearing a pair of snug Levis. Hanging on a wall far from the streets of terrorised Reykjavik, the puppet, and all ten videos, had come from a quiet, calm, cream office in an old manufacturing building in the East End of London. It had been produced by a place called the Viral Factory.

In 1976, the evolutionary biologist Richard Dawkins realised that it wasn't just living organisms that existed because they were good at surviving and reproducing. Ideas and fragments of human culture, he argued, are similarly wrapped up in the great blind race for survival. He urged us to think about cultural units – catchphrases, fashion, jingles – as 'memes', things whose existence is owed by their capacity to reproduce and spread like a gene. Matt Smith, the head of the Viral Factory, was an early witness to something that many more of us have now noticed. If cultural units also reproduce and spread, there is a certain kind that are particularly adept at doing so. Some information online grows and grows, getting louder and louder, spreading at incredible speed. In addition to the gene, another metaphor was increasingly used to describe such information. These kinds of cultural unit are infectious, so they are called 'virals', and it was specifically these that the Viral Factory existed to produce.

The Viral Factory is one of countless companies around the world that has arisen to control virals – things that only exist, of course, because of all of us pounding the 'share' and 'retweet' buttons on our phones. And here we see power again, not in the complexity of algorithms or the arcana of protocols, but in another discreetly hidden form. Behind many virals stand organisations like the Viral Factory, who can control them because they understand us better than we understand ourselves.

Matt Smith began his career in digital production, building websites for clients throughout the nineties as the world of commerce moved online. But they were 'like 'brochures', he said. Once made, they were static and boring. He wanted to make websites that were alive, dynamic, moving; not a paper brochure uploaded to the web.

Beginning in 1998, he started a website to put out a new video every day. 'Funny little content,' he said: vignettes, out-takes, bloopers. Some he'd find himself, and increasingly people would just send them in. Far different from the static brochures he was being paid to put together, this kind of content, he saw, sometimes took on a life of its own. It began to travel and be shared far beyond his own website. Before the days of social media, people were passing the videos around on email chains.

Soon his website – punchbaby.com – was getting 100,000 views every day. 'It dawned on me that millions of people saw the content,' said Matt. 'There were some very hardcore fans. Some wrote to me every day. One person had been badly injured in a car crash, and wrote to me to say, "Those videos got me through it."' His audience was mainly men, and a huge part was from the US military. Lots of bored people, sitting in front of powerful machines with really good internet connections.

For Matt, the commercial opportunity of mastering virals was obvious. While advertising paid for people's attention, a viral could get it for free. People would willingly pass it on to their friends, who were much more likely to pay attention to it than a message from a distant corporate. Overall, he thought, it made advertising more like a branch of the entertainment industry, and exactly at a time when people were getting better and better at ignoring advertising, or blocking it completely. 'I went to ad agencies, and they chucked me out. Agencies thought that virals couldn't be manufactured; they couldn't be made to order. Everyone was getting big media kickbacks, and these videos didn't need media spend.'

The existence of infectious ideas that spread across society certainly predates both punchbaby.com and the internet. Virals have spread through graffiti, through word-of-mouth, on paper. Chain letters date back to the late eighteenth century, and some printed pamphlets have been explosively popular. Thomas Paine anonymously published a pamphlet in 1775 called 'Common Sense' that set out the case for US independence. It sold over 100,000 copies a month, winning, by proportion, the largest circulation of any book in American history. Similarly, in London in 1942, queues of people formed overnight outside the government bookshop to receive a copy of the Beveridge Report, which laid the foundation of the modern welfare state in Britain.

Yet the force that Matt had been trying to master had found, in the internet, a particularly infectious new medium. Ideas can be transmitted more quickly, cheaply and frictionlessly than ever before. Now, with the rise of social media, virals routinely bubble in the online world, reaching out from the computer to change offline life.

Virals can bring with them both redemption and destruction. 'Neknominate' (neck-and-nominate) was a drinking game where players filmed themselves downing a drink in one go, and then nominated another person to do the same within twenty-four hours. It went viral, and as it spread it also escalated. People drank crazier concoctions in more extreme circumstances. Starting with pints of beer, players ended up downing pints of gin, vodka, vodka mixed with wine, and wine mixed with whiskey, vodka and beer. The videos became more and more outrageous: people were drinking beer out of toilets, on top of mountains, on a horse in a supermarket.[22] It was a textbook viral, one wrapped up in peer pressure, desire to conform, but also – in increasingly insane stunts – to stand out from the crowd. Five deaths in the UK and Ireland were eventually linked to the game.[23]

Virals can also save lives. Stacey Hewitt became the first recipient of an organ from a total stranger thanks to social media, after the donor – Louise Drewery – spotted her Facebook appeal. It can transform lives in less obvious ways too. Bill Palmer's wife had gone into a nursing home after a fall. Ninety-five years old, he phoned a local radio station, just to say how lonely he felt: 'Every day is hell. I feel so alone.' As the DJ invited him to come in for a cup of tea, social media lit up.

22 www.youtube.com/watch?v=Ak478QNWHQM
23 www.nbc15.com/home/headlines/Dangerous-new-drinking-game-uses-the-power-of-social-media-246463811.html

After tens of thousands of views, Bill received offers from Sunday lunch to a private concert from a ukulele orchestra. Virals can lift important needs that were previously invisible into the spotlight.

Virals are also forcing society to change the way it does things. In 2015, a picture of the limp body of a small child being carried from a Greek beach appeared on newspaper front pages across the world. The boy, Alan Kurdi, had drowned with his brother Galip and mother Rehan when their boat capsized in the open sea on the way to Greece and, they hoped, a new life in Europe. It was a photo that cut with an edge sharper than any statistic: a single icon of human loss that came to represent the worst refugee crisis since the Second World War. But newspapers almost didn't print it. When they did, a spokesman for Getty explained in an interview to *Time* magazine, they broke a 'social taboo that has been in place in the press for decades: a picture of a dead child is one of the golden rules of what you never publish'.[24] Newspapers printed it and channels broadcast it because the picture was already out there. Before any professional journalist or editor had made the call, it was already sweeping through social media. 'We got to this point', continued the spokesman from Getty, 'because individuals have had the balls to publish the pictures themselves on social media. I think that gave the mainstream media the courage and the conviction to publish this picture.' It had already gone viral, and that in itself had convinced media organisations to break one of their own previously sacrosanct rules.

24 http://time.com/4022765/aylan-kurdi-photo/

Taming Virals

Virality can feel like a wild force: an uncontrollable storm of information that suddenly comes from nowhere to flash around the internet. But perhaps this is a force that can be tamed, harnessed and domesticated.

For the Viral Factory, and companies like it, the receipe for a successful viral – something so infectious that it rises above the noise of online life – needs three key ingredients. First, the content itself must immediately have a powerful emotional effect. It can be funny, shocking, sad, surprising, cute – any content that elicits a strong response, basically. There is something primal here in how virals need to tap into hugely powerful emotions, driving the urge to share them. For the Peng! Collective, an organisation that uses virals to spread political messages, the response is key. Any ideas in their content have to be packaged in a particular way for them to go viral. 'Come on, of course tactical media work has some rules,' Peng!'s memberJean Peters said to me. 'The content needs a story, it needs to be exciting. If you tell your idea to three people and two say "wow" it might well become a viral.' You start with a purely viral idea, he told me, and strip back the message as much as possible. Anything too overt or complicated weighs the viral down, limiting its spread.

Viral content, however, is usually not enough. One of the ways that agencies like the Viral Factory have some control is through 'seeding'. Sometimes seen as the dark art of virality, seeding is how agencies inject the information into the ecosystem in a deliberate, clinical way. 'Seeding is graft. It's systematic and methodical,' said Matt. Viral agencies have a constituency of social media influencers. They often use specialists, freelancers, to identify the right seeds, whose followers (I suppose the 'soil') are likely to share the content and be influenced by it. 'You need to get ten or fifteen influencers, targeted at a particular industry,' said Matt.

'In one example, the client pulled the seeding budget,' Matt explained, shaking his head. 'They loved the content so much, they thought it would succeed on its own. It was perfect for the target audience. We put it out, and it died.' Four months later, it had bubbled up again, and been seen 20 million times. But, uncontrolled, the viral hadn't happened in the first few weeks of the product launch when it was needed.

The last ingredient is luck. Virality can be tamed, but never truly mastered. Like a good poker player, the Viral Factory can make intelligent bets and shape the odds in their direction, but they can't guarantee winning. There is always some chaos in the order.

Virals only exist because of us. Whether they are used by large companies to launch products, or by activists to destroy the reputations of those large companies, virals all share a common trait: their ability to draw us in. And whilst they seem organic, chaotic, totally grassroots, but behind some of them are people who are learning to control, formalise and proceduralise their production. Here, I was learning, was another kind of hidden power different again to algorithms or protocols or bots. In those phenomena, the power lay in how inhuman they were: complex beyond our comprehension, tireless beyond our endurance, arcane and machine-like. But the power of places like The Viral Factory was in their ability to create things that reflected – some might say *used* – our essential humanity and psychology to get us to share. Virals exist because of us.

Hooked

In the south-west corner of Seoul, on a road lined with small trees and high-rise blocks, some five minutes from the Han River is a small brick building called the Haja Centre. It is conspicuously low-tech compared to the mirrored skyscrapers and moving neon advertisements that surround it. But inside the Haja Centre is a colourful, friendly place, full of screens, workshops and noise: people doing woodwork and learning how to repair bikes. There I meet Choong-Han Lee, who everyone calls Akii. He is dedicated to helping a certain kind of patient that I'd never heard about before. They are called hikikomori, or 'the departed'.

Hikikomori are recluses who have retreated from offline life. Often seeking total isolation, some never leave their homes, or even hardly their rooms, for months or years on end. In Japan, where the phenomenon was first identified, the government estimates the average age of those affected is thirty-one, but many are adolescents or young adults who entirely rely on their parents for housing and food.

Akii has another term for hikikomori, one, he thinks, that better explains what is actually happening. He calls them 'gravity-free youth'. Young people across South Korea are in a dangerous situation, he told me; they have no 'gravity', no pull that gives their lives meaning. In part, Akii thinks this is due to a lack of national purpose. The previous generation of South Koreans built their country. They pulled it from the smoke and ashes of the 1950s civil war and turned it into one of the economic power-houses of the world. South Korea was a small dot of capitalism facing the huge expanses of communist Asia, of China and the

USSR. But as the Cold War came to an end, the generation now arriving into adulthood didn't have that guiding, driving, national purpose any more. In addition, the glittering example of capitalist society that South Korea became is also an individualistic one, and South Korean youth, Akii told me, feel little of the pull of community. They do feel the stigma of failure, however – of a society telling them that failure is their fault, that they haven't worked hard enough. Mixed in with all these overarching reasons, most hikikomori personally suffer some kind of traumatic moment when they withdraw: bullying, sexual abuse, a failure to graduate from school, a relationship breakdown, the loss of a job, a public humiliation.

The Haja Centre has a 'Come out and Play' Project, to reach out to hikikomori, and tries to start the long journey of bringing them back into society. They teach music as a way of bringing hikikomori back into groups, forming relationships with a mentor and peers, and building self-esteem. Eventually, Akii aims to bring them from social isolation to giving a gig in front of an audience.

Akii left the room, and there was a long pause. He finally came back, and with him was one of his students – a hikikomori currently being treated on the programme. We nervously sat around a table – myself, my translator Jihye Kim, Akii and his student.

The student met my gaze and took a breath. Then she started to tell me about his life. He was eighteen now, and sixteen when he'd withdrawn. 'I got into elementary school. I should have dropped out, but I stayed in. Then I dropped out in high school. After I dropped out, I had no real relationship or link to society or any other group. I just thought, "I am who I am." I wasn't in contact with any other person. One hundred per cent hikikomori,' he began.

She became nocturnal, and began to play online games more and more. 'I'd play whenever I wanted a relationship with others. It's connect and disconnect, that's why it's useful.' The game he played was called *MapleStory 2*, a scrolling cartoonish fantasy role-playing game. '*MapleStory* was the one thing I could enjoy doing during this time.' He played the game fifteen hours a day, every day, for two years. He broke off from the translation, looked at me with a big grin, put two thumbs down, and said directly in English: 'BAD GAME.'

'Did you become a famous gamer?' I asked.

He laughed. 'Do you know how much you need to play to become a famous gamer in South Korea? I wasn't even average.'

I had expected the hikkikomori to be downtrodden, downcast. I was afraid that talking to me would be a forced, painful experience for him. But the person I met was the opposite. He wore a black, tight-fitting leather coat over a white T-shirt and brown trousers. He had neat round spectacles, and a fashionable bowl cut, the colour of his hair browned and lightened a little. He was effervescent, kinetic, with the easy extroversion of the class clown; in fact he was downright animated, leaping about in his chair, responding in different voices, and accentuating points with a chopping motion of his hand.

'You were, uh, really a hikikomori?' I asked.

Again, he broke from the translation and responded directly to me, but this time with no grin. 'One hundred per cent. One hundred per cent hikikomori.'

'Respect the choice of the hikikomori,' he continued. 'We are affected by the problems of society very much. Everyone is; maybe we are just more sensitive to the pressures that most of society feels. The people who are behind are losers. The weak are blamed.

"They don't try hard" or "It's all their fault they are behind." Others try to accept this problematic social side. But hikikomori do not accept it. This is what we are turning away from.'

In Japan and South Korea, the phenomenon of hikikomori is a public health crisis. Shut away in bedrooms, it's very hard to know how many of them there are, but Akii thought between 30,000 and 300,000 in South Korea, between 70,000 and 700,000 in Japan, in varying degrees of departedness. Imagine, a city full of people who don't leave their house. A city of emptiness and silence, of darkened shopping malls, deserted roads. The only light comes from a million bedrooms, the only movement from the humming optic fibres sneaking under the quiet streets. An invisible, silent public health crisis.

'I was isolated anyway,' Akii's student finished, 'but the game made it so much worse. The isolation drove me into the game, but playing the game made me feel even more isolated, and so I became even more dependent on the game.' The rise of hikkikomori is a bigger one than simply technology itself, but as hikikomori feel a push from society, turning them away, many also feel a pull towards technology. Digital life feels like part of the problem because it provides a kind of gravity of its own, pulling people out of other orbits. 'The internet is like a black hole,' Akii told me later. 'There is some kind of community. Some kind of fun and values. But it's a false feeling. Your needs seem fulfilled, but they are not.'

On my way back from South Korea, I was reading a book by Nir Eyal called *Hooked*. 'Face it: we're hooked,' the book begins. 'The technologies we use have turned into compulsions, if not full-fledged addictions.' We are brought back to our devices again and again by the habits we form, Eyal explains, 'automatic behaviours triggered by situational cues; things we do with little or no conscious thought'. Companies produced 'little more than bits of code displayed on a screen [that] seemingly control users' minds'.

On the plane, I had hoped to read a whistleblowing account of how technology was being designed that caused people to be drawn so strongly and assuredly to them. But as I flicked through the pages, I realised I'd picked up something very different. The book was a step-by-step, how-to guide on building habit-forming products. 'Forming habits is imperative for the survival of many products,' Eyal warns would-be technologists. 'Others are already cashing in. By mastering habit-forming product design, the companies profiled in this book make their goods indispensable.'

At the heart of *Hooked* is Eyal's Hook Model. First, technologists need to find a 'trigger' to action. This could be an email alert, a notification, something to get the target to use your technology. Then comes the 'action' itself, whatever behaviour the target uses the product to do. However, 'what distinguishes the Hook Model from a plain vanilla feedback loop is the Hook's ability to create a craving.' Step three of the Hook Model recognises that predictable outcomes don't create desire. The key to forming habits is to create a variable reward: where using the product sometimes gives you an amazing experience and other times not, but either way does so in a manner you can't anticipate until you use it. Checking email is one example: most are boring, but one tells you you've won a cruise in the Bahamas. The last phase of the Hook Model is investment, when the user puts something into the product, such as time, data, effort, social capital or money. This increases the user's ties to the product, and makes them more likely to come back for more.

Nir Eyal's focus is on human psychology to make the Hook Model as hooky as possible. Finely dissecting what motivates humans to act is the first step in motivating humans to act. The book is full of discussion around dopamine surges, heuristics, cognitive biases, and the neuroscience behind cravings. '*Hooked* seeks to unleash the tremendous new powers innovators and entrepreneurs have to influence the everyday lives of billions of people. I believe the trinity of access, data and speed presents unprecedented opportunities to create positive habits,' Eyal argues. In one section he sketches out the 'Habit Zone', another is called 'Building the Mind Monopoly'. In another, he discusses how habit-forming technologies cause discomfort when they are not used. They create a constant 'itch', a feeling that stays there until it is scratched. 'Once we come to depend on a tool, nothing else will do . . . For those able to shape them in an effective way, habits can be very good for the bottom line,' he cheerfully concludes in one chapter.

The most frightening thing is that Nir Eyal is only stating what this burgeoning field is already doing. The principles he is pointing to are widely applied across the technologies that we use every day.

Scattered throughout tech giants and start-ups are graduates of the Persuasive Technology Lab at Stanford. It was founded in 1998 by behavioural psychologist B. J. Fogg, to systematically apply psychological insights to technology, with the aim of getting people to do things they otherwise wouldn't do. There was, Fogg argued, a new field that stood at the intersection between computer science and psychology, where persuasion and digital tech met. He called it 'captology' – the study of computers as persuasive technology–. And just like with Eyal, the academic framework that sits behind Fogg's own model is a grab-bag of applied psychology.[25] He draws on social cognitive theory, the heuristic-systematic model, the elaboration likelihood model, cognitive dissonance, Maslow's hierarchy of needs, attribution theory, behaviourism, and so on and so on.

In 2018, for the first time, gaming addiction was listed as a mental health condition by the World Health Organisation.[26] There is much about it as a psychological phenomenon that we do not understand and clinical evidence for it is still emerging.[27] Estimates of its prevalence range from around 1 per cent of ta population to over 10 per cent, with a 2014 meta-analysis across thirty-one nations giving a prevalence rate of 6 per cent within older adolescent populations.[28] Where it exists, it has been 'inversely associated with the quality of life, as reflected by both subjective (life satisfaction) and objective (quality of environmental conditions) indicators'.[29] Reasons for the formation of addiction are never straightforward and a great range of factors has been correlated with internet addiction and heavy use, including personality types, social networks, mental health and other forms of addiction.[30] But one of the reasons is simply that digital technology is designed to be addictive.

25 www.mebook.se/images/page_file/38/Fogg%20Behavior%20Model.pdf
26 www.bbc.co.uk/news/technology-42541404
27 Internet gaming disorder is listed in Section III, Conditions for Further Study, DSM-5, 2013.
28 Moreno, Jelenchick, Christakis, Problematic Internet use maogn older adolescents: a conceptual framework, Computers in Human Behaviour 29 (2013), 1879–1887.
29 C. Cheng, 'Internet Addiction: Prevalence and Quality of (Real) Life', *Cyberpsychology, Behavior and Social Networking*, December 2014
30 Kuss, Rooij, Shorter, Griffiths, Mheen, 'Internet Addiction in Adolescents: Prevalence and risk factors, Computers in Human Behaviour 29 (2013) 1987-1996'; H. Kang, 'Self-traits and Motivations as Antecedents of Digital Media Flow and Addiction', *Computers in Human Behavior*, November 2013

There may be nothing wrong in principle with being persuaded by machines. Fogg himself has written fairly extensively on the ethics of persuasive technology, and the Persuasive Technology Lab stresses the potential of technology to bring about positive change in all of us. To be fair to Nir Eyal, he also does include a chapter on ethics. Weight Watchers, one of Eyal's examples, creates habits and in doing so makes us healthier. He offers a thought experiment for every technologist where they should only create habits that they would want themselves and that materially improve lives.

The only other addiction identified that is behavioural, rather than substance-related, is compulsive gambling. And for that reason, UK gambling companies must carry socially responsible messages ('Don't let the game play you', 'Gamble for fun, not to win', 'Winners know when to stop').[31] Gamblers who recognise they have a problem can self-ban themselves from bookmakers. The industry funds research into problematic gambling, and in a review in 2017, the government announced plans to limit stakes, implement player protections, and consult on research, education and treatment.[32] There is work done on how to track compulsive behaviour like chasing losses, where the gambler's stakes constantly increase, and there is a mix of both voluntary and statutory measures that are being implemented. The extent to which these regulations are actually applied across gambling remains controversial, and by no means do I think that the gambling industry is perfect, nor the protections that are given enough, but at least it *is* regulated.

---

31 http://igrg.org.uk/wp/wp-content/uploads/2015/12/Gambling-Industry-Code-for-Socially-Responsible-Advertising-Final-2nd-Edition-August-2015.pdf
32 www.gov.uk/government/uploads/system/uploads/attachment_data/file/655969/Consultation_on_proposals_for_changes_to_Gaming_Machines_and_Social_Responsibility_Measures.pdf

Advertising has long concentrated on human psychology to try to change what we buy, and companies think about how their consumers feel all the time. Yet I still felt angry, even outraged, at the thought that the promotion of habits and compulsions were being woven into technology that surrounds us every day. Weight Watchers creates habits that people have explicitly decided they want. But Eyal was teaching technologists to promote habits that, for bald commercial reasons, they wanted us to have, not that we want to have. The step-by-step ethics guide that Fogg suggests, much like Eyal's thought experiment, make it a personal moral determination for each technologist or company to decide how far they will go in applying persuasive technology. And technologists undertaking their own private thought experiment for – asking themselves questions like whether they'd want to use their own product – did not strike me as a particularly effective safeguard. Outside of any kind of enforced moral code or regulatory framework, the formation of habits is a matter for technologists' private conscience rather than public control.

There was something so brazen and unapologetic about using human psychology to promote habits and even addictive behaviour. 'Let's admit it: we are all in the persuasion business,' Eyal argued. But this wasn't about persuasion at all. It wasn't trying to convince us on the level of argument and evidence. 'To initiate action,' he reminds the reader, 'doing must be easier than thinking. Remember, a habit is a behaviour done with little or no conscious thought.' This was about trying to influence us, like virals, in a more primal way: evoking deeply buried, primordial human traits in very subtle ways to get us to do someone else's bidding. This wasn't about persuasion, it was about compulsion.

Technology, so designed, I thought, isn't really about giving people more choices; it is actually about removing choice. This is all about using what is known about human vulnerabilities in order to engineer compulsion. And usually for profit. Whether influenced by Eyal, Fogg or the many graduates of the Persuasive Technologies Lab, technology is being built that activates our deeply buried, primitive and largely automatic psychology to make us behave in very dependable ways. Like smoking in the early twentieth century, I don't think we know how harmful, or disempowering, this can be.

Hidden Power

Through technology, power now operates in ways that are in one way or another inhuman , and sodifficult to see and to comprehend. Algorithms are sometimes too complex for even its creators to understand. Protocols enforce rules too arcane for us to pay attention to. Bots are just one example of automation doing things that previously only humans did. Each example is different, but each shows how the basic ways that our lives are shaped can be covered by things that are covered by a kind of technical camouflage that we can't, and don't, look under.

At the same moment, virals – and more broadly lots of different forms of 'persuasive' digital technology – are being designed in ways that more and more sophisticatedly reflect what humans are really like. There is something profoundly unsettling in how the deepest, most primitive heuristics and proclivities that we have are being activated to promote certain behaviours. The design of tech is becoming more efficient at reaching within us to manipulate our basest, most simple impulses. Below the level of argument, evidence and persuasion, this is a power over baser things: habits, responses, reflexes.

In each case, power is obscured for a different reason. But they are all examples of how our lives can be influenced in ways that are now difficult for us to even notice, let alone challenge. Power that isn't transparent is a form of power that isn't accountable. Regulation is difficult to apply. The law is often absent. Professional standards are often silent and public understanding is dropping too far behind. Hidden power isn't controlled by any of these external means. While power itself isn't evil, hidden forms of power have the greatest capacity to be used in abusive ways.

INTERLUDE

The Power of Life and Death

It was just before Christmas 2016, and the evening was damp and cold. I weaved through the packed streets of London's West End, the streetlights reflecting off the shining pavements, silently cursing myself for being outside. I had agreed to meet Chris in a pub wedged between shops and theatres, and inside it was hot and cramped. Perched on a stool in a corner, I tried to ignore the elbow digging into my back and the musty smell of wet clothes. Too hot, too loud. I hadn't wanted to stay for long, but soon after Chris arrived, I realised I couldn't leave. Leaning towards me, he held out his phone. It was playing a video.

On the screen: complete darkness, light breathing in the background. A torch is clicked on, a thin beam shining directly onto a sheet of white paper, crumpled, as if it's just been pulled out of a pocket. Printed across the paper in large, black font, was a message:

gang member for besa mafia on dark web
dedication to pirate london

The bright white centre of the torch drifts across the paper, and is clicked off. There is a much longer pause now: ten seconds, twenty, thirty. Then in the complete darkness, there is a metallic, scraping sound.

Suddenly the screen is full of light. Fire streaks across the ground, weaving away from the camera, and towards a dim shape in the background – a car. In a moment it is covered in flames, rolling out from the undercarriage and licking up around and over the roof.

The same scrap of paper is held back up to the camera, lit now by the car burning ferociously in the background. The 'dedication' is now clear, the sound of crackling from the torching car getting louder and louder until the video abruptly ends a few seconds later.

'What is this, Chris?' I whispered, comically glancing over my shoulder to see if anyone else had seen it.

'That was meant for me. I'm pirate london.'

We are all aware that we can use technology to profoundly affect the lives of others around us. That there is a power at our fingertips that didn't exist before. But how deeply could it affect our lives? And how easy is it to access? To use?

Over the next year, I followed Chris's story. Of all the examples of power I had come across in the course of researching this book this was, I confess, the one I have felt most uncomfortable writing about. At points I resolved not to. But over time it began to reveal – I thought – an answer to this question. And as it did so, it began to show what was happening to power, in similar ways, everywhere.

Until I met Chris, power had felt important but abstract. It was something that, to me, existed in grand theory, but not burning cars. But from the comfort of their own rooms, Chris and his nemesis had found a power at their fingertips that they wouldn't have dreamed of before. They used it in ways that, as we'll see, were both incredibly brave and horribly cruel, but also in ways that were hidden and strange to the rest of us. Power could be so near, so accessible, but also shrouded in shadows. Both liberation and oppression came in forms so unfamiliar, it was difficult to tell them apart, and they were far away from the traditional centres of power that used to control them.

Chris

Dark net researcher, ethical hacker, cybercrime investigator . . . I'm not sure there is yet a neat label for what Chris is. Chris is someone whose identity, politics – his *raison d'être* – is wrapped up in the technology that he uses. In his early thirties, by day Chris works as a sysadmin – an IT specialist – at a large company in central London. But the reason we met is because of what Chris does when he gets home from work. In his flat, with six screens in front of him, Chris plunges into the darkest and most dangerous places that exist on the internet in order to shine a light on them.

The area that Chris explores is known as the 'dark net'. These are websites, markets, file storage services, email exchanges that, contrary to the internet most of us use every day, are anonymous.

On the dark net, nobody knows who you are, and nobody knows where you go, and it has become a place where those who most benefit from anonymity have gathered. A place where drugs are openly bought and sold, a world of political whistleblowers and child abusers.

Chris had been drawn to the dark net because it was also a place of swirling rumours and hysteria. Behind this wall of anonymity, there were rumours that you could buy anything – *anything* – that you wanted. For $100,000, a dark net site offered day trips to an island 'somewhere near New Guinea' for the sport of hunting humans (trophies allowed, weapons not included). Somewhere on the dark net there was rumoured to be a 'Red Room', a website that hosted the live stream of the torture and murder of captured ISIS fighters for paying users. Then there were sites where major sports matches were purportedly fixed and thrown. But as Chris investigated each of these, he found they were rumours only. 'I'm trying to comprehensively document the major streams of bullshit,' Chris had told me, introducing himself.

I was fascinated by what Chris was doing. It felt like a new form of investigative journalism or police work, but one that demanded a level of technological savvy and cyber-cultural immersion that very few journalists or police officers possess. And on that night we first met, I learned that Chris was deep into the most serious of any of his forays into this strange, scary world. For over a year, Chris had been investigating one of the most pervasive of all the rumours about what the dark net could now provide: murder on demand. On the dark net were markets that claimed to connect would-be killers with dark net users who wanted someone dead, and were willing to pay for it.

Chris had thought that these assassination markets were just another myth, and he'd written a few blogs that publicly debunked them as fantasy. And now, a year later, here was the video.

For the first time in all of Chris's investigations, it was ambiguous whether he'd found a real operation. 'That doesn't happen to people,' said Chris, contemplating the video he'd just shown me. 'Scammers don't do that.' Murder, perhaps, really was now something that you could buy at the click of a button. And Chris thought he might have annoyed the people who provided it.

Besa Mafia

The website that Chris had targeted, investigated and publicly debunked was called Besa Mafia. 'Hire a killer or a hacker,' the website's slogan reads. 'We are the Albanian Mafia. We have members in each and every country and we have expanded online as many other organisations.'

'If you want to kill someone,' the website promises, 'we are the right guys. We have professional hitmen available through the entire USA, Canada and Europe. And you can hire a contract killer easily.' The main background colour of the website is, predictably, black, with stark white text. It's full of images: a man in a hoodie aiming a handgun right at you, a cityscape bathed in deep red and, at the bottom of the screen, a series of bodies lying prostrate on the pavement, covered in blood.

Like any other market, the website claims simply to be connecting up demand and supply. You can register either as a hitman or as a customer. Killings start from $5,000 for 'basic killers', 'suitable for normal persons', says the website. The hitman will use a stolen vehicle and shoot the target at close range, carried out 'usually by drug dealers and gang members who have financial issues'. But for $30,000 you can hire an 'ex-military trained hitmen with a sniper rifle on buildings' for harder targets: CEOs; business people; government officials and others who might have body-guards or be armed themselves. Non-lethal beatings start at $500, going up to $2,000 'if you want broken bones or cut body parts, such as nose, ears, etc'. Optional add-ons include 'make it look like an accident' (+$4,000).

The site's USP is similar to those of the illegal drugs markets that have genuinely flourished on the dark web. Technology now means that any transaction, whether drugs or contract killings, can be done distantly and anonymously. On the dark web, nobody would know that you are browsing the site. Use throwaway email addresses, the site warns, and never meet the killer in person. You pay in bitcoin, so there is no financial link that ties you to the hit. The site even offers anonymity advice in a section called 'Stay Safe'. 'Never tell anyone about the hit job that you ordered,' the site warns, 'and do not brag.' Risk-free, frictionless, anonymous murder for money – that is the proposition.

Like Ebay, the site purports to be an impartial, trusted middleman. Clients interested in these services are directed towards an online order form. You enter the target name (or nickname), their address, city, country, their job details and a picture. The client pays the money to the website, who holds it in trust while an assassin is assigned and tasked. There is a dispute resolution procedure for clients unhappy with their hit, and oppor-tunities to hire a different hitman or withdraw money if the issues can't be resolved. Only when the assassin uploads sufficient proof of the killing is the money released to them, with the website taking a 20 per cent cut.

The website has a login system, FAQs, bitcoin advice. There are lists of useful resources for buying bitcoin, using anonymous email, and finding other criminal services. But there are also touches that seemed like crude imitations of a credible and legal service, rather then the actual provision of an illegal one. 'Online copyright 201-2-2016 Besa Mafia. All rights reserved' ran at the bottom of the website, and likewise a 'Terms of Use and Disclaimer'. An online assassination site ready to assert its intellectual property rights through dry legal boilerplate seemed a little bizarre, to say the least.

The Hack

The site was launched in 2015, and Chris had learned about it a year later. When he'd browsed the website, he'd become convinced the whole thing was a scam.

'I know exactly how a dark net market works,' Chris had told me. The challenge faced by any dark net market is that neither buyer, nor seller, nor the people running the market itself are known to any of the other parties. In order to function, these kinds of markets need to establish trust without identity, and the normal way that this happens is through a reputation system. The seller's track record is made public, and each buyer provides feedback on what they've bought; whether it matched the product description, whether it arrived in a timely way, and so on. In a drug market, sellers typically start small, and work hard to build trust with their clients over time.

Reputation systems work for drug markets, but, in Chris's eyes, they couldn't work for assassination markets. Killings start, price-wise, a lot higher than drugs, and there are far fewer purchases. There simply wouldn't be enough examples of killings, he thought, for any seller to convince a possible buyer so that they'd go ahead with it.

Chris wrote about the site on his blog, publicly ridiculing it as a self-evident scam. But some months later, he'd received the video as a threat. But rather than scare Chris off, it both annoyed and intrigued him. So in the early months of 2017, he determined to launch a full-blown investigation of the site.

He tweaked and probed, trying to find a way of learning more about who else was using the site, and what was happening. And before long, a spectacular breakthrough led him deep into the workings of the site, much deeper than he suspected he could get. At the beginning of the investigation, he'd sent some messages to the site itself, and realised that each of the messages he received in answer had a specific number – a unique ID. Despite all the website's promises of security, it had a terrible flaw that allowed Chris to simply change the message ID, and read other messages – ones, of course never intended for him to see. With some custom tools – some scrapers and scripts – he downloaded the entire message database, and built a window into what was really happening there: who was registered, what they were saying to the site, even who was paying money.

'I'd be scrolling through the messages,' said Chris, 'troll, troll, troll, troll.' One person registered on the site in order to take out a hit on the celebrity chef Ainsley Harriott. A would-be assassin struggled to source A4 paper in order to write out a warning. One user tried to take a contract out on themselves: 'not a joke,' they assured the administrator, 'I am looking for a hitwoman to kill me.' 'Hitwomen are usually not pretty sexy women,' the administrator sharply replied, 'they are normal women that are crazy and mean, and will kill you with no remorce [sic].' Another spent a week arguing with the administrator, a conversation that descended into a CAPS LOCK TORRENT OF ABUSE FROM BOTH SIDES.

'A word that I hate to use, because it's used all the time, is disturbing,' Chris told me. But some of the messages Chris had taken from the site really were. Amongst the trolls were conversations that seemed more serious. Chris had tried to debunk a scam, but he had found instead people who were paying significant sums of money to have people killed . . .

'Hey there I am in south NJ and need a handgun with ammo because I lack the ability to obtain one myself legally,' read one message. 'How would getting this work and how much would it cost?' Then, almost in passing, 'Alternatively to a gun order, I could place a hit order. However, the target would be fourteen. Is that an acceptable age or too young? I can budget up to $20k for the order.' Following a discussion with the administrator, the user had ended up actually paying 40 bitcoin (£12,000 at the time) for the murder of their fourteen-year-old target. This wasn't trolling.

An ordinary-sounding American couple was targeted. 'They have many enemies. Many they do not know,' the client ominously pointed out. 'It's very important that they are taken care of together. This should not be hard as they live, travel, and spend most of their days and nights together.' Some requests were more opaque. 'Hello, There is one fucking guy I have only his name and the city he lives in, how can I hire a killer to kill him?' asked one user. The complex request became too expensive, so the client and administrator discussed ways of defraying the cost. 'If you allow them to take of the internal organs of the boyfriend to sell on the black market,' the administrator proposed, 'we can maybe reduce the cost of the operation.' 'The guy is healthy and still young also If they want more organs in I can arranging for them that,' the client replies, again eventually paying 7 bitcoin (around £2,000) for the hit and kidnap.[1]

All the conversations, however, directly confirmed the suspicions that Chris had had from the very start: it was a scam. The assassinations never actually happened. As he read the messages flowing between these clients and the administrator of the website, he realised that in each case an unforeseen problem blocked the hit. The hitmen had been arrested, or they'd been scared off, or a different team needed to be assigned.

As each hit was delayed, they also became more expensive. 'The second team is not interested to do the job for $5000,' the administrator told one client. 'If you don't add the 7 bitcoin today, the second team will abort and we will have to assign a 3rd team at a lower level, same as the first team.' The client paid more bitcoin (eventually about £6,000) and again the hit looked like it was about to be carried out: 'Our team is there in the parking lot. From time to time the [sic] drive around the area; they are looking for him.' Again the hit was missed. And again. 'I took chance and went with u,' the exasperated client wrote, 'truth be told – this wasted a lot of my time and effort. with no result.' It was a strange pang of

---

1 I have left the errors contained in quotes throughout this chapter, to give you an unvarnished sense of the kinds of chatter that passed through the site.

moral outrage from a person trying to commission a murder. 'i wont be one of your supporters on any forum after this.'

Eventually, the website would turn on these would-be murderers. 'Hi,' a typical message would read. 'I am sorry to disappoint you. Unfortunately, this site has been hacked'. We got all customer and target information and we will send it to law enforcement unless you send 10 bitcoin to this address.' Only if they received the money, they warned, would they delete the information. Given it was on the dark net, most people decided to take their chances, and didn't reply.

Around a dozen people also offered their services to the site as thugs or hitmen. One seemed to be trying to flee law enforcement in the States, and was looking for a new identity. An American posted his own price list to deliver a dog bite ($800), cut or beat ($750), arson (car, one-storey house, small office $1,200), break bones ($1,500), and killing (hand kill, sharp object kill: $7,500; small-calibre short-range kill: $6,000). It was impossible to tell lies from truths, whether any of these were genuine, or whether all of them were. The offers sounded fantastical, like the hitman claiming specialist kills involving blowpipe poisoning ($35,900), or death by arrow shot ($45,000). But the existence of the whole site was fantastical.

For the first eight months of 2016, Chris quietly waited, watching the site in operation and recording what he saw. Over that time, around 800 messages were exchanged between its users and a shadowy administrator. There were twelve significant targets for whom money had been paid, and about as many people again who had wanted, possibly, to sign up to carry out killings and other forms of violence. Overall about £65,000 of cryptocurrency had been paid to the site, and no money had been returned. But however serious the requests, they hadn't, as far as Chris could tell, resulted in anyone coming to any harm.

Then, in early 2017, Chris spotted something. 'This was where it all changed,' he said, pulling up a new message.

It began, by the site's standards, fairly normally:

'I am looking to hire you for a hit, but what is the recommended way to convert cash to bitcoin anonymously. If I pull $5,000 out for a hit, after the hit I would assume that the police would see that draw and wonder where it went, so even if the bitcoins are not traceable, that missing money would raise suspicion?'

'Hit and run is what I was thinking and that would work fine,' the administrator had responded. 'So can we say 15 bitcoin for hit with a car and ensure fatality?' Over several months, the user told the site where the potential hit was and where she was going. 'I heard that she will be there from 12–1 working on her computer, because she is watching some event,' one read. 'It looks like Monday might work. It sounds like the dad is taking the kid somewhere.' Another read: 'For reasons that are too personal and would give away my identity, I need this bitch dead, so please help me . . . I do want it done.'

Fifteen bitcoin (£11,000) was paid, but like all the other cases on the site, no hitmen were sent and no murder was forthcoming. 'I have gone out of my way to try and get you good information,' the user had written. 'I feel that I am at risk of being suspected if I ask too many more questions. You have had three good attempts and none of them have worked.'

Chris had read the messages, and marked them down as another successful scam. But then he spotted a news article mentioning an assassination market.[2] In November 2016, around the time that I had first met Chris, a man in America had summoned police to his house to report a suicide. A woman, his wife, was lying dead on the bedroom floor, a gun lying next to her outstretched hand. It had all the hallmarks of a suicide, but after the police had run the tests, another story emerged. The victim's hands had no residue of gunpowder or traces of blood, and the autopsy revealed she had been drugged before the shooting.

The US police had investigated, and found that the husband – an IT specialist – frequently visited the dark web, and had visited Besa Mafia. The messages on the website were the words of an actual murderer.

'When I found out, I was screaming,' Chris said. 'I didn't know what to do.'

'You need to go to the police!' I said. 'This is extremely serious. It doesn't matter whether or not the site is a scam. People are paying money to have other people killed.'

Chris looked at me like what I had suggested was the most obvious thing in the world. 'You think I didn't try?'

The Takeover

Throughout his investigation in 2016, Chris had tried to hand over all the information that he had about Besa Mafia to the police.

2 http://www.startribune.com/cottage-grove-man-charged-in-wife-s-murder/411079495/

He'd gone to his local police station. He'd phoned the National Crime Agency. He'd phoned the Los Angeles Police Department, then the FBI. From Chris's perspective at least, nobody was taking him seriously. An Albanian mafia group conducting murder-for-hire as an e-commerce venture? The dark net? Bitcoin?

'I knew for a fact the police were not looking into this,' Chris told me. So he decided to take matters into his own hands.

As Chris explored the site from the inside, he noticed that he had more information than just the messages that had been sent through it. He also managed to find the email login details for the site's administrator. Using them, every day, he crept into the administrator's email account, quietly watching the actual back office operation of the website: messages about building the website, using freelancers and social media marketing.

Suddenly, Chris's hand was forced. One day he logged into the administrator's email while the administrator was already logged in, and locked the administrator out. 'Who is this?' the administrator sent, in an email to himself, trying to communicate with Chris. 'I was clicking like hell,' Chris said, grinning now, excited at reliving the high drama of the digital takeover. 'Password reset, password reset, password reset. Boom. The operation was now mine.'

From there, Chris's next move was a strike on the assassination market itself, an attack as surreal as anything on the site. Chris called it Operation Vegetable. He uploaded something called a 'shim' to the website – a smuggled fragment of code. That fragment opened a tiny lever of control for Chris within the website. On 3 July 2016, he struck, using that lever to wrestle the website offline. People trying to visit the site were now diverted to a site that Chris had set up, with the message: 'Besa Mafia has closed for business. After six months of scamming bitcoins and stealing over 100 BTC ($65,000) the site has closed. No one was ever beaten up or killed.' In the background a song was playing. Goodbye, farewell, auf wiedersehen, goodbye.

The website was down, but the targets on it might still be in danger. And there was still no sign that the police had taken Chris's information seriously. I decided to do something I had determined not to do, here or in any of the other areas I was researching. I became involved. Chris wasn't, I thought, speaking to the right people within the police, so I arranged a meeting between Chris and some specialists there who would know what he was talking about.

A month went by, then another. That, I thought, was that. It was months later in 2017 before Chris wrote to me again. 'Hi Carl. I am doing very poorly indeed,' he said in an email. 'The police have raided my flat on Saturday on suspicion of incitement to murder. All my electronics are seized. I was in jail for thirty-six hours and accused of being the mastermind behind the site.'

'I was off ill,' Chris told me. 'I wasn't feeling very good. I was mooching around the flat. It was about 1 p.m., and then I could hear some people behind the door. Suddenly, they broke down my door, yelling, "Police, arms in the air, arms in the air!" These guys are wearing body armour and pads and stuff like that. They were ready for a fight.'

The irony was that they were now forcibly taking something that Chris had desperately been trying to give them: all the information about Besa Mafia. 'What services does Besa Mafia provide?' they'd interrogated him at a local police station. 'What do you use Tor for? . . . Have you had any part in the setting up of Besa

Mafia? . . . Were you involved in managing the website?' Chris was eventually let out and formally received a notification of 'no further action', but what could have been his triumph was instead his lowest moment.

An explanation lay in the shadowy presence behind the website. The administrator was someone whom Chris, in a strange way, had begun to talk to. After Chris had seized his email, the administrator had started sending messages to his old account, to learn more about the people trying to shut down his enterprise. He suspected it was law enforcement, and wanted to reassure them that the whole thing was a scam.

He had introduced himself to Chris as Mark, 'but friends call me Yura'. While in private Yura was keen to admit the site was a scam, he had publicly tangled with Chris to demonstrate that it was authentic. Once he'd lost control of his own website, Yura – the administrator of a dark net assassination site – went on a PR offensive.

'Besa Mafia admins exposed,' one article read. 'The site is owned by Eileen Ormsby [a journalist and colleague of Chris who had become involved in the investigation] . . . and by Chris from London, UK.' Probably working through others, Yura sprayed articles across the internet that told a story very different from the one myself and Chris knew. It sought to implicate Chris as the person *really* behind the site. 'The Besa Mafia drama continue [sic], after its founders Eileen O. Chris and Yura D. are fighting with each other,' another article starts.

There were dozens of articles, invariably written on the popular blogging platform blogspot. And although crude, the articles had been deliberately tailored to dominate search engine results. The counter-narrative that these articles summoned was ingenious.

Chris was using 'a special camouflage technique to resist to FBI and law enforcement'. His exposé was deliberate, the articles claimed: calling it a scam was both a way to promote the site and to deflect any interest from law enforcement. The articles posed as an exposé of the exposé. They claimed that calling the site a scam was itself a scam. One of them was even called fightingbe-samafia.blogspot.com. 'We condemn Besa Mafia and their illegal activities,' the article thundered. 'The crazy world with the today's technology makes it all happen.'

The administrator had created a smokescreen of misinformation that itself purported to identify a smokescreen of misinformation. If the police or anyone else had put Besa Mafia into a search engine, they would have found a tangle of different articles, all apparently from different writers, and all pointing to Chris as the mastermind behind it.

In private Yura was far more conciliatory. 'I love animals, I love people, I love life and liberty,' he said. Yura was obviously nervous about being arrested, and took pains to stress that it was a humble scam that didn't justify a large, expensive investigation. In his own eyes, he also saw Besa Mafia as a righteous act:

'I consider that instead of doing credit card fraud as other people on deep web, is better to scam criminals who want to do murder . . . I tried various things before, like credit card fraud, etc. but I don't like it. I saw that there is a niche in the murder sites online, there was no credible site so we tried to do besa mafia credible.'

It wasn't only Chris, but also Yura who considered himself a vigilante of sorts, taking on the criminals who used the site:

'my plans were to ask for more and more and more money each time to deplete their financial resources and time and hopes until they give up stalling the murder for months both for my benefit to get as much bitcoin as possible but for the target benefit as well, as the more time passed the customer lost more faith that he can do it after the murder was not done, I asked for more bitcoins for a more expensive hitman and then more and more this could make the customer think that hitman are not to be trusted in the end and he would not hire a hitman in real life either after this because he would be afraid of being scammed again.'

The New Global Power Grab

Chris's journey into the heart of an assassination market is so otherworldly, and so bizarre, that at first it feels unconnected from all of us who do not choose – as Chris does – to spend time in the darkest recesses of the internet. It is frightening but also distant, a window into life at the fringes of society, but certainly not most people's everyday reality.

Yet at its heart, this story shows a truth about power that is far more general. The people who know how to harness this technology can become powerful in ways that would have been impossible a few years ago. Yura had made £65,000 scamming would-be murderers, actual murderers, villains-for-rent and crime syndicates simply by setting up a website. Chris came home after a long day at work and was transformed into a superhero of sorts: taking down predators and criminals single-handedly. But to all intents and purposes, their lives didn't change. Yura could only resort to spreading rumours online when he was caught. Chris couldn't even convince the police of the seriousness of the crimes he was investigating.

Unrecognised, unknown, shadowy. Power is now working outside of the places where traditional centres of control – the law, the police, public opinion, general knowledge – can recognise it, let alone control it. The final part of Chris's story highlights, I think, this key struggle. The old gods are dying, and the new ones are wild, and for most of us, unknowable.

EPILOGUE

The New Gods

I had started my journey with a stranger holding a knife to my throat, as I held one to his. It had all begun with a moment of stillness, and terror. 'Power', the technologist said, 'is this. My life in your hands. Your life in mine.' I think he was right. I was keeping an open mind about where I might find power, or what it would be like when I found it, but this was really what it came down to: our lives in the hands of others. But I knew power could manifest itself in ways entirely different to the crude edge of a blade. It was never going to be that simple.

As we stood there, perfectly still, the technologist's phone began to beep. It beeped, paused, and beeped once more. Then it began to ring. Then it stopped and again started to beep insistently. The technologist lowered his knife and walked over.

When I'd arrived at his house, a fully automated LiDAR-enabled vacuum cleaner had been humming around our ankles. The technologist had pointed it out with pride. 'Soon everyone will have one of these,' he'd said, beaming. It certainly seemed efficient, quietly and methodically cleaning every inch of floor in a choreographed circuit. But while we were preoccupied with the knives it had got lost. It had somehow motored out of the front door, closed it, and trundled off. And now it was calling for help.

It seemed to me that the technologist was right, but perhaps not in the way he meant. We all know about the power of a knife. But in the last decade or so a huge number of new influences have appeared in our lives, and are becoming increasingly important and more central to them. Influences that we haven't expected, and that we don't properly understand. Influences that are shaping our lives in a number of different ways, sometimes without us knowing why, or how. Power today can easily come in the form of a vacuum cleaner, as well as a knife.

Those early hackers at the Tech Model Railroad Club had felt it first. As soon as the computers arrived in the hallway, a new form of power fizzled at their fingertips. Power over computers, power over people ... eventually power over the world. It was a dizzying, intoxicating realisation, to see the potential so close, so accessible. A power that few people could comprehend was being unleashed. And across almost every single walk of life today, I had found people who felt something similar. Who had come to their own intoxicating realisations. There were new opportunities, new freedoms, new systems that would have been unthinkable a generation ago.

Eliot Higgins had launched world-changing investigations from the living room of his house in Leicester, with little more than some intelligent research and a well-connected network. At his fingertips were new ways of finding the truth and challenging lies.

He had faced off against the Russian state, and won. Audrey Tang had progressed from being a high-school drop-out to being one of the most important government ministers in a country of 23 million people, motivated by a belief that technology can make democracy better. Mrs Grimmenstein, a semi-retired flute teacher from rural Germany, had forced the deputy chancellor to amend a key policy with an online petition. tFlow had run amok in another liberation of sorts, fighting corruption, abuses of power and despotic governments online. Chris and Yura were superhero and super-villain, battling in a world of anonymity and unlimited possibility. All of them living a life they never could have dreamed of without computers.

Technology is offering a new kind of power, and new routes to power. The individuals and organisations that have noticed and embraced these opportunities have helped to change the world. And, like the early hackers, each has found power outside of its normal channels. Eliot didn't need to go to the mainstream press to get his stories heard. Audrey didn't need to follow a traditional career trajectory to get a government position. Soldiers don't need to fight to win wars. The cybercriminal doesn't need to leave his house to step outside of the law. Whether for good or bad, these people have found a power freed from its usual centres and bindings. Each of these people has taken on, or simply ignored, the rules, structures and organisations that are much bigger, richer and conventionally more powerful than they are. Many of the old hierarchies are getting weaker. Some are disappearing altogether.

So power is both more available and more fluid than it once was, spilling out from old rigidities of privilege that once contained it. We have more freedoms than ever before. But are we more controlled? Are we just locked in a different kind of prison? The undermining of traditional centres of power isn't simply a question of power changing hands. It also changes how power itself is controlled.

Traditional institutions and centres of authority have been badly undermined. Some of these institutions haven't adapted quickly enough, some can't adapt, and for others it still isn't clear how they *should* adapt to embrace the realities they are confronted with today. As technology weakens the very structures and institutions that determine where power sits, they weaken the rules for how power can be used. It is the law that sets the frameworks for how power can be legitimately used. The authorities hold special powers in order to effectively confront crime and injustice. Journalists have held power over our attention, but have long used it to stand up to abuses of power. Regulations perform the same function. Political institutions manage how power is transferred. Across our lives, power is operating in ways either without any rules, or in places where the rules are harder to enforce. Power had been tamed by these rules. Now it is not.

Liberation and control, I realised, are not in conflict. We are living through an onset of tremendous liberations and potent new forms of control at exactly the same time. Working outside of these rules, technology has made it easier to shape the lives of others in so many positive ways. But it has also presented the opportunity to exploit, manipulate and harm.

Criminals break into our most personal data with relative impunity. The dark net offers a haven for anyone with the skill and motivation to commit a multitude of crimes. Police forces the world over are experiencing an enforcement crisis. Algorithms shape our behaviour in ways their creators don't even understand. Technology is not only transforming democracy, it is rapidly outpacing it. At exactly the moment when power is becoming more available, it is also concentrating. We are yet to properly comprehend the impact of the pooling of wealth in Silicon Valley. Three of the world's richest people are self-made tech billionaires, all capitalising on the power inherent in the world they operate in. We are only beginning to realise that alongside the freedoms now available to us, there is also a network of control and dominion.

Perhaps more importantly, the old hierarchies are not all disappearing. The stories in this book are connected by more than technology. Like those early hackers, the individuals that are benefiting most today are those with the technical nous, skill and education to take the opportunities available. At least the ones I found were disproportionately white, disproportionately male, disproportionately middle class (as far as I could tell) and disproportionately from western or high-income countries. In part, this says something about who I am, and who I know. But in part I think it says something else, too. Liberation exists, but certainly not for everyone.

Power itself has changed. Beyond the access we now have to it, and the new forms of control that have access to us, there is a larger truth. When power operates through technology, it is often hidden, and often unchecked. Sometimes it is buried in the technical arcana of an algorithm. Sometimes within proprietary technology. Sometimes the code is open and visible, but only a tiny number of people can actually interpret and understand it. And that means we know less about what influences our lives today than we did in the past. With each passing day, we know less, not more, about the tools of information warfare that are used to manipulate online spaces, about the skills of hackers, about how psychology is applied to promote habit-forming technology. About the use of data to understand everything from our political to commercial preferences. The gap between the power others have over our lives through the use of technology, and our ability to understand and recognise that power, is ever-widening. Power these days rests on technical capabilities that are getting further away from public awareness and consciousness, not closer to it.

Weird and hidden, these new forms of power together have something in common which older, visible, more recognisable forms of power typically do not. They are far less constrained by rules. These forms of power are not only new; they are also wild. They are untamed by the web of laws, professional standards, norms, moral codes, ethical frameworks and public scrutiny that used to limit what power was able to do.

This end is really only the beginning. We are stepping into a world where power is, I think, more accessible to each of us. We are all a little closer to the gods than we were before. But the gods are closer to us too. And they hold forms of power that we can't always see. We now face a world beset by the onrush of both liberation and control together. A world where technology is allowing the more perfect expression of those conflicting qualities that humans have always carried inside themselves: the desire to dominate and control, and also the potential to be brave and selfless. The new gods have broken out of their cages, and we are only beginning to comprehend the world they are making.